Signpost Guides

# FLORIDA

The best of Florida's stunning
beaches and wildlife havens, plus
a full guide to the theme parks
of Orlando, the art deco buildings
of Miami Beach, the wilderness of
the Everglades and the relaxed
ambience of the Florida Keys

Mick Sinclair

The
Globe
Pequot
Press

Guilford, Connecticut

Thomas
Cook

Publishing

Published by Thomas Cook Publishing
The Thomas Cook Group Ltd
PO Box 227
Thorpe Wood
Peterborough PE3 6PU
United Kingdom

Telephone: 01733 503571
E-mail: books@thomascook.com
Advertising sales: 01733 503568

The Globe Pequot Press
PO Box 480
Guilford, Connecticut USA
06437

Text: © 2000 The Thomas Cook Group Ltd
Maps and diagrams: © 2000 The Thomas Cook Group Ltd

**ISBN 0-7627-0681-3**

**Library of Congress Cataloging-in-Publication Data is available.**

Publisher: Stephen York
Commissioning Editor: Deborah Parker
Map Editor: Bernard Horton

Series Editor: Christopher Catling
Copy Editor: Karen Pieringer
Written and researched by: Mick Sinclair

Although every care has been taken in compiling this publication, and the contents are
believed to be correct at the time of printing, The Thomas Cook Group Ltd cannot accept
responsibility for errors or omissions, however caused, or for changes in details given in the
guidebook, or for the consequences of any reliance on the information provided.

The opinions and assessments expressed in this book do not necessarily represent those of
The Thomas Cook Group Ltd.

Readers are asked to remember that attractions and establishments may open, close or
change owners or circumstances during the lifetime of this edition. Descriptions and assessments are given in good faith but are based on the author's views and experience at the time
of writing and therefore contain an element of subjective opinion which may not accord
with the reader's subsequent experience.

We would be grateful to be told of any changes or inaccuracies in order to update future
editions. Please notify them to the Commissioning Editor at the above address.

# About the author

Mick Sinclair first visited Florida when Miami was more synonymous with retirement homes than art deco architecture and Mickey Mouse was still a recent arrival. Since then, he has witnessed Miami's transformation into a trendsetting modern city, Orlando's evolution into a theme park capital, and Florida itself becoming one of the world's most-visited but least-understood regions.

Intimately familiar with the state's top tourist attractions, best beaches and most scenic roads, Mick is also an initiate of rural Florida. He knows the wayside towns and villages, has canoed rivers and lakes, and hiked through prairies and swamps.

Between trips to the Sunshine State, Mick has written guidebooks to California, Chicago, New York, San Francisco and Scandinavia. His writing career began in 1980 with reviews and features on music, film, books and contemporary culture. Such work continues to appear in newspapers, magazines and books, and on websites, throughout the world.

# Contents

# About Signpost Guides

Thomas Cook's Signpost Guides are designed to provide you with a comprehensive but flexible reference source to guide you as you tour a country or region by car. This guide divides Florida into touring areas – one per chapter. Major cultural centres or cities form chapters in their own right. Each chapter contains enough attractions to provide at least a day's worth of activities – often more.

### Star ratings
To make it easier for you to plan your time and decide what to see, the main sights and attractions are given star ratings. A three-star rating indicates an outstanding sight or major attraction. Often these can be worth at least half a day of your time. A two-star attraction is worth an hour or so of your time, and a one-star attraction indicates a site that is good, but often of specialist interest. The stars are intended to help you set priorities, so that travellers with limited time can quickly find the most rewarding sights.

### Chapter contents
Every chapter has an introduction summing up the main attractions of the area, and a ratings box, which will highlight the area's strengths and weaknesses – some areas may be more attractive to families travelling with children, others to wine-lovers visiting vineyards, and others to people interested in finding castles, churches, nature reserves, or good beaches.

Each chapter is then divided into an alphabetical gazetteer, and a suggested tour. You can select whether you just want to visit a particular sight or attraction, choosing from those described in the gazetteer, or whether you want to tour the area comprehensively. If the latter, you can construct your own itinerary, or follow the author's suggested tour, which comes at the end of every area chapter.

### The gazetteer
The gazetteer section describes all the major attractions in the area – the villages, towns, historic sites, nature reserves, parks or museums that you are most likely to want to see. Maps of the area highlight all the places mentioned in the text. Using this comprehensive overview of the area, you may choose just to visit one or two sights

One way to use the guide is simply to find individual sights that interest you, using the index, overview map or star ratings, and read what our authors have to say about them. This will help you decide whether to visit the sight. If you do, you will find plenty of practical information, such as the street address, the telephone number for enquiries and opening times.

Symbol Key

❶ Tourist Information Centre

❷ Advice on arriving or departing

❷ Parking locations

❷ Advice on getting around

➔ Directions

❸ Sights and attractions

❶ Accommodation

❶ Eating

❷ Shopping

❷ Sport

❷ Entertainment

## Practical information

The practical information in the page margins, or sidebar, will help you locate the services you need as an independent traveller – including the tourist information centre, car parks and public transport facilities. You will also find the opening times of sights, museums, churches and other attractions, as well as useful tips on shopping, market days, cultural events, entertainment, festivals and sports facilities.

Alternatively, you can choose a hotel, perhaps with the help of the accommodation recommendations contained in this guide. You can then turn to the overall map on page 10 to help you work out which chapters in the book describe those cities and regions that lie closest to your chosen touring base.

## Driving tours

The suggested tour is just that – a suggestion, with plenty of optional detours and one or two ideas for making your own discoveries, under the heading *Also worth exploring*. The routes are designed to link the attractions described in the gazetteer section, and to cover outstandingly scenic coastal, mountain and rural landscapes. The total distance is given for each tour, as is the time it will take you to drive the complete route, but bear in mind that this indication is just for the driving time: you will need to add on extra time for visiting attractions along the way.

Many of the routes are circular, so that you can join them at any point. Where the nature of the terrain dictates that the route has to be linear, the route can either be followed out and back, or you can use it as a link route, to get from one area in the book to another.

As you follow the route descriptions, you will find names picked out in bold capital letters – this means that the place is described fully in the gazetteer. Other names picked out in bold indicate additional villages or attractions worth a brief stop along the route.

## Accommodation and food

In every chapter you will find lodging and eating recommendations for individual towns, or for the area as a whole. These are designed to cover a range of price brackets and concentrate on more characterful small or individualistic hotels and restaurants. In addition, you will find information in the *Travel facts* chapter on chain hotels, with an address to which you can write for a guide, map or directory. The price indications used in the guide have the following meanings:

| | |
|---|---|
| $ | budget level |
| $$ | typical/average prices |
| $$$ | de luxe |

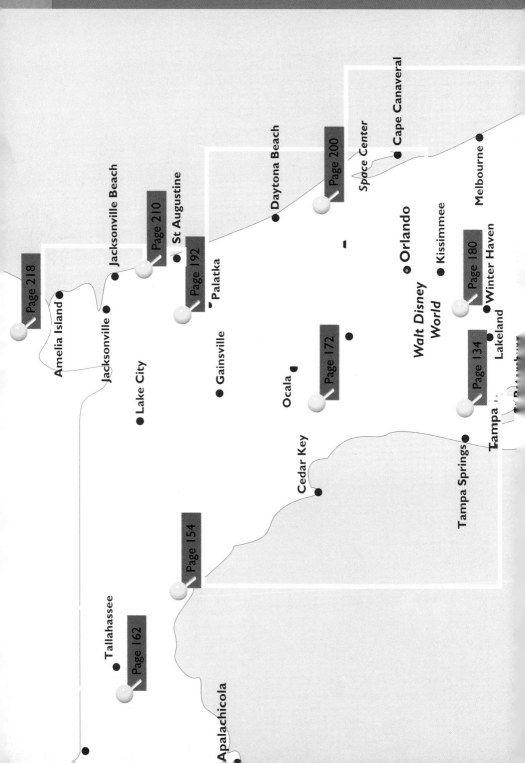

Page 218

Page 210

Jacksonville Beach

St Augustine

Page 192

Daytona Beach

Page 200

Space Center

Cape Canaveral

Melbourne

Amelia Island

Jacksonville

Palatka

Orlando

Walt Disney World

Kissimmee

Page 180

Winter Haven

Lake City

Gainsville

Ocala

Page 172

Lakeland

Page 134

Tampa

Cedar Key

Tampa Springs

Page 154

Tallahassee

Page 162

Apalachicola

Fort Pierce

Page 88

Page 74

Lake
Okeechobee

Fort Lauderdale

Page 42

Page 52

Miami City and Miami Beach

Key Largo

Everglades
National
Park

Florida Keys

Page 64

Page 114

Punta Gorda

Page 124

Naples

Page 94

Page 226

Key West

Page 104

Page 162

Tallahassee

Page 244

Apalachicola

Panama City

De Funiak Springs

Page 254

Page 264

# Introduction

Subtropical sunshine, a thousand miles of beaches and the best theme parks human ingenuity can devise make Florida one of the world's greatest tourist destinations. Forty million people come here each year and very few leave disappointed. Not many among them, however, really make the most of what this extremely varied and rewarding state has to offer.

At the heart of Florida is Orlando, the state's tourism linchpin. The major theme park complexes of Walt Disney World and Universal Studios are based here, as is every other conceivable attraction from 'haunted' houses to crazy golf courses. Yet small towns and historic communities also lie well within Orlando's sway, as do immense stretches of coast where deservedly popular areas such as Daytona Beach and Clearwater Beach lie alongside isolated tourist-free strands lining pine-fringed barrier islands.

Orlando's sprawling form denies it the character that many Florida cities possess. A large Latin-American population brings vibrancy to Miami, where Cuban restaurants delight the culinary adventurous and the Art Deco District is one of the state's architectural treasures. Miami Beach draws the young, fashionable and affluent to its smartest hotels, but no Florida city is more conspicuously wealthy than the long-time millionaire's playground of Palm Beach.

Different again is Florida's homely capital, Tallahassee, nestling amid the oak-filled hillsides of the Panhandle. And at the end of the Florida Keys, few places combine history, relaxation and scenic splendour – notably intensely dramatic sunsets – as effortlessly as Key West.

While tourism underpins the Florida economy, efforts are under way to ensure that visitor numbers, and a continually expanding permanent population, do not destroy the state's many unique environments. With its sawgrass prairies and cypress swamps, the Everglades are the best known of the many natural areas that come as a revelation to Florida first-timers. State parks and wildlife refuges are common, providing user-friendly introductions to denizens such as alligators and manatees. Even Florida's plants and trees can be stunning; many wild areas harbour glorious stashes of wild flowers while the state can also claim vast pine forests and several hundred species of palm.

Natural Florida also includes beaches, quickly revealed as much more than merely places to laze in the sun. Ranging in colour from golden brown to dazzling white, the sands might be favoured by surfers, prized for their shells, provide a venue for weekend barbecues or romantic escapes, or enable sea turtles to creep shyly ashore after dark to lay their eggs.

Despite its strong links with theme parks, it was not Walt Disney who discovered Florida but 16th-century Spaniards, who encountered a Floridian population established for tens of thousands of years. Although major pre-European remains tend to be confined to museums, plenty survives of Florida's colonial past. Spanish-founded St Augustine is one of the oldest cities in the US, while Pensacola was fought over by the British, Spanish and French before becoming a strategically important US base.

Florida's diverse cultural strands are evident throughout the state. The Cross Creek cottage of writer Marjorie Kinnan Rawlings reveals the deprivations of 1930s Florida as well as the landscapes that inspired the writer. The Koreshan State Historic Site, near Fort Myers, recalls a time when Florida, for some, represented the earthly Garden of Eden. And the Cuban presence, past and present, is strongly felt in Miami, Tampa and Key West.

Perhaps the most remarkable aspect of Florida is how much can be seen and enjoyed so effortlessly. The quality and comfort of American cars, the relatively low cost of petrol and an excellent and easily navigated road system with frequent scenic stretches makes getting around simple and pleasurable. Each of the 25 driving, walking and city tours in this book is designed to maximise time and minimise effort in discovering the best of Florida in all its forms.

Sleeping and eating are also good news. Hotels, motels and evocative bed-and-breakfast inns are found at every turn in all price ranges, as are the restaurants that suit all tastes and budgets. Whether ordering American staples such as milk shakes and burgers or Florida specialities like conch fritter, heart-of-palm salad, grilled mahi-mahi or fried catfish, you can rest assured that it will be served fresh and with a smile.

**Right**
The Biltmore Hotel, Miami

# Travel facts

## Accommodation

**Florida Room Reservations**, part of a nationwide organisation based at 595 Federal Road, Brookfield, CT 06804; tel: (203) 775-4466; fax: (203) 775-4599; toll-free: (800) 847-4835. Web: www.stayusa.com

**Florida Hotel & Motel Association** 200 W College Avenue, Tallahassee, FL 32301; tel: (850) 224-2888.

**Bed & Breakfast Scenic Florida** Box 3385, Tallahassee, FL 32315; tel: (850) 386-8136.

Several web sites detail specific bed-and-breakfast inns throughout the US and beyond including **International Bed & Breakfast Pages** (www.ippb.com) and **Bed and Breakfast Online** (www.bbonline.com).

Most tourist offices will have details of accommodation in their area.

From luxury hotels with in-room Jacuzzis to simple motels beside the Interstate, Florida is well served by accommodation of all kinds in all price ranges. National hotel chains such as Best Western and Holiday Inn (typically $60–$90 per room) are prevalent, as are motel chains such as Days Inn and Super 8 (usually $40–$65 per room). Most provide clean rooms with bathrooms and TV (usually with a range of cable channels to complement the nationally networked channels). Some offer rooms with kitchenettes, known as 'efficiencies', usually adding $15–$25 to the room price. In general, the more you pay, the bigger the room and more plentiful the facilities will be. Increasingly, many hotels and motels offer a rudimentary free breakfast.

Usually with much more charm than the chains are the many independently run hotels and motels, such as the Art Deco hotels of Miami Beach (likely to charge $90–$140) and those beside rivers and lakes catering primarily to boating and fishing enthusiasts (typically $45–$75).

Reservations are easily made by phone (most chains have a toll-free number) or fax and in some cases by e-mail, ahead of arrival. Only during peak periods (this may mean a local sports event or festival, a national holiday or simply the main tourist season) is space likely to be in short supply.

More individual lodgings are offered by bed-and-breakfast inns (usually $90–$150), often century-old homes with a handful of guest rooms liberally filled with antiques and scented with potpourri. The hosts usually provide a full breakfast; some also offer afternoon snacks and complimentary wine or sherry. The hosts are well acquainted with local points of interest and driving and dining details. Many inns are booked well ahead for weekends, and there may be a minimum two-night stay over busy periods.

All accommodation is usually paid for by credit card, which can also be used to secure a reservation confirmation (be sure to acquire a reference number) ahead of arrival and not debited if you cancel the booking with reasonable notice. A reservation without confirmation will usually be held until 1600 or 1800 on the day of arrival. Sales tax and any local accommodation taxes are rarely part of the quoted price.

**Above**
Nassau Hotel, Miami Beach

## Airports

See pages 32–3.

## Children

With theme parks, zoos, wildlife parks, beaches and many kid-orientated museums and attractions, Florida could be designed for children. Most obviously, Orlando's theme parks are the stuff of youngsters' dreams, even though only Disney's Magic Kingdom really has a lot to appeal to younger ones.

Theme parks are large and often crowded, and it is very easy to become lost and separated. Most have a supervised Lost Kids Area, a mini playground with sufficient amusements for them to forget that they are lost until their parents show up to reclaim them. It is a good idea for kids to be given ID bearing their name so that park staff can contact parents over the PA system. For children old enough to explore on their own, parents should fix a time and place to meet later. At all parks, pushchairs ('strollers') can be rented for the day.

Along with theme parks, Florida also has over a hundred state parks. These are well-managed natural areas, most with walking trails and picnic tables, some with swimming and canoeing facilities. The park visitors' centre arranges park ranger-guided activities, many of them intended to introduce youngsters to the joys of wild Florida. Most activities take place at weekends and during US holidays.

Miami's MetroZoo (*see page 58*) boasts white Bengal tigers and komodo dragons among several hundred species spread over 300 acres of replicated habitats. Near Palm Beach, Lion Country Safari (*see page 81*) is a drive-through, 500-acre park holding not just lions but elephants, rhinos, antelopes, giraffes, chimpanzees and a host of other creatures.

In many towns and cities, museums encourage young visitors with hands-on, interactive exhibits designed to entertain as they educate. Two of the biggest are Tampa's Museum of Science and Industry (*see page 138*) and Fort Lauderdale's Museum of Discovery and Science (*see page 80*).

In all but the most formal restaurants, children are not only welcome but presented with their own menu as soon as they sit down, together with assorted small toys, colouring sets and picture books. Kids' menus are likely to feature burgers, hot dogs, pizzas and French fries in child-sized portions at parent-pleasing prices. Most restaurants have high chairs and kids' seats readily available.

Florida does have it pitfalls for children, though. Young skin is especially susceptible to sunburn, while heat and humidity (most intense during the south Florida summer) can quickly cause irritability. Long car drives bring problems, too, although roadside amusements, be it crazy golf or a stand selling boiled peanuts, can provide a welcome diversion.

## FLORIDA

### with

### THOMAS COOK HOLIDAYS

- Excellent prices - kids from £189 and adults from £399.

- Free regional domestic flights.

- Great value accommodation including **Walt Disney World**® Resort Hotels and self catering homes.

- *Disney Cruise Line.*

- Twin/Multi Centre Holidays including the Caribbean.

- Pre-bookable attraction tickets.

- Wedding packages.

- Thomas Cook's Connections - savings on getting to the airport.

*To make a booking call*
# 01733 418100

*To order a brochure call*
# 01733 417979
*and quote* **AFLO1199**

ABTA: V6434  ATOL: 265
The Thomas Cook Group Ltd.

Internet site: www.tcholidays.com

## Thomas Cook Foreign Exchange Facilities

Thomas Cook Travellers Cheques free you from the hazards of carrying large amounts of cash. Thomas Cook Foreign Exchange Bureaux are listed below. They all provide full foreign exchange facilities and will change currency and travellers' cheques (free of commission in the case of Thomas Cook Travellers Cheques).

They can also provide emergency assistance in the event of loss or theft of Thomas Cook Travellers Cheques.

## Thomas Cook Foreign Exchange Bureaux

Thomas Cook Currency Services
3526 North Ocean Boulevard, Fort Lauderdale, Florida. Tel: 954 566 2771

Thomas Cook Foreign Exchange
Southwest Florida International Airport, Suite 8638, 16000 Chamberlin Parkway, Fort Myers, Florida. Tel: 941 561 2204

Thomas Cook Currency Services
80 North Biscayne, Boulevard, At the Columbus Bazaar, Miami Downtown, Miami, Florida. Tel: 305 381 9260

Thomas Cook Currency Services
55 West Church Street, Suite 120, Orlando, Florida. Tel: 407 481 8238

**Above right**
Miami Beach sunbathers

## Climate

South and much of central Florida have a subtropical climate. The region has mild winters and hot and humid summers with frequent short but severe thunderstorms.

Winter is the peak tourist season. In northern Florida, summer is the busiest tourist period with hot, sunny days but usually much less humidity than experienced in the south. Winter days range from mild to cool, with occasional freezing night-time temperatures. The high moisture content of Florida's air can cause heavy morning and evening fogs from late autumn to early spring. The Panhandle very occasionally sees snow in winter.

Hurricanes may strike from June to November, though these are closely tracked and warnings are issued.

## Currency

There are 100 cents to the dollar. Most commonly used are the $1, $5, $10 and $20 notes, and the 1 cent, 5 cent, 10 cent and 25 cent coins (respectively known as a penny, nickel, dime and quarter). A dollar coin is also in circulation and is infuriatingly similar to a 25 cent coin.

Visitors are strongly advised to carry the bulk of their money as US dollar travellers' cheques. In most transactions, such as paying a restaurant bill, these may be used as cash (ID is rarely required in this situation, but should always be carried). The most useful cheque sizes are $10, $20 and $50; anything larger used to pay a relatively small bill will not be appreciated.

It is common, and expected where large sums are concerned, for bills to be paid by credit card. Credit card holders who know their PIN numbers may also be able to get cash (for a fee added to the

**Festivals**

Festivals occur throughout Florida at the slightest excuse. A day of special events may mark anything of local interest – such as seashells, arts and crafts, sandcastle-building or seafood – or be major film and book festivals of the kind staged annually in Miami. Local tourist information centres will have full details.

next statement) from a cash dispenser (ATM) usually outside banks. Most are part of the Cirrus or Plus networks accepting MasterCard and Visa.

## Customs regulations

Customs allowances for visitors aged 21 or over include one litre of alcohol and 200 cigarettes. Prohibited items include lottery tickets, chocolate liqueurs and fresh fruit. Check with customs officials at home for returning duty-free allowances, but don't buy duty-free. Alcohol, tobacco, perfume and similar items are cheaper at supermarkets and department stores than at airport and downtown duty-free shops.

## Drinking

Whether you are driving, walking or doing anything else in the Florida heat, bottled drinking water (readily available in shops and petrol stations) is always useful and in some situations essential to avoid dehydration. Many public areas also have drinking water fountains, invariably safe and refreshing. Soft drinks are also readily obtainable, as are various flavoured iced-teas and iced-coffee in bottles and cans. As in the rest of the US, most diners serve (hot) coffee with limitless refills.

## Eating out

Simple diners and coffee shops that Americans take for granted but which overseas visitors relish for their good value and attentive service (especially towards children) are plentiful throughout Florida. Some, such as Denny's and Waffle House are ubiquitous national chains. Alongside them are many local independents. Some establishments are open around the clock; nearly all serve breakfast (rarely provided by hotels and motels), lunch and, in many cases, dinner.

As well as internationally known burger outlets and pizzerias, every town has a number of ethnic restaurants – Italian and Thai being particularly plentiful – and coastal regions in particular have many eateries specialising in seafood. Also widely found are buffet restaurants, such as Shoney's, which may not offer the world's best food but do offer it in unlimited amounts.

For top-class dining, most towns have a sprinkling of French restaurants and others, especially common in Miami Beach, where ground-breaking chefs explore the various avenues of new American cuisine. In general, prices in an ordinary restaurant will range from $6–$10 for breakfast, $8–$15 for lunch and $12–$20 for dinner. An evening meal in the leading local restaurant will usually be $25–$40 per person, without drinks.

## Electricity

America uses 110-volt 60-hertz current with two- or three-prong plugs. Power and plug converters are seldom available.

Beware of buying electrical equipment – it probably won't operate on your voltage at home. Exceptions are battery-operated items such as radios, cameras and portable computers.

## Entry formalities

Citizens of most European countries and Australia, provided they have a full passport valid for more than six months, their trip is for less than 90 days' duration and they hold a return ticket, do not require a visa to visit the US, but must complete the visa waiver form provided on the plane.

## Food

Traditional Florida rural fare includes gator tail (the only edible part of the alligator), frog's legs and turtle, though these dishes (especially the latter) are relatively hard to find. Much more plentiful is beef from the state's farms and the produce of its rivers and coast such as grouper, tuna, mahi-mahi (also called dolphin, but the fish, *not* the mammal), mullet, trout, catfish, oysters, shrimps and crab.

Eagerly devoured by locals during their April to October season are the creamy claws of stone crabs, usually served as an expensive appetiser. Less costly and available year-round is the sea snail known as the conch, frequently served as a chowder and, particularly in the Florida Keys, as deep-fried fritters.

As a result of its large Cuban population, Miami has many Cuban restaurants serving pork, beef, chicken and seafood dishes in traditional Cuban styles, accompanied by black beans, rice and plantains. Stands offering Cuban sandwiches – large rolls generously stuffed with meat, cheese and various pickles – and thimble-sized cups of potent Cuban coffee, are another Miami speciality. Cuban fare also inspired the nuevo-Cuban cuisine that was the talk of the city during the early 1990s.

Traditional dishes of the Southern US appear throughout Florida and especially in the Panhandle, where common side-dishes are grits (ground corn) and hush puppies (fried corn balls). Other regional fare includes heart-of-palm salad, using the vegetable at the centre of Florida's official state tree, and Key Lime Pie, a dessert common in the Florida Keys.

## Health

Travellers are unlikely to encounter any unusual health problems in Florida. However, the strength of the sun should not be underestimated. Spend only a few minutes on the beach or beside the hotel pool during your first few days, and increase this time gradually. Always apply a strong sunscreen (SPF 25 at least). Remember that kids are especially vulnerable. Wear lightweight, light-coloured clothing, always carry a sun-reflecting hat and good-quality sunglasses. Avoid dehydration by drinking plenty of water: bottled water is easy to find and there are safe drinking fountains in many public places.

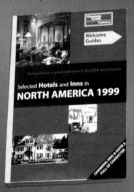

## Information

Leaflets, brochures and maps of all kinds are freely available from Florida's many Welcome Centers, Chambers of Commerce and Convention and Visitor Bureaux. Many hotels and motels also have racks of local and statewide tourist literature. Further details are given in the local sections of the book.

## Insurance

For overseas visitors in particular, travel insurance is an important consideration. Besides covering lost items, delayed travel and other possible expenses, insurance is an essential safeguard against potentially astronomical medical bills in the event of illness or injury. A reasonable policy from a specialist insurer (identical policies offered by travel companies are usually much more expensive) should cost around £30–£40 for two weeks per person.

## Maps

The grandly titled Official Transportation Map, issued by the Florida Department of Transport, is free from many tourist information centres and provides a good general overview of the state and its road system. Local tourist information centres also offer free maps of their area, but these are of variable quality and not always as useful as they first appear. The most detailed road maps are those of DeLorme's *Florida Atlas & Gazetteer*.

## Museums

Florida might be known as the home of Walt Disney World but it does have some remarkably good cultural museums. They include a major collection of the work of Spanish surrealist Salvador Dali (in St Petersburg), a noted Rubens stash (in Sarasota) and commendable museums of state history in Tallahassee and Miami. Smaller museums devoted to local history often reveal fascinating insights into Native American and frontier-era life. The largest of numerous child-friendly museums with interactive exhibits are in Miami, Fort Lauderdale and Tampa.

## National and state parks

Much of Florida's distinctive scenery and the wildlife that lives in it is protected by several national (*www.nps.gov*) and over a hundred state parks (*www.dep.state.fl.us*). The former include Everglades National Park which protects a section of the Everglades – a remarkable area of sawgrass and swamp occupying almost all of south central Florida –

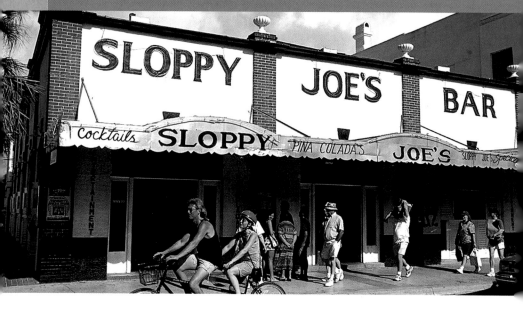

## Packing

Be sure to pack lightweight cotton clothing that includes a hat, swimwear, sunscreen, good quality sunglasses, a jacket or sweater for possibly cool evenings and winter mornings, travel documents, including driving licence, currency as US dollar travellers' cheques and a small amount of cash.

and the Canaveral National Seashore area close to the Kennedy Space Center. State parks tend to be less dramatic but offer tremendous wildlife-watching, walking trails and hiking routes, canoeing, swimming and much more. Almost all parks have informative visitors' centres and operate ranger-led activities such as guided walks and canoe rides.

## Opening times

Regular shop opening times are weekdays 1000–1800, but many keep longer hours and open on weekends. Some, including many supermarkets, never close. A number of restaurants are open around the clock but most that serve breakfast do so from 0600 and typically stay open until 2200 or 2300. Some restaurants serve only breakfast and lunch but do not close in between; up-market establishments usually open only for lunch and dinner, from 1100–1400 and 1600–2300 respectively. Major theme parks are open every day of the year, usually from 0900 or 1000. Theme park closing times are adjusted seasonally with longer hours, sometimes until midnight or later, over holiday periods and many weekends.

## Postal services

Stamps are sold by post offices, usually open 0900–1630/1700 on weekdays; major branches also open on Saturday. Stamps are also sold through vending machines in some hotels, supermarkets, shopping malls and petrol stations. Post boxes are blue and sited on street corners.

**Above**
Sloppy Joe's Bar, Key West

## Reading

The ups and downs of modern Florida and its tourist industry have been ably and entertainingly chronicled by Carl Hiassen in a series of novels that includes *Double Whammy*, *Tourist Season* and *Native Tongue*. Alexander Stuart captured the ascent of Miami's South Beach into one of the world's trendiest places in *Life on Mars*, while from an earlier period, *Cross Creek* found Marjorie Kinnan Rawlings (better known for *The Yearling*) describing everyday life in 1930s rural Florida.

Architecture buffs will enjoy Hap Hatton's *Tropical Splendor*, a spirited and lavishly illustrated tale of good and bad Florida buildings, while Barbara Beer Capitman's *Deco Delights* is a fine companion to viewing Miami Beach's Art Deco District from the person who did most to save it. Saving the Everglades, meanwhile, was the preoccupation of Marjory Stoneman Douglas whose *Everglades: River of Grass*, published in the 1940s, remains the most erudite eulogy to this amazing natural area.

## Public holidays

Banks and all public offices will be closed on all the following holidays; shops may be open on some of these days: New Year's Day (1 Jan), Martin Luther King Jnr's Birthday (third Mon in Jan), Presidents' Day (third Mon in Feb), Memorial Day (last Mon in May), Independence Day (4 July), Labor Day (first Mon in Sept), Columbus Day (second Mon in Oct), Veterans' Day (11 Nov), Thanksgiving Day (fourth Thur in Nov), Christmas Day (25 Dec). Good Friday is a half-day holiday and Easter Monday is a full day holiday. Actual dates may vary if the holiday falls on a weekend.

## Public transport

Long-distance public transport is limited to Greyhound buses (*tel:* (800) 231-2222) and Amtrak trains (*tel: (800) 872-7245*), both of which operate limited services within Florida. Although many cities and larger towns have a bus service, this is usually of little use to visitors and often closes down in the early evening with a skeletal service operating at weekends. Only in Miami, where buses are complemented by the elevated Metrorail and the Metromover serving the Downtown area, is public transport more comprehensive. Wherever you are, a rental car really is essential.

## Safety and security

Crimes against Florida's tourists have received far greater publicity than their frequency deserves but there are a number of safety tips that should be observed to ensure you leave the Sunshine State with nothing but good memories.

Do not open your hotel door to strangers. Leave valuables in the hotel safe when you go out. In crowd situations, be alert for pickpockets and in cities avoid walking on dimly lit streets. Be wary of discount tickets offered for major tourist attractions; some are genuine, many are fakes.

When driving, lock doors and keep windows closed. Stop only in populated, well-lit areas and do not stop to offer assistance to other drivers. Do not stop if flagged down by anyone other than a police officer: police cars use flashing blue and red lights to signal you to stop. Legally, you should stop if involved in an accident but do not do this if you are rammed from behind; instead continue to a well-lit, populated area. Always lock valuables in the boot.

## Sales tax

A state sales tax of 6 per cent is added to the marked price of most purchases, with additional local taxes applied in some areas.

**Above**
Key Largo diving mural

## Sport

### Spectator sports

Florida claims three professional football teams – the Miami Dolphins, Tampa Bay Buccaneers and Jacksonville Jaguars. The Miami-based Florida Marlins brought professional baseball to the state in 1993, although other pro teams use Florida as a spring training centre, bringing many fans with them to watch pre-season matches. Professional basketball comes from the Miami Heat and Orlando Magic, and professional ice-hockey courtesy of the Miami-based Florida Panthers and Tampa Bay Lightning.

College sports, notably football, are highly popular. Matches featuring the Gators, from Gainesville's University of Florida, or their arch-rivals the Seminoles, from Tallahassee's Florida State University, often draw bigger crowds than their professional counterparts. Anyone wearing green and yellow in Miami is likely to be a fan of the Hurricanes, the nickname of all Miami University's sports teams.

Florida also hosts several major tennis and golf tournaments, top motor sports events such as the Daytona 500, and an important annual surfing competition at Sebastian Inlet.

### Participant sports

Diving (a certificate is necessary; tuition is readily available) and snorkelling are immensely popular in the Florida Keys and wherever else conditions are suitable. State and national parks often have designated areas for canoeing and swimming. Horse-riding is offered at several places, including on the sands of Amelia Island. With more than a thousand courses, a third of them open to the public, golf is played widely and avidly throughout Florida.

Information on spectator and participant sports is available from any tourist office, or from the Florida Sports Foundation, 107 W Gaines Street, Suite 466, Tallahassee FL 32399-2000; tel: (850) 488-8347.

## Stores

Many leading nationwide shops and department stores have outlets in

Florida, usually gathered together on the outskirts of cities and towns into large shopping malls; Miami and Orlando each having a particularly large number. Factory outlet stores (and entire factory outlet malls) are also common, although increasingly these offer merchandise at little if any savings on regular retail prices. Around Orlando, especially, there are also many smaller roadside outlet malls, sometimes comprising no more than market stalls inside tents, selling assorted souvenirs and household items of variable quality at knock-down prices.

The latest Disney souvenirs are available from the shops at Disney West Side, part of Walt Disney World, as well as from the Disney parks.

## Telephones

Public telephones are reliable and local calls are inexpensive. Hotel and motel lobbies, restaurants, petrol stations, shopping malls and many other places have public telephones and are usually safer and shadier places for making calls than public phones on the street. Hotel rooms are always equipped with telephones, though charges are higher than on public phones. Many tourist attractions have toll-free numbers prefixed 1/800, which require no money to be inserted, although these calls are often charged for if made from a hotel room. Card-operated public phones are increasingly common; phone cards are sold in many shops. Major credit cards can also be used to make phone calls.

## Time

Most of Florida is on Eastern Standard Time (EST), five hours behind the UK and six behind the rest of Western Europe. The Panhandle west of the Apalachicola River uses Central Standard Time (CST), an hour behind the rest of the state.

## Toilets

Most public buildings, museums, theme parks and tourist attractions, shopping malls, restaurants and petrol stations (where you will probably need to ask for the key) have free public toilets, usually maintained in good condition.

## Tipping

Florida's service industry wages are notoriously low and most employees who serve the public rely on tips for a good proportion of their pay. In restaurants and taxis, tip 15–20 per cent of the bill; if a hotel porter carries your bags, tip at least $1 per piece.

# Driver's guide

## Accidents

Legally, you must stop if involved in an accident and report it to the police if there is injury to people or damage to property. If you are hit by another vehicle, particularly from behind, do not leave the vehicle but indicate for the other driver to follow your car to a populated, well-lit area where the authorities can be contacted and the damage inspected.

If it is safe to do so, stay at the scene of the accident and await the arrival of police. Accidents can be reported, if appropriate, using the emergency number (tel: 911) or contacting the Florida Highway Patrol (tel: FHP). Most rental cars carry accident report forms which must be completed in the event of any accident.

## Auto clubs

There are benefits, such as free maps and booklets, and sometimes discounted accommodation available to members of overseas motoring organisations affiliated to similar organisations in the US, such as the American Automobile Association (AAA) which is linked to the UK's AA. Check with your organisation for the details and latest offers.

## Breakdowns

Most rental cars are of a good standard and breakdowns are rare. None the less, drivers are provided with a toll-free number to use in the event of a breakdown. If possible, move the broken-down vehicle away from traffic and into a safe, well-lit area. Emergency phones are sited along major roads. Most rental companies have outlets throughout Florida and will provide a replacement car swiftly.

## Car hire

Florida offers some of the least costly car rental charges in the US with all major companies having outlets in the main cities and airports. Time and money can be saved by arranging car hire before arriving in the US, but look for an 'all inclusive' price that provides adequate insurance coverage (see *Insurance*) and includes local taxes and surcharges. Fly-drive deals are often good value but be wary of prices that do not include insurance or local taxes.

Cars are usually rented for a specific period with unlimited mileage. In most cases, the car must be returned with a full tank of petrol; if it is not, then steep surcharges apply. Additional charges often apply if the car is not returned to the point where it was collected, although 'drop-offs', such as leaving the car in a different city, are easily arranged.

Payment is usually by credit card; customers paying cash will need to leave a sizeable deposit. The minimum age for renting is 21, though drivers aged under 25 will often face a surcharge. Further fees are payable for additional drivers and child safety seats (legally required for children of certain ages, see *Seat belts*).

Cars can usually be collected from on or near airports. After a long flight is often the worse time to be driving on unfamiliar roads, especially if you arrive during or just before the hours of darkness. In this case, arrange to collect the car the following day.

All rental cars have automatic gears and air-conditioning, a necessity in Florida's climate. A manual or leaflet detailing the car's main controls should be found in the glove compartment.

Recreational vehicles (RVs), the US equivalent of campervans, should be rented in advance; it is difficult to rent an RV in Florida. Although RVs can offer savings and convenience, these tend to be offset by fuel costs and the fact that RVs must use designated RV campsites.

## Drinking and driving laws

Driving Under the Influence (DUI) is regarded extremely seriously in Florida and can result in a large fine, imprisonment and possible suspension of you licence if you refuse a roadside test or are found to have a blood alcohol content of 0.10 or higher. Remember that if you drink alcohol on the plane prior to arrival in Florida you may be over the limit if you pick up a rental car once you have landed. It is strongly recommended that drivers do not drink alcohol at all. Any alcoholic beverages in the car must be carried in the trunk.

**Below**
Key West milemarker

## Driving conditions

Traffic drives on the right. On a multi-lane road, overtaking is permitted on either side although slower-moving traffic should generally keep to the right.

Traffic lights are hung above the centre of the road. If not prohibited by a sign, drivers may turn right on a red light provided they first stop and check that it is safe to do so. When turning left, a green arrow gives right of way; a green light means you may turn but oncoming traffic has right of way. Flashing amber lights indicate proceed but with caution; flashing red lights mean stop and then proceed with caution.

# VISIT FLORIDA™

*"Official Tourism Promotion Corporation for the State of Florida"*

## 24 HOUR CONSUMER INFORMATION LINE
## **09001 600555** (Calls cost 60p per minute)

*TELEPHONE 0207-630-6602  FAX 0207-630-7703  www.flausa.com*

## Insurance

It is extremely important to be adequately insured while driving a rental car. Apart from all-inclusive deals (see *Car hire*), most standard rental agreements include only the legal minimum levels of insurance.

Loss Damage Waiver (LDW) insurance, sometimes called Collision Damage Waiver (CDW), is strongly recommended and covers damage to and theft of your vehicle. Without this, the rental company may impose a very large deposit on the vehicle. Also strongly recommended is Supplementary Liability Insurance (SLI), which raises third-party liability well above the barely adequate legal minimum.

School zones, indicated by road markings and signs, have a marked speed limit when lights are flashing. Yellow school buses drive with flashing yellow lights that change to flashing red when stopping to pick up or drop off. When this happens, vehicles behind the bus must stop and on a two-lane road (if not divided by a central reservation) traffic in both directions must stop.

At four-way stops (signposted as such), vehicles approaching from any direction must stop at the junction and proceed across in order of arrival.

Although Florida is usually warm and sunny, heavy rainstorms can occur with little warning causing visibility to be reduced and road surfaces to become slippery, requiring reduced speed and greater caution than usual.

## Fuel

Petrol stations are plentiful on all but the most remote roads. Many are open around the clock with pumps equipped with credit-card machines enabling payment to be made at the car-side. In others, payment can be made in cash or by credit card at the counter. In a few, pre-payment is necessary. On most pumps, step-by-step instructions are given. Use the pumps labelled 'Self' for self-service, otherwise it will be assumed you require refuelling, an oil-check and a windscreen wash from an attendant.

Petrol in the US is considerably cheaper than in many comparable countries and Florida has some of the lowest petrol prices in the nation.

## Lights

Headlights must be switched on at dusk and during fog or rain. Many rental cars have day-use headlights which automatically come on when the engine is started and operate during daylight at reduced power.

## Parking

Theme parks and major tourist attractions have ample parking space, though many charge up to $5 per car. Make a note of where you are parked (Disney parks provide a ticket with tear-off segment for doing this) to help find the car later. In city centres during weekdays, street parking can be difficult although there is widespread metered parking (often with a time limit) and public car-parks.

Parking is free at shopping malls and supermarkets; many restaurants have parking space for customers. Most hotels and motels have adequate car-parks; parking at bed-and-breakfast inns is sometimes more limited. National and state parks have free car-parks (provided an admission fee is first paid).

**Above**
Key West

When parking during the day, look for a shaded area to prevent the car interior becoming unbearably hot on your return. If you are returning at night, ensure the car is parked in a well-lit area.

## Police

If stopped for a simple mistake while driving, police will probably take a tolerant attitude once it is established you are a tourist. Stupidity, recklessness and drunken driving (*see page 27*) are different matters and may be severely punished. Stop only for marked police or highway patrol vehicles.

## Security

Lock doors and keep windows closed when driving. Do not stop to offer assistance to any motorist who appears to have broken down and do not leave the vehicle if hit from behind (see *Accidents*). Stop only for marked police or highway patrol vehicles which will flag you to a halt with blue and red flashing lights. Park in accessible, well-lit areas. Be suspicious of anyone lingering in a car-park.

## Seat belts

Seat belts must be worn by drivers and front-seat passengers. Children aged four or under must use a child's car seat; those aged four or five must be in a safety seat or wearing a seat belt in the back seat.

## Speed limits

Speed limits, indicated by signs, are usually 15mph to 30mph in towns and 55mph to 70mph on Interstates, which often have a 40mph minimum speed. Other traffic will rarely observe the speed limit but you should: police frequently stop speeding drivers and fines are high. In school zones, indicated by road markings and signs, reduced speed limits are indicated and apply when lights are flashing.

## Tolls

Florida has a few toll roads, particularly around Orlando, and bridges. Tolls are usually 50c–$1.50, more for the long-distance Florida Turnpike according to miles travelled. Tolls are paid at booths; correct change is not necessary.

# Typical road signs in Florida

## INSTRUCTIONS

Stop    Give way    Wrong way - often together with 'No entry' sign    No right turn    No U-turn

  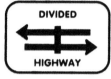  

One-way traffic    Two-way left turn lanes    Divided highway (dual carriageway) at junction ahead    Speed limit signs: maximum and maximum/ minimum limits

## WARNINGS

Crossroads    Junction    Curve (bend)    Winding road

Stop ahead    Two-way traffic    Divided highway (dual carriageway)    Road narrows on right    Roadworks ahead

 Railway crossing     No-overtaking zone

# Getting to Florida

Most visitors from outside the US, and many from within, arrive in Florida by air. None the less, the state is easily accessed by road from the southeastern US (the main Interstates routes being I-10 from Alabama, I-75 and I-95 from Georgia) and by rail with long-distance train services linking Orlando and Miami, and smaller Florida communities, with the major cites of the northeastern US.

## Airports

Although almost every sizeable Florida community has an airport, the chief points of entry for airborne arrivals are Miami, Orlando and Tampa. Sanford (near Orlando) is the point of entry for many British charter operators. International visitors can often continue their journey on a domestic flight at little extra cost on the standard scheduled fare. All American and many major international scheduled airlines serve Florida, as do a number of charter companies.

Major car-hire companies are well represented at most airports and will transport pre-booked customers to their waiting cars. Alternatively, car hire can be arranged on the spot although this can be costlier and more troublesome than pre-booking (see *Driving*).

**Below**
National Museum of Aviation, Pensacola

If arriving during rush hours or during the hours of darkness, it can be sensible to spend a night near the airport and collect your rental car the following day. This is especially true in Miami, where the road system can be confusing and some neighbourhoods are dangerous. Most companies will collect customers from airport area hotels free of charge; many airport hotels will collect guests free of charge from the airport.

Other than rental cars, transport from airports includes taxis and shuttle buses. Public bus services to and from airports are very limited.

### Miami International Airport
Seven miles west of Downtown and 14 miles west of Miami Beach,

Miami International Airport (tel: (305) 876-7000) is Florida's major international airport and an important hub for routes between the US and South and Central America. On arrival passengers may face lengthy queues to clear immigration. The airport is equipped with a wide range of restaurants and shops, including those offering duty-free sales for departing international passengers.

Super Shuttle (tel: (305) 871-2000) is one of several minibus companies operating between the airport and any destination in the city; fares are calculated according to the postal zip code of the destination and are displayed on notice-boards. Public buses also serve the airport but are not recommended for passengers with luggage or anyone unfamiliar with Miami.

Taxis are plentiful and charge a fixed fee (not including tip) to specific destinations. All forms of ground transportation from the airport, including the courtesy buses of car-rental companies and major hotels, can be found directly outside the arrivals area.

### Orlando International Airport

Orlando International Airport (tel: (407) 825-2001) is approximately 9 miles east of International Drive, 13 miles northeast of Kissimmee and 14 miles east of Walt Disney World. Large, modern and exceptionally user-friendly with a full range of facilities, the airport's only drawback is the sheer numbers of passengers who pass through it.

The courtesy buses of car-rental companies and major hotels collect arrivals from the clearly indicated Ground Transportation area, which is also the place to find shuttle buses or taxis. A considerably cheaper (and safer) alternative are the local buses operated by Lynx (tel: (407) 841-8240) between the airport and International Drive, though this option is not well suited to passengers with bulky luggage.

### Tampa International Airport

Serving Tampa and the beaches of the St Petersburg and Clearwater areas, Tampa International Airport (tel: (813) 870-8700) is 6 miles north of Downtown Tampa and 13 miles from the Gulf beaches. A bright and modern airport, Tampa is generally less crowded than Miami and Orlando airports, receiving far fewer international flights.

The courtesy buses of car-rental companies and major hotels collect customers from outside the arrivals area, which is also the departure point for shuttle buses and taxis.

### Sanford International Airport

British charter flights are the only international arrivals at Sanford International Airport (tel: (407) 322-7771), 30 miles north of Orlando and 50 miles southwest of Daytona Beach. The small airport has been tailored to the needs of British holiday-makers. Alamo and Dollar car rental companies have a large reception area directly opposite the terminal; others collect their customers with courtesy buses.

**Above**
The 1740 Castillo de San Marcos,
St Augustine

# Setting the scene

A trendsetter in international tourism, with the world's most advanced theme parks and seemingly endless stretches of sunkissed beach, Florida is also a rapidly expanding and increasingly economically powerful state. Its is fast losing its reputation as a retirement centre, and nowadays enjoys a reputation for the cosmopolitan lifestyles and dynamic multiculturalism epitomised by Miami.

Yet as it embraces the new, Florida also keeps much from the past. The state harbours some of the US's most precious natural areas, and many of the endangered creatures that are distant memories elsewhere are seen here in the wild. Florida history, too, is accessible – Native Americans, European explorers, frontiersmen, millionaires, architects, artists, writers, and all manner of eccentrics have left a mark on this beguiling region.

### The first Floridians

Until they were devastated by European diseases to which they had no immunity, several diverse groups of native people inhabited the area from around 10,000 BC. Traditionally thought to have arrived from the north, recent theories suggest that at least some of these first Floridians originated in Central America and the Caribbean. By around 5000 BC, nomadic hunter-gatherer existence was giving way to semi-permanent settlements, and by the time Europeans arrived, Florida held an estimated 100,000 people split into four geographically distinct main groups – the Apalachee, the Tequesta, the Timucua and the Calusa. Evidence of their existence is provided by archaeological finds, shell mounds and the mysterious ceremonial stones near Crystal River.

### European discovery

Although Florida had been sighted in 1498, it was not until 1513 that a Spaniard, Juan Ponce de León, former governor of Puerto Rico, made the first known European landing. Arriving on Easter Sunday, de León named the land 'La Florida' to mark the Spanish festival Pascua Florida. In search of the fabled 'fountain of youth' and to curry favour with the Spanish king, de León returned to Florida in 1521 with 200 would-be settlers intending to colonise it. The attempt was thwarted by strong native resistance, however, which drove the expedition back to Cuba where de León died from his wounds.

### European exploration and settlement

Subsequent attempts at colonisation also ended dismally for the Spanish, due to native opposition and the treacherous nature of the land. An expedition led by Hernando de Soto, lasting four years and beginning in 1539 with a landing on the west coast (the precise location is unknown but documented by a site at Bradenton), also ended in tragedy but did include the first European sighting of the Mississippi River and provided important written records of Florida at that time.

The arrival of a group of French Huguenots in 1562 and their building of Fort Caroline (near Jacksonville), encouraged the Spanish, fearful of losing their dominance of shipping routes, to renew their interest in Florida. The result was a Spanish massacre of the French and the creation of St Augustine, which became the base for a string of missions established by the Spanish across northern Florida, none of which were particularly successful and none of which survive.

### British Florida
The already weak Spanish mission system in Florida was further undermined by native attack, often encouraged by the British who were now established in American colonies of their own. The British demonstrated their interest in Florida in 1568 when Sir Francis Drake led a bombardment of St Augustine. The 1763 Treaty of Paris, which was intended to end disputes over North America between Britain and France, forced Spain to cede Florida to Britain in return for Havana, Cuba.

### US rule
Although the British began turning Florida into a productive colony, the Spanish regained control in 1783, largely through Britain's all-consuming involvement in the American War of Independence which led to the creation of the self-governing United States of America. Ostensibly to pursue Seminoles (*see below*) alleged to have attacked land owned by US citizens, General Andrew Jackson, later to become US president, made an illegal foray into Florida in 1818, sparking what became the First Seminole War and intentionally destabilising the region's colonial government. As a result, Florida formally become part of the US in 1821.

### The Seminole and Miccosukee
Steadily pushed south from their traditional lands in Alabama, South Carolina and Georgia by European settlers, the Native American Seminole and Miccosukee people (sharing many cultural traits but speaking separate languages) began arriving in Florida during the 18th century. In Florida, too, came conflict between natives and white settlers, sometimes over the former's providing of sanctuary to the escaped slaves of the latter.

When Florida became part of the US, increasing white settlement heightened tensions, as did the US policy of enforced re-settlement of Native Americans to reservations in the American Midwest. Two further Seminole Wars followed. The capture of a celebrated Seminole

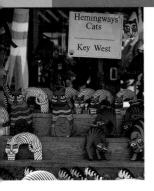

chief, Osceola, in 1837 led to the Seminoles' surrender and the exodus of many Seminoles to Oklahoma. Several hundred, though, remained in Florida and moved into the uninhabited Everglades.

Around 14,000 Seminole and Miccosukee remain in Florida today, many on reservations in the south and central areas of the state. Some Miccosukee remain in the Everglades, living in the traditional open-sided, thatched-roof houses, raised on stilts from the ground, known as 'chickees'.

### The Florida cracker

Some of the most evocative historic homes in Florida are 'cracker cottages', simple wood-framed structures of the mid-1800s to the early 1900s. Designed to make the most of breezes and often built with Dade County pine, a local wood resistant to the termites that ate many early Florida homes, the cottages were occupied by 'crackers', typically rugged and individualistic settlers who forged a living from the land or the sea, or a combination of both, in the days when Florida was still an isolated outpost of the US, barely penetrated by roads or rail. Sometimes used today as a term of abuse to denote an unsophisticated and usually racist white person, the term 'cracker' is of disputed origin but is thought by many to be derived from the crack of the cattle whip used by early settlers.

### Railroads and developers

Apart from a few isolated settlers in the south, Florida's population was, by the late 1800s, concentrated in the north and northern central areas, and mostly concerned with cattle and citrus farming. A few rich tourists, however, were beginning to visit the state, largely for its natural springs. Seeking to turn this trickle into a flood were two millionaire entrepreneurs.

Standard Oil mogul Henry Flagler steadily extended his railroad from Jacksonville to Key West making the state's east coast accessible for the first time, building a series of luxury hotels, creating Palm Beach from scratch and stimulating the growth of Miami. Florida's west coast, meanwhile, was opened up by Henry Plant, who brought his railroad to Tampa, turning a sleepy town into a major port city and paving the way for a cigar industry that brought settlers from Cuba and Europe.

The advent of affordable cars found more Americans vacationing in Florida. In the 1920s, Carl Fisher turned an uninhabited island into Miami Beach, importing its sand and building the hotels that quickly become major tourist magnets, helping cement Miami's soaring reputation as the US's fun and sun capital.

### Walt Disney's World

Florida's emergence as a modern pacesetter in global tourism is largely attributed to Walt Disney. The ground-breaking animator opened his first theme park, Disneyland, in Los Angeles in 1955 only to find that the park's success stymied its growth as non-Disney businesses quickly surrounded the park.

In the 1960s, the Disney Company began secretly purchasing plots of land close to the agricultural town of Orlando. By the time the Magic Kingdom opened in 1971, Walt Disney World, as the area was named, had its own roads, power supply and police force. It expanded with EPCOT Center in 1982, Disney-MGM Studios in 1990, Animal Kingdom in 1998 and a series of smaller recreational areas together with Disney-run hotels, restaurants, and shopping and entertainment areas.

As Walt Disney World put Orlando on the world tourism map, other major attractions such as SeaWorld and Universal Studios arrived, stimulating a statewide tourism boom.

## Florida architecture

Many of Florida's older towns and cities, notably Key West and Fernandina Beach, have large numbers of well-preserved Victorian homes, the decorative carpentry of Queen Anne and Edwardian dwellings highlighting the break from the simplicity of the cracker era (*see opposite*) to reflect increased affluence.

Florida also found itself breaking new ground with luxury hotel architecture. Although put to new uses, those built by Henry Flagler in St Augustine and by Henry Plant in Tampa remain, as do 1920s resort hotels such as the Biltmore in Miami, the Don Cesar in St Petersburg Beach and the Breakers in Palm Beach. Miami Beach gained landmark hotels in the 1940s with the Eden Roc and Fountainbleau as part of the Florida hotel building tradition which continues into the present with the ever-more imaginative hotels of Walt Disney World.

From the 1910s Florida also became dotted with palatial millionaire's homes, often apeing the styles of the most lavish European palaces. Notable survivors include Henry Flagler's Whitehall in Palm Beach, the Ringling Estate in Sarasota and Villa Vizcaya in Miami.

A 1920s land boom encouraged the creation of entire towns in mock-Mediterranean Revival style, demonstrated by Palm Beach and Boca Raton. A decade later, when Miami Beach needed fast and cheap buildings, what is now the celebrated Art Deco District began taking shape.

The re-discovery of its art deco buildings, narrowly escaping demolition and, through the 1980s, given pastel colourings and accentuation of their period details, helped fuel Miami's emergence as a pacesetting style centre. Among Miami's modern landmark buildings was the Atlantis, a much-photographed bayside condominium built with a 'missing' central section occupied by a palm tree and red spiral staircase, designed by the local, world-famous firm of Arquitectonica.

Such innovation was rare, however, in a fast-growing state creating living space with tract housing and providing anodyne chain hotels for tourists. One coastal exception was Seaside, a town begun in 1981 using a mixture of old Florida and traditional New England styles to create wooden homes framed by picket fences and narrow walkways.

### Florida people

The fourth most populous state in the US, Florida's population has been expanding since the 1920s. Of its 13 million people, 85 per cent live in urban areas. Revealing the shift in population from north to south, the state capital, Tallahassee, is located in the Panhandle with a population of just 124,000, while Florida's major city, Miami, holds two million in the state's heavily populated southeast corner.

Traditionally, Florida has attracted retirees, but while they once headed for Miami or St Petersburg they now tend to move to smaller towns in north and central Florida. A growth in white-collar job opportunities has brought many younger settlers from other parts of the US, serving to greatly reduce the average age of Florida residents and spicing up the state's previously staid image.

While most who settle in Florida are US citizens, the state has also gained sizeable ethnic groups, particularly from Central America and the Caribbean. In Miami, over half the population have a mother tongue other than English. Around 300,000 Cubans arrived in Miami during the early 1960s. They and their descendants are now highly influential in the city and beyond. Other Miami communities include significant numbers of Dominicans, Haitians, Jamaicans, Salvadorians and Nicaraguans.

Florida lifestyles range from the urban sophistication of multicultural Miami to the traditional Deep South mood and manners found in the Panhandle, geographically, historically and culturally linked to Alabama and Georgia. Central Florida possesses the state's major theme parks and is the dynamo that drives the state's tourist industry. Yet it also has small towns, some dominated by cattlemen working on the local farmlands and others, such as Micanopy, by the antiques shops in restored Victorian buildings that do most to draw visitors to otherwise forgotten communities.

### Florida at work

With 40 million visitors yearly, tourism is the state's major source of revenue and directly or indirectly employs almost a third of the Florida work force. Other long-established industries include the state's 39,000 farms, predominantly in central Florida's grasslands which raise cattle and thoroughbred horses, and produce 70 per cent of all the citrus fruits sold in the US.

While fishing is a popular recreational pursuit throughout Florida, it is also a major employer in some areas. Shrimp, lobster, oyster, Spanish mackerel and grouper form just part of a catch worth $200 million annually.

Established ports and manufacturing cities such as Tampa and

Jacksonville have thrived and evolved into important financial centres, while a knock-on effect of NASA's presence on the Space Coast has been the rise of electronic and high-tech engineering industries.

## Florida's forests

Around 40 per cent of Florida is covered by forest. Although the state has over 300 tree species, it is various types of pine that predominate, particularly in north and central Florida, and which provide the raw material for the state's sizeable lumber industry. Live oaks are common throughout Florida, as in certain areas are various dogwoods, maples and palms such as cabbage palmetto, sable palm and the majestic royal palm.

Discovering unusual trees can be a highlight of a visit to a natural area. South Florida has the gumbo limbo, strangler fig and the swamp-dwelling bald cypress with its exposed root or 'knee' poking above water. South Florida coastal areas also have the hard-working mangrove, allowing new land to form by collecting debris around its tangle of exposed roots.

## Florida's creatures

Among the immense variety of wildlife that inhabits the state's diverse terrain are several exotic species that are particularly loved, feared or simply fighting for survival as human impact upsets Florida's fragile ecosystems.

Florida's alligators have made a tremendous recovery since being hunted almost out of existence. An estimated two million now inhabit the state's rivers, lakes and swamps. Alligators rarely threaten without being provoked but are known to attack dogs and small children. While alligators are easily found, the same is not true of the Florida panther. Part of the cougar family, the Florida panther chiefly resides in the Everglades but hunts over wide areas. Though once prevalent, mercury contamination of wetlands is thought to have helped reduce numbers to around 30.

In the Florida Keys, Big Pine Key holds around 300 Key deer. This dwarf species of deer, usually reaching just 2ft in height, lives in pine woods but commonly appears in resident's back gardens looking for food. South Florida is the only part of the US where the snail kite survives. This small species of hawk lives only on apple snails, opening their shells with its pointed beak.

Between February and August, five species of sea turtle come ashore to lay their eggs on Florida beaches, the only time the creatures leave the security of the ocean. Just a few of the hundred or so eggs will produce a hatchling that survives to adulthood. Many eggs will be eaten by racoons while young turtles often become fatally disorientated when trying to find their way to the ocean. Guided tours lead visitors to watch the night-time egg-laying.

Florida's warm rivers and springs are ideally suited to the manatee (*see page 155*).

# Highlights

## Two days

Be it history, nature, scenery or theme parks, the drives and walks in this book cover many varied aspects of Florida. Some are especially suited to particular interests, however, and there are those that should not be missed if you only have two days to spare.

From Miami: **The Florida Keys, Key West**
From Orlando: **St Petersburg and its Beaches, The Space Coast**
In northern Florida: **St Augustine, Amelia Island and the Northeast Corner**

## Beaches

**The Space Coast** (*see pages 200–209*)
**The Culture Coast** (*see pages 162–171*)
**The Pensacola area and its beaches** (*see pages 272–281*)
**St Petersburg and its beaches** (*see pages 144–153*)
**From Orlando to Daytona Beach** (*see pages 192–199*)

## Theme parks and major attractions

**Orlando and its theme parks** (*see pages 180–191*))
**The Space Coast** (*see pages 200–209*)
**Tampa** (*see pages 134–143*)

## History

**St Augustine** (*see pages 210–217*)
**Pensacola** (*see pages 264–271*)
**Around Tallahassee: the Old South** (*see pages 236–243*)

## Nature

**South Miami and Everglades National Park** (*see pages 64–73*)
**Coast to coast across the Everglades** (*see pages 114–123*)
**The Space Coast** (*see pages 200–209*)
**Fort Myers and the Lee County Islands** (*see pages 124–133*)

## Children

**South Miami and Everglades National Park** (*see pages 64–73*)
**Orlando and its theme parks** (*see pages 180–191*)
**The Space Coast** (*see pages 200–209*)

## Homes of the rich and famous

Miami Beach (*see pages 42–51*)
Palm Beach (*see pages 86–93*)
The Gold Coast (*see pages 74–85*)
The Culture Coast (*see pages 162–171*)

## Off the beaten track

The Nature Coast and rural Florida (*see pages 154–159*)
Between Tampa and Orlando (*see pages 172–179*)
Tallahassee to the Forgotten Coast (*see pages 244–253*)

## Small towns

The Nature Coast and rural Florida (*see pages 154–159*)
Tallahassee to the Forgotten Coast (*see pages 244–253*)
Crossing the Panhandle (*see pages 254–263*)
From Orlando to Daytona Beach (*see pages 192–199*)

**Below**
Walt Disney World:
Magic Kingdom

# Miami Beach

### Ratings

| | |
|---|---|
| Architecture | ●●●●● |
| Beaches | ●●●●● |
| Nightlife | ●●●●● |
| Food | ●●●●○ |
| Outdoor activities | ●●●●○ |
| History | ●●●○○ |
| Museums | ●●●○○ |
| Art | ●●○○○ |

**L**ong and slender Miami Beach has 7 miles of beach and several distinctive neighbourhoods, but the place everybody wants to see is super-chic South Beach, home of the wonderful Art Deco District. The visual appeal of the art deco buildings made the area a venue for fashion shoots and TV commercials in the 1980s, stimulating the interest that quickly turned this once neglected quarter of Miami into a buzzing place-to-be, with recording studios, model agencies, trendy cafés and celebrity-owned nightclubs catering to the style-conscious rock, film and fashion superstars who arrived to sample the South Beach vibe.

Yet as trendy as it is, South Beach has plenty to offer even the most unfashionable visitor. Good-value hotels and restaurants abound, the beach and the art deco buildings really are stunning, there are several classy museums and the vibrant atmosphere is enhanced by warm ocean breezes rustling the palm trees.

## Sights

ⓘ **Art Deco Welcome Center**
*1001 Ocean Drive; tel: (305) 672-2014. Open daily 1100–2100.*

**Miami Beach Chamber of Commerce** *1920 Meridian Avenue; tel: (305) 672 1270. Open Mon–Fri 0900–1700, Sat 1000–1600.*

**Art Deco District***
The 16 blocks of shops, apartments, single-storey homes and hotels in the heart of Miami Beach that display the distinctly American Streamline Moderne form of art deco design, based on the geometric ideas underpinning car, plane and ship design, were the result of fast and cheap building during the 1920s and 1930s. Narrowly escaping demolition in the late 1970s, many of the buildings acquired pastel colours and neon illumination through the 1980s and became the favoured backdrop for fashion photographers. Joined by a batch of new buildings in similar style, they became part of the unmistakable Miami Beach look.

Some of the best examples are the hotels on Ocean Drive, such as the **Breakwater**, the **Cardozo**, **Park Central** and **Waldorf Towers**, with its imitation lighthouse topping one corner. The **Leslie** is one of the more lauded attempts to turn an art deco original into an emblem

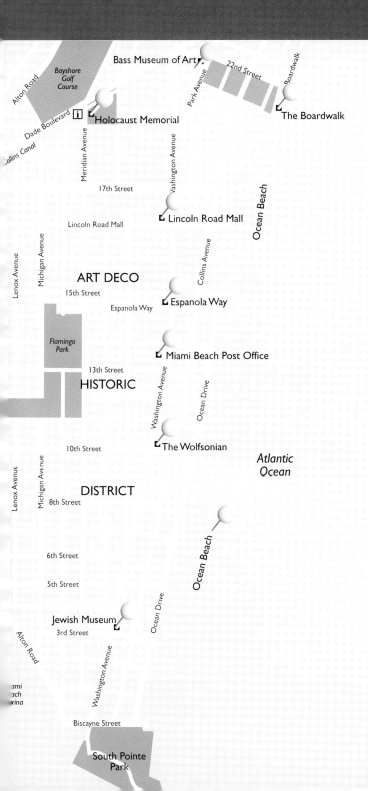

Alton Road

Bayshore
Golf
Course

Bass Museum of Art

Park Avenue

22nd Street

Boardwalk

Dade Boulevard

i

Holocaust Memorial

The Boardwalk

Collins Canal

Meridian Avenue

Washington Avenue

17th Street

Lincoln Road Mall

Ocean Beach

Lincoln Road Mall

Lenox Avenue

Michigan Avenue

ART DECO

Collins Avenue

15th Street

Espanola Way

Espanola Way

Flamingo
Park

13th Street

Miami Beach Post Office

HISTORIC

Washington Avenue

Ocean Drive

10th Street

The Wolfsonian

Atlantic
Ocean

Lenox Avenue

Michigan Avenue

DISTRICT

8th Street

6th Street

Ocean Beach

5th Street

Jewish Museum

Ocean Drive

3rd Street

Alton Road

ami
ach
rina

Washington Avenue

Biscayne Street

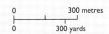

South Pointe
Park

**Art Deco District tours** Immensely informative 90-minute guided tours ($) of the Art Deco District begin at the Art Deco Welcome Center (see page 42) on Saturdays at 1030 and Thursdays at 1830. Bicycle tours ($) of the same area take place on the first and third Sunday of the month from the Miami Beach Bicycle Center, 601 5th Street; tel: (305) 674-0159.

**Art Deco Weekend** A weekend each January is devoted to the celebration of the district's architecture with lectures and many other special events.

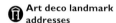

**Art deco landmark addresses**

**Breakwater** 940 Ocean Drive.

**Cameo Theater** 1445 Washington Avenue.

**Cardozo** 1300 Ocean Drive.

**Colony Theater** 1040 Lincoln Road.

**Delano** 1685 Collins Avenue.

**The Leslie** 1244 Ocean Drive.

**Lincoln Theater** 555 Lincoln Road.

**Park Central** 640 Ocean Drive.

**Shelbourne** 1801 Collins Avenue.

**Sterling Building** 810 Lincoln Road.

**Waldorf Towers** 850 Ocean Drive.

of 1990s Miami Beach. Along Collins Avenue are the towering **Delano** and **Shelbourne**, while Washington Avenue highlights include the **Cameo Theater** and the **Post Office** (see page 47).

Throughout the district, you need do no more than stroll to discover many art deco features such as porthole windows and imitation ships' funnels used to disguise rooftop storage tanks, and the Florida motifs such as sunburst friezes and pelican-decorated wrought-iron gates.

**Bass Museum of Art**✦✦

Among the more individual of Miami Beach's early art deco landmarks was the coral rock building adorned with Mayan motifs and bas-reliefs that once held the public library and is now the home of the Bass Museum of Art. The museum provides a welcome chance to escape the sun and ogle what is among the foremost art collections in the state, always bolstered by temporary exhibitions, usually on contemporary themes.

The museum's permanent holdings stem from a private collection of European art. While major names such as Rubens and Sir Thomas Lawrence are represented, the stand-out canvases tend to be from lesser-known names such as artist Marcellus Kofferman, notably with his *Holy Family*, and the Dutch artist Cornelis Cornelisz van Haarlem, whose intense *Crucifixion Triptych* occupies the centre of one gallery. *The Tournament*, a 16th-century tapestry created by the Flemish School, also captures the imagination.

**Beaches**✦✦✦

Some of the world's finest physiques can be seen tanning on the golden sands at Miami Beach. Seven miles long and in places 100yds wide, it is very much the focal point of daytime activity. Hit the sands shortly after dawn and you might also spot fashion-model photo shoots, commercials or music videos being filmed with the Art Deco District as a backdrop before the sunlight becomes too intense and the crowds too large.

It may be a surprise to learn that the beach is not natural but stemmed from an unlikely alliance between a Quaker farmer, who settled here in 1907, and developer Carl Fisher. They devised a scheme to plant palm trees and bring sand to what was then a swamp-filled island. Incredibly, Miami Beach became America's vacation capital by the 1920s.

The sand (often replaced following major storms) is pleasantly soft underfoot and uniformly yellow but the beach's social mixture is more varied. Around 1st Street would-be surfers lament the (usual) lack of suitable waves; the 21st Street area is predominantly gay; further north, is the rugged vegetated **Haulover Beach Park**.

Miami Beach as the world knows it, however, is between 5th and 18th streets, around **Lummus Park**. This is the place to work on your tan or simply admire everybody else's, take dips in the ocean watched by life-guards from the historic art deco life-guard station opposite 11th Street or simply laze in the sun as the music spills over from the bars across Ocean Drive. Incidentally, this in one of few places in the US where topless bathing is tolerated.

### The Boardwalk**

Formed of raised wooden planks and accessed from most adjoining streets, the Boardwalk lies between 21st and 46th streets carrying walkers and joggers along the beach's edge. There are rest points with shady seats and pathways providing access to several hotels noted for their architectural excesses, such as the Fontainebleau and the Eden Roc, and open-air bars tempting Boardwalk users with ice-cold drinks.

### Española Way*

Created in 1925, two-block-long Española Way has the barrel-tiled roofs, bell towers and striped awnings of a Mediterranean village that derive from the designer's plan to re-create a European artists' colony. In keeping with its would-be artistic heritage, Española Way has commercial art galleries and small apartments on its upper floors that property brokers describe as 'artists lofts' in the hope of selling them.

On the corner with Washington Avenue, the **Clay Hotel** was a popular nightspot during the 1930s. It was here that Cuban band leader Desi Arnaz helped create the rumba craze that spread across the US. Arnez is perhaps better remembered as the real-life husband of comedienne Lucille Ball, and her partner in the *I Love Lucy* TV series.

**Below**
Art deco landmark: The Leslie, at 1244 Ocean Drive

## Holocaust Memorial❖❖

Miami Beach has one of the world's largest communities of holocaust survivors and in 1990 gained a lasting memorial to the atrocities of the Nazi era with this affecting work by Kenneth Treister.

The memorial begins with a historical display on Jews in Europe, leading up to the rise of anti-Semitism in Germany. Visitors continue along the Lonely Path and through a tunnel, symbolising an individual's loss of identity and marked with the names of concentration camps, into the heart of the memorial. Here, a 42-ft-high bronze arm, etched with a concentration camp tattoo, reaches forever upward in a forlorn attempt to reach freedom. In the foreground many individual figures, contorted and bearing expressions of horror and torment, surround the visitor.

Although reactions to the memorial have been mixed, for many it is an emotionally draining experience. The final section, the Reflective Pool, provides an area of calmness, a chance to gather thoughts while gazing across a lily-decorated pond.

🛈 **Holocaust Memorial**
*1933–1945 Meridian Avenue; tel: (305) 538-1663. Open daily 0900–2100.*

**South Florida Arts Center** *810 Lincoln Road.* Individual studios keep own times; see notice board in entrance for details.

## Lincoln Road Mall❖

Packed with clothing and jewellery stores, Lincoln Road was labelled the 'Fifth Avenue of the South', a comparison with the fashionable shopping strip of New York, during the booming 1950s. After years of decline, the area is again on the rise with a pedestrianised section that has become a thriving centre of creativity and culture.

Sidewalk restaurants give the area further appeal, as do the excellent restoration of art deco buildings such as the **Colony Theater** and the **Lincoln Cinema**, both performing arts venues, and the impossibly long and slender **Sterling Building**. The latter is partly occupied by the **South Florida Arts Center**, created in the 1980s to provide studios and exhibition space for contemporary artists, many of whom display their work during weekends and evenings.

**Miami Beach Post Office** *1300 Washington Avenue. Open Mon–Fri 0600–1800, Sat 0600–1600.*

**Sanford L Ziff Jewish Museum of Florida $$** *301 Washington Avenue. Open Tue–Sun 1000–1700.*

**The Wolfsonian $$** *(free Thur evenings) 1001 Washington Avenue. Open Tue–Sat 1000–1800, Thur until 2100, Sun 1200–1700.*

## Miami Beach Post Office**

The 1939 Miami Beach Post Office is a splendidly restored example of deco federal, an architectural style that evolved during the federal-government building programme of the Depression. Classical motifs and subdued decoration distinguish the post office from the neighbouring art deco buildings. Within the rotunda, housing the public area, are original stamp tables and mail boxes; an eye-catching mural by Charles Hardin showing scenes of Cavalry and Indians fills one wall.

## Sanford L Ziff Jewish Museum of Florida*

'Always a view, never a Jew' was one marketing slogan used by hotels in Miami Beach during the 1930s, a period when anti-Semitism forced local Jewish people to have homes only in the area south of 5th Street. Such prejudice is one issue documented by the exhibitions of this museum, housed in a 1936 synagogue designed by art deco luminary Harry Hohauser. The influx of European Jews into Miami Beach during the 1940s following the rise of Nazism and anti-Semitism led to the election of Miami Beach's first Jewish mayor in 1943.

The core exhibits are drawn from the Mosaic project, created in 1984 to travel through Florida charting the state's Jewish communities and gather items of historical interest. Objects such as a shell-covered dress made for a Purim party in Jacksonville in 1916, a Florida citrus label in Hebrew, items from Cuban Jews who arrived following the Castro-led revolution, and countless family and business photos make for engrossing browsing.

The building itself is a bonus. The loss of its congregation as the population moved north through the 1940s, and damage inflicted by Hurricane Andrew in 1992 led to a two-year restoration project that returned this art deco landmark to its former glory.

## The Wolfsonian**

The son of the first Jewish mayor of Miami Beach, Mitchell Wolfson Jnr stored his expanding collection of items of design interest in a warehouse, until he decided to cut his losses on storage charges and buy the building. Now simply called the Wolfsonian, this fine museum is also a research centre devoted to the study of objects and their social and political context.

With ceramics, books, posters, paintings, industrial items and much more, the permanent collection includes 70,000 articles, mostly from the late-19th to mid-20th centuries. Selections are displayed to illustrate a particular theme and might feature anything from 1920s art deco ashtrays to 1960s experimental kitchens.

The first exhibit, however, is the 1927 Mediterranean-style building itself, its entrance decorated by Spanish-style bas-reliefs. Immediately inside are the stained-glass windows and green and gold terracotta façade salvaged from a 1929 theatre in Philadelphia.

**Above left**
Miami Beach Holocaust Memorial

# Accommodation and food

Miami Beach's many hotels range from the decadently appointed lodgings at fashion's cutting edge to plain and simple rooms ideal for those on a budget but with a hankering to be near the action. Food is no less varied and plentiful, with Cuban cuisine particularly worth sampling.

**Clay Hotel $** *1438 Washington Avenue; tel: (305) 534-2988 or (800) 379-CLAY.* A landmark on the corner with Española Way, the Clay holds the local youth hostel and also offers private rooms at extremely good rates.

**Delano $$$** *1685 Collins Avenue; tel: (305) 672-2000 or (800) 555-5001.* Devilishly trendy and wickedly expensive, the Phillipe Starck-designed interiors draw ultra-fashionable faces from around the world.

**Indian Creek Hotel $$** *2727 Indian Creek Drive; tel: (305) 531-2727 or (800) 491-2772.* Authentically restored to its 1936 appearance, the lobby makes a winning first impression; the inviting atmosphere and friendly staff make amends for the nice but slightly small rooms.

**Park Central $$** *640 Ocean Drive; tel: (305) 538-1611 or (800) 727-5236.* Once a favourite of gangster Al Capone, it has been renovated to bring out the best of its art deco features. Comfortable rooms, some with a fine view of the beach.

**Raleigh $$$** *1775 Collins Avenue; tel: (305) 634-6300 or (800) 848-1775.* Art deco landmark given a post-modern restyling to please a discerning, and very chic, clientele.

**Larios on the Beach** $$ *820 Ocean Drive; tel: (305) 532-9577.* Serves mouth-watering Cuban fare and, on Saturday nights, is enlivened by a Cuban band encouraging impromptu dancing.

**News Café** $ *800 Ocean Drive; tel: (305) 538-6397.* With a few tables and a small menu of classy fare, this round-the-clock eatery has been the place to see and be seen for years.

**Pan Coast Café** $$–$$$ *At the Indian Creek Hotel, 2727 Indian Creek Drive; tel: (305) 531-2727.* Make a reservation because this small dining space has a very popular Caribbean/Pan-Asian menu that changes twice weekly.

**Publix** $ *1046 Dade Boulevard; tel: (305) 534-4621.* Small food shops are found all over Miami Beach but this enormous supermarket not only has the lowest prices but incredible 1960s architecture.

**Van Dyke Café** $ *846 Lincoln Road; tel: (305) 534-3600.* Excellent for people-watching while munching on king-sized sandwiches or other inexpensive dishes.

**Yuca** $$$ *501 Lincoln Road; tel: (305) 532-9822.* Nuevo-Cuban cuisine took off in Miami largely thanks to this restaurant which is still earning rave reviews after several years.

# Nightlife

South Beach is the vibrant heart of Miami's nightlife, whether for Cuban music, trendy nightclubs or just bars with original art deco furniture. Read the free *New Times* for the latest happening places. The in-vogue spots may not operate a dress code but do have a simple fame code: if you lack it, you won't get in. The long-running bars and clubs listed below, however, generally have a more tolerant policy towards unknown faces.

**Abbey Brewing Company** *1115 16th Street; tel (305) 538-8110.* Small bar with a variety of independently brewed ales and a convivial atmosphere.

**Bash** $$ *655 Washington Avenue; tel (305) 538-2274.* Local boy Mickey Rourke is one of the celebrities who co-own this perennially popular nightspot; less trendy than it once was.

**Clevelander** *1020 Ocean Drive; tel (305) 531-3485.* Open-air hotel bar with regular live music at night and during weekend afternoons.

**Club Deuce** $$ *222 14th Street; tel (305) 673-9537.* A bizarre mix of locals, tourists, drag queens and cops frequent this likeably scruffy neighbourhood bar.

**Groove Jet** $$ *323 23rd Street; tel (305) 532-2000.* Good dance sounds and a lively atmosphere attract many South Beach faces.

# Suggested tour

**P** Parking is difficult and expensive throughout Miami Beach, although there is metered parking along many streets. Traffic is particularly heavy at weekends. Many hotels have parking areas for guest use. If you are arriving from elsewhere in Miami, it is worth while checking local bus routes (mostly good) to avoid parking problems. As in the rest of Miami, buses have a flat-fare and correct change is necessary. If requested, drivers issue free transfers.

**Length**: Main tour 1 mile; with both detours, 4.5 miles. Buses are frequent along Washington Boulevard and can be used as a supplement to the walking tour.

**Duration**: Half a day is sufficient for a good sampling of the Art Deco District but allow a full day to cover the main tour and one or both detours, and to pause for meals and refreshments. Parking is difficult and traffic can be heavy, particularly at weekends.

**Links**: Using any of the causeways joining Miami Beach to mainland Miami, this route links easily with Miami (*see pages 52–63*). Heading north, the coastal Hwy-A1A continues for 23 miles and makes a scenic link to The Gold Coast (*see pages 74–85*).

The **ART DECO DISTRICT ❶** is most impressively revealed by the hotels on Ocean Drive between 14th and 5th streets. While exploring these seductive few blocks, make a point of calling into the **Art Deco Welcome Center ❷** on the beach facing 12th Street. From here, continue two blocks inland along 12th Street for the **MIAMI BEACH POST OFFICE ❸** on Washington Avenue. The immediate area is lined with interesting shops and small restaurants and cafés. A short stroll north is **ESPAÑOLA WAY ❹**, between 14th and 15th streets. Continue north on Washington Avenue to **LINCOLN ROAD MALL ❺** and another inviting spot for lunch or a snack.

**Detour**: Two blocks south on Washington Avenue from the Post Office, the imposing façade of the **WOLFSONIAN ❻** marks the junction with 10th Street. Continuing south, crossing the major traffic artery of 5th Street, leads into a largely residential area and finds the **JEWISH MUSEUM ❼** on the corner with 3rd Street.

**Detour**: While exploring Lincoln Road, turn northwards along Meridian Boulevard for the **HOLOCAUST MEMORIAL ❽**, three blocks ahead just before the junction with the busy Dade Boulevard. Return to stroll the rest of Lincoln Road and turn north along Washington Avenue, noting the impressive profile of the Delano hotel beside the ocean at the eastern end of 17th Street. Passing the enormous Miami Beach Convention Center, Park Avenue forks to the right off Washington Boulevard to the **BASS MUSEUM OF ART ❾**. Cross the museum's sculpture-decorated gardens and turn right along 22nd Street for the southern end of the **BOARDWALK ❿**, continuing to 46th Street.

## Also worth exploring

At the southern tip of Miami Beach, the well-kept trees and lawns of the 17-acre **South Pointe Park** provide a respite from the crowds that mill through much of South Beach. Here, the calm is usually disturbed only by the bluster of ocean breezes and the crashing of waves against the shoreline as cruise ships and cargo vessels move through the slender Government Cut, a channel dredged in the 1970s to provide smooth passage between the Port of Miami and the Atlantic.

Placed at intervals beside the winding pathways are benches perfect for picnics and ship-watching. Walk to the west edge of the park to admire the pricey private yachts moored at the marina. The park bandshell sometimes hosts concerts.

# Miami: the City

**Ratings**

| | |
|---|---|
| Architecture | ●●●● |
| Children | ●●●● |
| History | ●●●● |
| Nature | ●●● |
| Shopping | ●●● |
| Beaches | ●● |
| Museums | ●● |
| Scenery | ●● |

**M**iami Beach steals the show but there is much more in this fast-growing city than art deco architecture, scantily clad roller-bladers and swathes of crowded beach. Scattered throughout are distinctive neighbourhoods, such as the sedate Mediterranean-style Coral Gables and fashionable Coconut Grove, that have long been cities in their own right. Meanwhile, even the briefest look around Little Havana reveals the strongly Latin-American element in a city where around half the population is Cuban or of Cuban descent.

For beach lovers, Key Biscayne has miles of tempting sand where tourists are usually outnumbered by locals and neither are much in evidence during the working week, making this a perfect retreat for beachcombers and hopeless romantics. One-of-a-kind sights include the immeasurably grand Vizcaya and a misplaced 12th-century Spanish monastery. More predictable but none the less excellent stops are the Metrozoo and Seaquarium. City driving on generally easily navigated freeways and local roads is simple if unspectacular.

## Sights

**ⓘ Greater Miami Convention & Visitors Bureau** *701 Brickell Avenue, Suite 2700; tel: (305) 539-3064. Open daily 0830–1700; web site: www.miamiandbeaches.com*

**🏠 The Barnacle $** *3485 Main Highway; tel: (305) 448-9445. Tours Fri–Sun 1000, 1100, 1330, 1400.*

**Bayside Marketplace\***
Though no more than a collection of shops, Bayfront Marketplace is a surprisingly enjoyable place to pass an hour. Besides the obvious opportunities for buying and browsing – the stores sell everything from luggage and books to lingerie and gourmet chocolate – the walkways are pleasantly shady with views of the Downtown skyline and Biscayne Bay. Live music and other entertainment is common and there are several restaurants and a large food court.

**The Barnacle\*\***
One of Miami's earliest and most ingeniously designed homes, the Barnacle was erected by Massachusetts-born yacht builder Ralph Middleton Monroe in 1891. Monroe purchased 40 acres of bayside land in Coconut Grove, which at that time lacked even a road link with the separate community of Miami, and created the Barnacle from wood salvaged from shipwrecks.

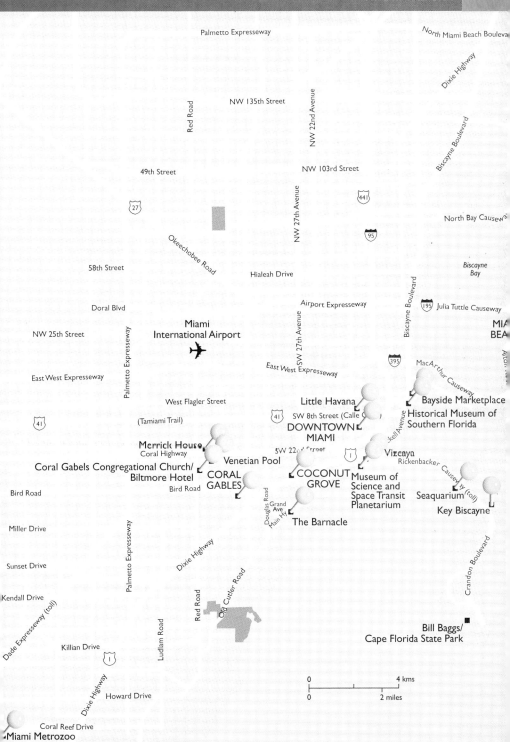

Palmetto Expresseway

North Miami Beach Bouleva

Dixie Highway

NW 135th Street

Red Road

NW 22nd Avenue

Biscayne Boulevard

NW 103rd Street

49th Street

NW 27th Avenue

27

441

North Bay Causew

95

Okeechobee Road

58th Street

Biscayne Bay

Hialeah Drive

Doral Blvd

Airport Expresseway

Biscayne Boulevard

195 Julia Tuttle Causeway

NW 25th Street

MIA
BEA

Palmetto Expresseway

SW 27th Avenue

Miami
International Airport

✈

East West Expresseway

East West Expresseway

395

MacArthur Causeway

Aton n

West Flagler Street

Little Havana

Bayside Marketplace

41

SW 8th Street (Calle

Historical Museum of
Southern Florida

(Tamiami Trail)

DOWNTOWN
MIAMI

Brickell Avenue

Merrick House

Coral Highway

SW 22nd Street

Vizcaya

Rickenbacker Causeway (toll)

Coral Gabels Congregational Church/
Biltmore Hotel

Venetian Pool

1

CORAL
GABLES

COCONUT
GROVE

Museum of
Science and
Space Transit
Planetarium

Seaquarium

Bird Road

Bird Road

Douglas Road

Grand
Ave

Key Biscayne

Miller Drive

Main Hy

The Barnacle

Sunset Drive

Dixie Highway

Crandon Boulevard

Kendall Drive

Red Road

Old Cutler Road

Dade Expresseway (toll)

Palmetto Expresseway

Killian Drive

1

Bill Baggs/
Cape Florida State Park

Ludlam Road

Dixie Highway

Howard Drive

| 0 | | 4 kms |
|---|---|---|
| 0 | | 2 miles |

Coral Reef Drive

Miami Metrozoo

**The Biltmore** *1200 Anastasia Avenue; tel: (305) 445-1926. Guided tours Sun 1330, 1430, 1530.*

**Coconut Grove Chamber of Commerce** *Peacock Park, beside MacFarlane Road; tel: (305) 444-7270. Open Mon–Fri 0900–1700.*

**Miami City Hall** *3500 Pan American Drive; tel: (305) 250-5300. Open Mon–Fri 0800–1700.*

To improve air circulation and avoid flooding, he raised the house 8ft above ground, vented the roof and covered the porch to enable windows to be opened during storms. These and a host of other unique features made life bearable in the heat and humidity of the south Florida summer. Monroe continued to be inventive when his family expanded. Rather than build a new house, he simply raised the Barnacle and slid in a new storey underneath.

The fine points are revealed on the guided tour, the only way to see inside the Barnacle and discover the wonderful collection of Monroe memorabilia, including photos of early Coconut Grove luminaries.

### The Biltmore❖❖

Its elegant wings brought together by a 315-ft-tall tower, loosely modelled on the Giralda in Spain, and surrounded by palm trees, the Mediterranean-style Biltmore hotel oozes luxury from every stone. Architects Schultze & Weaver, better known for Manhattan's renowned Waldorf Astoria, gave the hotel crystal chandeliers, custom-loomed rugs and a lobby ceiling decorated with gold leaf to reflect the flames from over-sized fireplaces.

Completed in 1926, the Biltmore's first guests, including Judy Garland and the Duke and Duchess of Windsor, amused themselves in the hotel grounds with tennis, golf, fox-hunting or rides along mock-Venetian canals in mock-Venetian gondolas. Yet the Biltmore's glory days were short. A hurricane and financial disaster hit Miami just months after the hotel opened. It became a military hospital in 1942 and was empty for 20 years before undergoing a $5-million renovation and re-opening in 1993.

Entering the lobby of the hotel, marketed as 'the last word in civilisation', reveals leering gargoyles above the staircases, the chirping of caged birds, and a terrace loggia with views across the golf course. Don't leave without seeing the pool where guests were once coached by Johnny Weissmuller, Olympic champion and future Hollywood *Tarzan*, who broke his first swimming record here in the 1920s.

### Coconut Grove❖❖

Smart art galleries, trendy shops and some of Miami's most expensive apartments are all features of Coconut Grove. One of Miami's oldest areas, it was settled in the 1840s by Bahamians who salvaged shipwrecks, and later by New Englanders, such as Charles and Isabel Peacock who opened Miami's first hotel on what is now Peacock Park.

The heart of Coconut Grove is around the junction of Main Highway and McFarlane Road, where the **CocoWalk** is a popular grouping of shops, cinemas and restaurants. The sloping, tree-lined **Peacock Park** is the venue of numerous well-attended festivals and brings views of the Dinner Key marina, where Coconut Grovers tether their yachts. The Streamline Moderne structure beside the key was once the terminal for PanAm's seaplane service to Latin America. The modest size of the building makes it hard to believe that it is now **Miami City Hall**.

**Plymouth Congregational Church** 3429 Devon Road; tel: (305) 444-6521. Open usually Mon–Fri 0830–1600.

**Coral Gables City Hall** 405 Biltmore Avenue; tel: (305) 446-6800. Public areas open Mon–Fri 0900–1700. Closed holidays.

**Coral Gables Chamber of Commerce** 50 Aragon Avenue; tel: (305) 446-1657. Open Mon–Fri 0830–1700.

**Plymouth Congregational Church** is another link with Coconut Grove's past. Built with mock medieval features and a 400-year-old door from a Pyrenean monastery, by a single Spanish mason, the church was completed in 1917.

**Right**
Coral Gables: the Biltmore Hotel

### Coral Gables✦✦✦

Coral Gables is a 12-square-mile enclave of Miami with an appearance and character all its own. Dotted by Mediterranean-style fountains and plazas, bisected by quiet leafy streets lined by stucco-fronted homes and claiming some of Miami's most attractive buildings, Coral Gables was conceived in the 1920s by George Merrick, son of a local farmer, and marketed with the most expensive advertising campaign then known. It is a tribute to Merrick, and a 1970s conservation plan, that Coral Gables today probably looks as good as it ever did.

The commercial centre-piece is the **Miracle Mile**, lined by chic boutiques, and antiques and bridal shops. The western end is anchored by **Coral Gables City Hall**, with 12 columns fronting a semicircular rotunda topped by a three-tier clock tower. Inside, items from Coral Gables' history line narrow corridors while the interior of the dome carries a mural by Denman Fink, an artist who worked closely with Merrick.

### Coral Gables Congregational Church*

This sturdy Mediterranean-Revival church stands on land donated by George Merrick (*see Coral Gables, page 55*) and was completed in 1924. It is claimed that some of the interior wood furnishings date from the 16th century and were recovered from shipwrecks.

### Downtown Miami*

Bustling by day and deserted by night, Downtown Miami has little to merit a lengthy stop save for the exhibits of the Historical Museum of Southern Florida (*see below*). The museum occupies one side of the 1980s Philip Johnson-designed **Miami-Dade Cultural Center**, facing the city's main library and the Center for Fine Arts. Much of the rest of Downtown is a conglomeration of jewellery and electrical shops, many of its customers on shopping trips from Latin America. One enjoyable way to view Downtown is from the **Metromover**, which navigates a circular route just above the rooftops.

### Historical Museum of South Florida**

This small museum does a fine job in weaving together the diverse strands that underpinned South Florida's rise from mosquito-infested outpost to the US's fastest-growing region inside 80 years.

**Above**
The Coral Gables
Congregational Church

**Bill Baggs Cape Florida State Park**
$ 1200 S Crandon Boulevard; tel: (305) 361-5811. Open daily 0800–sunset; lighthouse tours Wed–Sun 0900, 1030, 1300, 1430, 1530.

Except for decimating the indigenous Tequesta people, the 16th-century Spanish who colonised other parts of Florida made little headway here. Not until the mid-19th century, when Key West boomed as a salvaging centre for shipwrecks and gained a cigar industry, was there major economic expansion. Displays and re-created buildings record the first boom era.

Another re-creation is of a 'chickee', a type of raised, open-sided hut used by Seminoles, a Native American group forced into the Everglades (where many still remain) by the 19th-century Seminole Wars. Inside are items describing traditional handicrafts and lifestyles.

Miami's inexorable rise, stimulated by oil tycoon Henry Flagler extending his east-coast railway to the newly emerging city in 1896, is charted by engrossing posters, photos and other artefacts, as is the 1920s property boom and the creation of Miami Beach. A segregated tram from 1925 provides a reminder of Miami's ethnic divisions.

The impact of Cubans in shaping Miami, of TV's *Miami Vice* in changing perceptions of it, the restoration of the Art Deco District and the devastation of 1992's Hurricane Andrew are among exhibits detailing more recent times.

### Key Biscayne**

Key Biscayne is a desirable Miami address and the very tidy residential section is bordered by two of the city's most attractive natural areas. A 3-mile-long beach fringes **Crandon Beach Park**, lining a patch of shallow and very calm water. Until they were destroyed by Hurricane Andrew in 1992, rows of Australian pines added to the beauty of the setting. Despite the lack of shade, the park remains a popular venue for weekend barbecues.

Also much depleted by Hurricane Andrew, **Bill Baggs Cape Florida State Recreation Area** is crisscrossed by footpaths and has a boardwalk beside its inviting beach. Another draw is the **Cape Florida lighthouse**. Decommissioned in 1978, the lighthouse's fascinating history stretches back to the Civil and Seminole wars and is described on guided tours.

### Little Havana**

Historically strong links between Florida and Cuba became firmer still when Miami became the point of arrival for approximately 300,000 Cubans fleeing the Caribbean island following the 1959 revolution. Many settled in what became Little Havana until their increasing prosperity financed a relocation to larger homes across the city. The humble dwellings here now accommodate 1970s and 1980s arrivals from strife-torn South and Central American countries.

Totems of Cuban culture predominate along **Calle Ocho** (SW 8th Street). Street counters dispense shots of sweet and strong *café Cubano*, Cuban men play dominoes in **Máximo Gómez Park**, and the eternal flame of the **Brigade 2056 Memorial** remembers those killed in the

**ⓘ Merrick House $**
907 Coral Way; tel
(305) 460-536. Open Sun
1300–1600; or by
appointment.

**Metrozoo $$** 12400 SW
152nd Street; tel: (305)
251-0400. Open daily
0930–1730.

**Museum of Science and
Space Transit
Planetarium $$** 3280 S
Miami Avenue; tel: (305)
645-4247. Open daily
1000–1800.

**Seaquarium $$** 4400
Rickenbacker Causeway; tel:
(305) 361-5705. Open daily
0930–1800.

1963 attempt to re-take Cuba by force which floundered at the Bay of Pigs. Close by are tributes to 19th-century Cuban heroes such as José Martí and Antonio Maceo.

## Merrick House✦✦

Coral Gables (*see page 55*) took its name from the boyhood home of its creator George Merrick, so-named for the coral rock used in its construction and its gabled roof. The Merrick house stood at the heart of the 160-acre citrus and vegetable farm, developed by George's father, on which the city arose. An introductory video tells the extraordinary story of Merrick and the Coral Gables he created before the guided tour continues around the house, highlighting design features and oddities such as the amusingly amateurish paintings by George's mother.

## Metrozoo✦✦

White Bengal tigers prowling a re-created Khymer temple and a pair of komodo dragons, the world's most powerful lizard and rarely seen outside its native Indonesia, are among the most photographed inhabitants of the 290-acre Miami's Metrozoo. Moats rather than bars divide animals and humans, and a full circuit of the 3 miles of pathways (a monorail allows short cuts) should bring sightings of giraffes, zebras, gazelles, ostriches, rhinos, bears, and lots more.

Cleverly constructed artificial tunnels and caves enable many creatures to be observed at close quarters. The koalas and other cuddly creatures are perennial child pleasures, as are the elephant rides offered in PAWS, the children's section of the zoo.

## Museum of Science and Space Transit Planetarium✦✦

Entertaining, interactive, multimedia exhibits make this an enjoyable place for kids to experiment with perspective, gravity, light and other scientific fundamentals, while exhibits describe Everglades' wildlife and invite visitors to shoot cyber hoops on a virtual reality basketball court.

There is more to enjoy in the Wildlife Center, where owls, hawks and falcons are among the creatures being nursed after sustaining injuries in the wild. Other menagerie members include tortoises, tarantulas and turkey vultures. Mounted insects and butterflies can be seen in the Collection Gallery, arranged beneath several somewhat morbid rows of animal skulls.

## Seaquarium✦

Touted as the home of TV's *Flipper*, the Seaquarium's shows demonstrate the abilities of dolphins and killer whales to respond to their trainers and entertain crowds. Elsewhere are pools of sharks, seals, sea lions, stingrays and manatees, an ungainly but much-loved creature found in Florida's waters. Alligators can also be seen, as can the much rarer American crocodile.

### Venetian Pool $
*2701 De Soto Boulevard; tel: (305) 460-5356. Open Tue–Fri 1100–1730. Sat–Sun 1000–1630.*

### Vizcaya $$ *3521 S Miami Avenue; tel: (305) 250-9133. Open daily 0930–1730.*

## Venetian Pool**

Few public swimming-pools can match the grandeur of the 1924 Venetian Pool or provide an excuse to swim and sightsee at the same time. Ingeniously conceived to fill a quarry that provided the rock used in the building of Coral Gables, the pool maintains the Mediterranean theme of the neighbourhood with Venetian-style lampposts, tiled loggias and palm tree-lined walkways, and uses a limestone outcrop as a diving platform.

## Vizcaya***

Opulent homes are two-a-penny in Miami but none have the history or the grandeur to match Vizcaya, a pseudo-Italian villa costing $15 million, completed in 1916. With a fortune made from farm machinery, James Deering commissioned Vizcaya in what was then a jungle-like setting on the edge of Miami. Architect Paul Chalfin frequently exceeded the owner's expectations, causing Deering to lament 'must we be so grand' as yet more shipments of antiques arrived from Europe.

Intended to reflect 400 years of occupation, Vizcaya intentionally combines architecture and furnishings from the Renaissance, baroque, rococo and neo-classical periods, while contemporary domestic comforts, such as elevators and a bowling alley, were included but discreetly concealed.

**Above**
The Venetian Pool, Coral Gables

Guided tours unravel a wealth of detail about Deering and the construction of Vizcaya as they pass through some of the 34 ground-floor rooms. These include a Robert Adams library, the beautiful rococo Music Room, and the Banquet Hall, decorated by two Ferrara tapestries that once belonged to English poet Robert Browning.

Visitors can wander at leisure around the upper floors, which include Deering's luxurious marble-walled bathroom, and stroll a few of the 25 miles of pathways that wind around the gardens, created over seven years using Italian and French formal landscaping methods.

**Above**
Vizcaya's opulent architecture

# Accommodation and food

Miami Beach generally offers greater choice in accommodation than the rest of the city. None the less, there are hotels scattered all over and the pick of the bunch, listed below, are in Coral Gables. Along with Coconut Grove and Little Havana, Coral Gables also holds some the city's best dining options but, again, there is greater choice at Miami Beach.

**The Biltmore $$$** *1200 Anastasia Avenue, Coral Gables; tel: (305) 445-1926 or (800) 727-1926.* The luxury evident in the public areas (*see page 54*) spreads to the rooms, although the ones to aspire to are the suites on the upper storeys of the tower, costing up to $1800 nightly.

**Hotel Place St Michel $$** *162 Alcazar Avenue, Coral Gables; tel: (305) 444-1666 or (800) 848-HOTEL.* Dating from 1927 and with just 27 rooms, this piece of neighbourhood history makes a wonderful romantic hideaway.

**Riviera Court $** *5100 Riviera Drive, Coral Gables; tel: (305) 666-3528 or (800) 368-8602.* Welcoming small motel within easy reach by car of all Coral Gables' attractions; half the rooms have cooking facilities.

**Cafe Tu Tu Tango $–$$** *CocoWalk, 3015 Grand Avenue, Coconut Grove; tel: (305) 592-2222.* Designed as an artist's garret, offering a tapas-style menu, daily specials and scrumptious pizzas.

**Bayside Marketplace** *401 Biscayne Boulevard; tel: (305) 377-4091. Open Mon–Thur 1000–2200, Fri–Sat 1000–2300, Sun 1100–2000.*

**Restaurant St Michel** $$$ *at the Hotel Place St Michel, 162 Alcazar Avenue, Coral Gables; tel: (305) 446-6572.* Coral Gables had many fine restaurants but this is the best bet for immaculately presented New American cuisine with a tropical twist.

**Versailles** $ *3555 SW 8th Street, Little Havana; tel: (305) 592-2222.* It's almost a crime to visit Little Havana and not eat at this long-running favourite of Miami Cubans, who come here for the festive mood as much as the Cuban food.

## Suggested tour

**Length**: Main tour, 8 miles; Downtown and Little Havana detour, 6 miles; Key Biscayne detour 10 miles. Metrozoo is 15 miles from the main tour.

**Duration**: The main route can comfortably be covered inside a day but allow at least another half-day for one or more of the detours. Of these, Downtown Miami and Little Havana are worth seeing but dispensable if time is tight; Key Biscayne is ideal for a leisurely break and the Seaquarium is a good destination for kids, as is the Metrozoo. Vizcaya is less interesting for kids but adults might allocate two or three hours to it and could do so while the youngsters enjoy the nearby Museum of Science and Space Transit Planetarium.

**Links**: Miami Beach (*see pages 42–51*), South Miami and Everglades National Park (*see pages 64–73*).

Take any route to Brickell Avenue. As it runs south from Downtown, this street is lined by sleek high-rise office buildings and on the left is the much-photographed Atlantis apartment building, a gap in its centre decorated by a palm tree. Just under a mile ahead, the entrances to **VIZCAYA ❶** and the **MUSEUM OF SCIENCE AND SPACE TRANSIT PLANETARIUM ❷** are on the left and right respectively.

Continuing south for 3 miles, the route becomes S Bayshore Drive and passes some of Miami's most exclusive homes (hidden behind effusive foliage) before reaching the driveway leading to **Miami City Hall ❸** and swinging right to become McFarlane Road and enter the heart of **COCONUT GROVE ❹**. Amid trendy boutiques and restaurants, a short footpath on the eastern side of Main Highway leads to the secluded **BARNACLE ❺**. Less than half a mile further on Main Highway is Devon Road and the **Plymouth Congregational Church ❻**.

Leave Coconut Grove headed west for 1.3 miles along Grand Avenue, passing through an undistinguished area until turning north on to Le Jeune Road (close to the busy junction with Dixie Highway). After 1.5 miles, the route reaches SW 22nd Street, locally called the Miracle Mile and the retail centre of **CORAL GABLES ❼**.

**Ancient Spanish Monastery** $ *16711 W Dixie Highway; tel: (305) 945-1461. Open Mon–Sat 1000–1600, Sun 1200–1600.*

The single-carriage Metromover runs on a loop circuit above Downtown Miami, an enjoyble break from exploring on foot and bringing elevated views of the skyline. Board from the Government Center terminal, adjacent to the Miami-Dade Cultural Center.

Coconut Grove and Coral Gables have limited metered street parking in their main areas and several well-signposted parking garages. The city's major attractions all have ample car-parking space for visitors' use. On weekdays, Downtown parking can be expensive; an incentive for using the centrally placed Metro-Dade County Garage is a discount at the Historical Museum of South Florida. Another option is to park at Bayside Marketplace. Crandon Beach Park and Bill Baggs Cape Florida State Recreation Area have their own car-parks.

The immediate area is best explored on foot but return to the car to drive west to Coral Way and the **MERRICK HOUSE** ❽, then south along the curving De Soto Boulevard for the **VENETIAN POOL** ❾ and **CORAL GABLES CONGREGATIONAL CHURCH** ❿, within sight of the splendid **BILTMORE** ⓫ hotel.

**Detour:** At the meeting point of several freeways, **DOWNTOWN MIAMI** ⓬ is an easy detour and the site of the **HISTORICAL MUSEUM OF SOUTH FLORIDA** ⓭. **BAYSIDE MARKETPLACE** ⓮ is just north of Downtown beside Biscayne Boulevard, travelling between the two by foot is easy. By car, turn right along SW 8th Street, just south of Downtown, for **LITTLE HAVANA** ⓯, 2 miles west.

**Detour:** To reach **KEY BISCAYNE** ⓰, take the Rickenbacker Causeway (toll), the multi-laned approach to which is off Brickell Avenue between the Atlantis and Vizcaya. The causeway makes a 3.5-mile crossing of Biscayne Bay, passing the entrance to the **SEAQUARIUM** ⓱ before reaching Key Biscayne itself. **Crandon Beach Park** ⓲ is on the left and the road continues for 1.5 miles through the island's residential section before reaching the **Bill Baggs Cape Florida State Recreation Area** ⓳.

**Detour:** The **METROZOO** ⓴ is 18 miles from Downtown Miami and most easily reached by taking any route to the Florida Turnpike (toll) and travelling south to the 152nd Street exit, from which the zoo is signposted.

## Also worth exploring

On a trip to Spain in 1925, multimillionaire William Randolph Hearst so liked an abandoned 12th-century Cistercian monastery that he bought it for $500,000, had it dismantled and shipped to the US. With tax demands biting into the Hearst fortunes, the dismembered monastery stayed in a New York warehouse until the 1950s when two entrepreneurs decided it would make a perfect Florida tourist attraction.

The reassembled monastery, known as the **Ancient Spanish Monastery**, regained a religious function in 1964 when purchased by the Episcopalian church and makes an incongruous Gothic addition to an unprepossessing area in the northern part of Miami. Items such as a lambskin parchment hymnarium, a walnut cabinet used by Pope Urban VII (1623–44) and a Christ the King statue believed to have been carved by one of the original monks are dotted about, and the peaceful gardens are a delight to stroll.

The monastery is best reached from the centre of Miami with I-95, exiting on to North Miami Beach Boulevard and following the signs after crossing Biscayne Boulevard. The monastery is also simple to reach from Miami Beach, crossing from Sunny Isles.

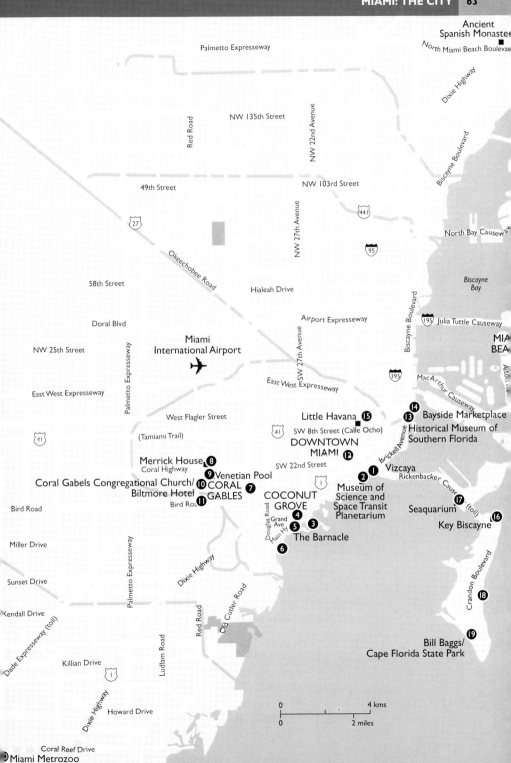

Ancient
Spanish Monaster
North Miami Beach Boulevar

Palmetto Expressway

Dixie Highway

Red Road

NW 135th Street

NW 22nd Avenue

49th Street

NW 103rd Street

Biscayne Boulevard

NW 27th Avenue

441

95

North Bay Causew

27

Okeechobee Road

58th Street

Hialeah Drive

Biscayne
Bay

Doral Blvd

Airport Expressway

195    Julia Tuttle Causeway

NW 25th Street

Miami
International Airport

Palmetto Expressway

SW 27th Avenue

Biscayne Boulevard

MIA
BEA

East West Expressway

East West Expressway

395

MacArthur Causeway

Alton R

West Flagler Street

41

Little Havana    15

14    Bayside Marketplace

13    Historical Museum of
Southern Florida

(Tamiami Trail)

SW 8th Street (Calle Ocho)

DOWNTOWN
MIAMI

Brickell Avenue

41

Merrick House    8
Coral Highway

SW 22nd Street    12

9    Venetian Pool

Coral Gables Congregational Church/    10    CORAL    Vizcaya
Biltmore Hotel    GABLES    7    2    1

Museum of    Rickenbacker Cause

Bird Road    11

Bird Roa

COCONUT
GROVE    4    Science and
Space Transit
Planetarium

17    (toll)

Miller Drive

Douglas Road    Grand
Ave    5    3

Seaquarium    16

Key Biscayne

Main Hwy

The Barnacle

Sunset Drive

Dixie Highway

6

Crandon Boulevard

East West Expressway

1

Kendall Drive

Red Road

18

Dade Expressway (toll)

Old Cutler Road

Killian Drive

Ludlam Road

Palmetto Expressway

19    Bill Baggs/
Cape Florida State Park

1

Dixie Highway

Howard Drive

0                    4 kms

0        2 miles

Coral Reef Drive

Miami Metrozoo

# South Miami and Everglades National Park

**Ratings**

| | |
|---|---|
| Diving and snorkelling | ●●●●● |
| Nature | ●●●●● |
| Boating | ●●●●○ |
| Children | ●●●●○ |
| Scenery | ●●●●○ |
| Photography | ●●●○○ |
| History | ●●○○○ |

**P**etrol stations, supermarkets and motels quickly give way to sawgrass prairies, alligators and beautifully plumaged birds as the suburban sprawl of South Miami becomes the wide-open natural expanse of Everglades National Park.

The section covered on this route is just one of the park's main areas (others are covered on pages 114–23) but it does provide a representative sample of the area's many diverse features and offers canoeing and boating opportunities. The natural world of the Everglades is matched by the coral reefs and tropical fish of Biscayne National Park, best enjoyed by snorkelling or scuba-diving but also accessible by glass-bottomed boat. The route also includes one of Miami's quirkiest sights, the Coral Castle.

Think twice about visiting the Everglades during the hot, humid and mosquito-infested summer, when much of the park is flooded. In winter temperatures are milder, mosquitoes fewer and park wildlife is at its most abundant.

## ANHINGA TRAIL✦✦✦

This simple half-mile trail begins as paved track before becoming a boardwalk traversing part of a sawgrass marsh. During winter, this is a particularly good place to spot birdlife – herons, great and snowy egrets (spot the latter by their yellow feet) and the characterful anhingas. Sometimes called the 'snakebird' for its style of swimming with only its neck exposed, the anhinga spears fish on its pointed beak before breaking surface and tossing the fish upwards to catch it in its mouth. After feeding, the anhinga can often be seen drying itself perched on a rock with its white-tipped wings at full stretch. Alligators, turkeys, marsh rabbits and various other creatures may also be viewed on this popular route.

## BISCAYNE NATIONAL PARK✦✦✦

Few places in Florida are better able to reveal the wonder of coral reefs than Biscayne National Park, 95 per cent of its 275 square miles being

**ℹ Tropical
Everglades
Visitors Center** *160
Hwy-1, close to the junction
of Hwy-1 and 344th Street
(Palm Drive); Florida City;
tel: (305) 245-9180 or
(800) 388-9669.* Run by
local chambers of
commerce, this large and
very informative stop is
packed with brochures,
leaflets and discount
coupons for local services;
the knowledgeable staff
dispense the latest
practical information.
More specific Everglades
National Park information
is provided by the visitor
centres within the park
(see page 68).

beneath the waves. Clear, clean waters make this a perfect spot for scuba-diving and snorkelling, or simply staying dry and enjoying the aquatic splendour from a glass-bottomed boat.

About 10 miles offshore, the coral reefs provide a home for turtles, lobsters, sponges, crabs and an array of other creatures, such as the stoplight parrotfish, the goosehead scorpion fish, the princess venus and the peppermint goby whose names are almost as exuberant as their colouring. The coral itself might look like a large lump of rock but is actually composed of billions of polyps, small soft living creatures that spend their days inside hard, rock-like skeletons and emerge at night to feed on plankton.

The park also holds 15th- and 16th-century Spanish shipwrecks, the target of many divers, and 44 small islands. The most northerly of the Florida Keys chain, the islands appear as vivid dots of green in this otherwise azure expanse of sea and sky. The islands' dense vegetation supports bald eagles, egrets, herons and other birds, and two are protected as nesting areas. Another, Elliot Island, which can be reached by boat, beckons visitors with hiking trails and the promise of utter tranquillity.

The reefs are the highlight of the park but don't overlook the mangrove forest that marks the shoreline. Blurring the distinctions between land and ocean, it protects the shore from extreme weather and forms a barrier to prevent pollutants entering the ocean. As the unwanted material trapped around the mangrove roots decomposes, it provides food for marine life and birdlife. The surprisingly fascinating life of the mangrove is described on the glass-bottomed boat tours.

# CORAL CASTLE✧✧

**Coral Castle $**
28655 S Dixie Highway;
tel: (305) 248-6344. Open
daily 0900–1800.

One of Miami's greatest mysteries, the Coral Castle was created by Latvian émigré Edward Leedskalnin, using coral rock dug from the ground on an acre of land he bought in 1918 for $12. Working alone with rudimentary hand tools, the uneducated Leedskalnin not only managed to move chunks of rock weighting several tons without assistance but created rock sculptures, many resembling pieces of furniture, to exact dimensions (the Florida-shaped table, for example, is a precise scale model of the state) seemingly using advanced mathematics to do so.

Twenty years in construction, the Coral Castle provided a home for Leedskalin until his death in 1951. His visitors would enter by the Three Ton Gate, a rock that did indeed weigh three tons but which, due to Leedskalin's mechanical skills, could be opened by finger pressure. The entrance used today is less interesting but the 1000-pound armchairs, the 25-ft-long telescope and the photogenic crescent moon, and many other objects, remain as curious to visitors now as when they first appeared. Still nobody can explain how or why Leedskalinin created them.

# FLAMINGO✧

**Flamingo Visitor
Center** Located 38
miles from the main entrance,
at the southern end of the
park.

Flamingo, the last stop on the road through Everglades National Park, once held a community of smugglers, fishermen and hunters, many of them making a living by killing roseate spoonbills and selling their feathers. Like many present-day tourists, the settlers thought the spoonbills were flamingos and named their community accordingly.

A hundred years on, Flamingo's sole permanent residents are a handful of official personnel who organise the only food and accommodation (other than camping) available in this section of the park. They also run the boat, canoe, walking and tram tours originating here. All the details can be found at the Flamingo Visitor Center alongside exhibits on local ecology. Among several trails in the vicinity is the easy route to **Eco Pond**, an artificial freshwater pond overlooked by an observation platform. During winter, early mornings and late afternoon egrets, woodstorks and many other birds are likely to be seen.

# GUMBO LIMBO TRAIL❖❖

**Above**
Coral Castle

A half-mile round-trip trail on a paved road, this begins close to the Royal Palm Visitor Center and weaves through what was, before being ravaged by Hurricane Andrew in 1992, a very shady hardwood forest. Many of the gumbo limbo and royal palm trees support epiphytes, such as orchids, that grow on other plants without damaging them, taking water and nutrients from the air. By contrast, the strangler fig, also seen here, usually begins as a wind-carried seed and steadily wraps itself around a host tree until the latter, deprived of light and water, dies.

Popularly known in Florida as the 'tourist tree' because its peeling red bark resembles sunburnt skin, the gumbo limbo tree sometimes plays host to the rare liguus tree snail, distinguished by the intense colouring of its shell, anything from deep orange or yellow to green and blue.

**Right**
The Mahogany Hammock
Trail

# MAHOGANY HAMMOCK TRAIL*

A hardwood hammock similar to but much denser than the Gumbo Limbo Trail (*see page 67*), the Mahogany Hammock Trail passes an observation tower giving views over many miles of sawgrass prairie, before disappearing into the cave-like interior of the forest. The damp conditions are ideal for ferns and epiphytes, many of which are found amid palms and gumbo limbo trees. Also here are the mahogany trees that give the trail its name, including the largest example in the US. Brittle mahogany wood, however, is particularly susceptible to hurricanes: these were badly affected by Hurricane Andrew in 1992.

# MAIN VISITOR CENTER***

🏛 **Everglades National Park $** *tel: (305) 242-7700; Main entrance daily 24 hours; Main Visitor Center daily 0800–1700; Flamingo Visitor Center Nov–Apr, daily 0730–1700.*

The first and largest of several visitors' centres in the park, this is an essential stop for the latest weather and mosquito information, and for listings of the day's park activities; any guided tour is well worth joining. Also here are park maps and exhibits and displays on the Everglades' unique ecology; grasping even a little of which will greatly enhance your visit.

# PA-HAY-OKEE OVERLOOK✢✢✢

A celebrated naturalist and writer, Marjorie Stoneman Douglas did much to encourage conservation of the Everglades and bestowed it with a lasting epithet: 'river of grass'. The description seems entirely apt from the 12-ft-high observation tower on this short trail which overlooks a sawgrass swamp stretching to the horizon.

Covering 8 million acres of the Everglades, the sawgrass plain is flooded each year as summer storms bring water spilling south from the vast Lake Okeechoobee. The shallow waters (average depth is around 6ins) move imperceptibly slowly through the sawgrass towards the sea. The stillness of the setting and knowledge that everything in the Everglades depends on this natural cycle (greatly affected over the years by human attempts at drainage and demands for drinking water) help make this an awesome sight.

# PINELANDS TRAIL✢

Formed by limestone ridges, the highest elevations in the Everglades are between 3 and 7ft above sea-level. Height keeps the ridges dry while sufficient soil gathers in their hollows to enable slash pine to grow. Also called Dade County pine, these trees have a strong and durable wood with a resistance to termites that made them the preferred building material for many early Florida homes.

During the wet season, the pinelands provide shelter for wildlife usually not seen elsewhere in the park, such as racoons, reef geckos, the cotton mouse and the five-lined skink, a type of lizard. The sharp edges of the limestone ridges generally make pineland exploration tricky, but this trail provides a safe way to explore this branch of the Everglades' ecosystem. A further bonus is the wonderful array of wild flowers.

## Alligators: the keepers of the Everglades

Widely misunderstood and often unreasonably feared, alligators are prevalent throughout Florida and are nicknamed 'the keepers of the Everglades' for the crucial part they play in sustaining wildlife during the Everglades' dry winter months.

During the winter, alligators are able to locate the water hidden beneath ground following the subsiding of the summer floods, digging with their powerful tails to create small ponds or 'gator holes'. Besides providing a habitat for the alligator, these holes allow fish, snails and turtles to survive, and provide sustenance to bobcats, otters, the occasional deer and other creatures. Everglades' birdlife depends on the gator holes' provision of food as part of their reproductive cycle.

When the summer rains return, the pathway worn by the alligator between the pond and its nest becomes a creek, speeding the flow of water and easing the movement of wildlife from the gator holes across the quickly flooded Everglades.

# Accommodation and food

Besides camping at three sites (*tel: (800) 365-2267*), accommodation within Everglades National Park is limited to the hotel at Flamingo. There are many motels in and around Homestead and Florida City, within a few minutes' drive of the park entrance, which make a feasible base if you are taking this route between staying in Miami and crossing the state to the Gulf coast. Food in the park is similarly limited to the winter-only restaurant and café at Flamingo (the marina store is open year-round and sells provisions). Again, there is more choice around Homestead and Florida City.

**Everglades Motel $$** *605 S Krome Avenue, Homestead; tel: (305) 247-4117.* Clean rooms and reasonable prices make a good combination and the location is ideal.

**Flamingo Lodge $$** *Flamingo; tel: (800) 600-3813 or (941) 695-3101.* Open year-round with comfortable rooms and a few cottages with

**Below**
Sunset over mangroves

cooking facilities. During summer the hotel restaurant is closed and guests need to provide their own supplies.

**Hurricane Andrew Motor Inn** $ *100 Highway 1, Florida City; tel: (305) 247-8833 or (800) 521-6004.* Large and unpretentious motel that takes its name from the natural disaster that caused it to be rebuilt with one of the most photographed inn signs in Florida.

**Capri Restaurant** $–$$ *935 S Krome Avenue, Florida City; tel: (305) 247-1542.* Full menu of American and American–Italian fare; often has good seafood. Closed Sun.

**El Toro Taco** $ *1 S Krome Avenue, Homestead; tel: (305) 245-8182.* Embarrassingly inexpensive Mexican food in a friendly setting; some of the ingredients are home grown.

**Flamingo Restaurant and Café** $–$$ *Flamingo; tel: (941) 695-3101 or (800) 600-3813.* The former has a full lunch and dinner service; the latter provides snacks. Both are open only during the winter.

# Suggested tour

**Length**: The entrance to Everglades National Park is 42 miles from Downtown Miami; the distance from the park entrance to Flamingo is 38 miles.

**Duration**: Driving time from the park entrance to Flamingo and back is 2–3 hours. Biscayne National Park and the Coral Castle are each 20-minutes' drive from the park entrance.

**Links**: Miami: the City (*see pages 52–63*), the Florida Keys (*see pages 94–103*).

From Miami, take Hwy-1 (S Dixie Highway) southbound. This is a fairly uninspired journey through the bland suburbia of South Miami. An alternative is to head west to link with the speedier, but no more interesting, Florida Turnpike (toll). Both roads meet south of Perrine at South Miami Heights.

On either route, turn right on to 344th Street (Palm Drive), taking Hwy-27, the well-signposted main route into **Everglades National Park**. Inside the park, Hwy-27 becomes known simply as Main Park Road and this is the route that continues for 38 miles to Flamingo. Stop first at the **MAIN VISITOR CENTER ❶** immediately to the right on entering the park to check the park conditions and daily events such as guided tours which may require advance booking.

Two miles ahead, a left turn leads to the Royal Palm Visitor Center and the start points of the **ANHINGA TRAIL ❷** and **GUMBO LIMBO TRAIL ❸**. Returning on the main route, 4.5 miles ahead is a left turn for Long Pine Key, the limestone ridge which holds the **PINELANDS TRAIL ❹**. From here, the flatness of the Everglades becomes apparent as Main Park Road passes through an immense expanse of sawgrass.

After a further 6 miles comes the right-hand turn for **PA-HAY-OKEE OVERLOOK ❺**, a chance to leave the car and absorb the dramatic sawgrass vista at first hand. The only disturbances to the pancake-flatness are the tree islands called hammocks; one of the densest lies 7 miles further on Main Park Road and can be explored on the **MAHOGANY TRAIL ❻**, accessed by a signposted side road. Main Park Road continues for 20 miles to **FLAMINGO ❼**, the centre of visitor services in this section of the park and starting point for guided tours.

**Detours**: Two miles north of Homestead, turn off Hwy-1 heading east along SW 288th Street for the **CORAL CASTLE ❽**, close to the junction with 157th Avenue. Further south off Hwy-1, **BISCAYNE NATIONAL PARK ❾** can be reached by turning east on to SW 328 Street and continuing to the end of the route at Convoy Point, park headquarters and departure point for boat tours. Bear in mind that boat tours should be booked prior to arrival, particularly during the peak winter season.

**Fruit and Spice Park** $ *24801 SW 248th Street; tel: (305) 247-5727. Open daily 1000–1700.*

**Monkey Jungle** $ *14805 SW 216th Street; tel: (305) 235-1611. Open daily 0930–1700.*

## Also worth exploring

The Homestead area is very much a rural, agricultural counterpart to modernistic Miami. While many people spend a night in the plentiful motels, few take the trouble to explore a bit deeper and discover some of the low-key charms and nearby attractions. Krome Avenue is the commercial heart of Homestead, with a pleasant small-town America atmosphere. The area bore the brunt of Hurricane Andrew in 1992 and some of the scars are still visible. One of the worst affected spots was the **Fruit and Spice Park**, which lost many of its exotic herbs, spices, plants and trees but has made great efforts to restore its former glory; delights such as the panama candle tree remain. Slightly further north, **Monkey Jungle** gives various species of primates space to roam through replicated rain-forest habitats as humans view them from caged walkways.

LAS OLAS

# The Gold Coast

## Ratings

| | |
|---|---|
| Beaches | ●●●●● |
| Scenery | ●●●●○ |
| Architecture | ●●●○○ |
| Museums | ●●●○○ |
| Nature | ●●●○○ |
| Sport | ●●●○○ |
| Children | ●●○○○ |
| History | ●●○○○ |

**K**nown as the Gold Coast supposedly for the sunken treasure lying offshore, the nickname commonly attached to this section of Southeast Florida also suggests the large amount of money needed to live in some of the state's most expensive coastal communities. Prized for their location within commuting distance of Miami as much as the proximity of superb beaches, Fort Lauderdale and Boca Raton, the former with a glorious shoreline and several excellent museums, the latter known for its Mediterranean Revival architecture, dominate the area.

Around these major towns, however, are many undeveloped beach tracts that make this route an attractive combination of unspoilt nature and stylish urban areas. Remnants of pioneer-era Florida are surprisingly easy to find as most communities here began as farming settlements – an unusual one is remembered by the Morikami Museum and Japanese Gardens – that battled the scrub and swamp that still asserts itself in the region's inland portions.

## BOCA RATON❖❖❖

**ⓘ Boca Raton Chamber of Commerce** 1800 N Dixie Highway; tel: (561) 395-4433. Open Mon–Thur 0830–1700, Fri 0830–1600.

**ⓘ Mizner Park** 400 N Federal Highway.

**Boca Raton Old Town Hall** 71 N Federal Highway; tel: (561) 395-6766. Open daily 0900–1700.

**Boca Raton Resort and Club** 501 E Camino Real; tel: (561) 395-3000. Guided tour $ Wed 1330.

Wealthy and conservative, and typically populated by boat-owning forty-somethings with a penchant for fine dining, Boca Raton is immediately recognisable for its Mediterranean appearance. Red barrel-tiled roofs, fake bell towers and tile-walled courtyards appear at every turn, a style originally introduced by legendary architect Addison Mizner in the 1920s.

Mizner's scheme to create an entire community on the 1600 acres he had purchased with the proceeds of his Palm Beach work (*see pages 86–93*) was ended by a collapse in the property market. None the less, a resurgence of interest in his work has led to new buildings in the same style in the Downtown area, such as the pink stucco open-air shopping mall, **Mizner Park**.

One of the few Mizner-designed buildings that remain is the greatly restored 1927 **Old Town Hall**, now owned by the local historical society who operate a library and mount modest displays in the interior. Much more spectacular is the **Boca Raton Resort and Club**, originally the Cloister Inn, a luxury resort built by Mizner to lure

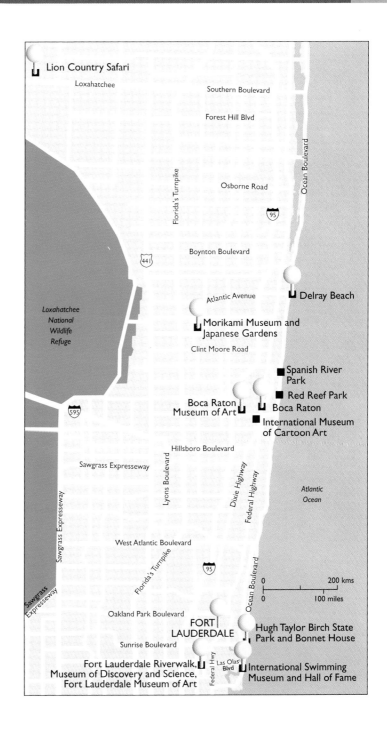

Lion Country Safari

Loxahatchee

Southern Boulevard

Forest Hill Blvd

Florida's Turnpike

Osborne Road

Ocean Boulevard

95

Boynton Boulevard

441

Loxahatchee
National
Wildlife
Refuge

Atlantic Avenue

Delray Beach

Morikami Museum and
Japanese Gardens

Clint Moore Road

Spanish River
Park

Red Reef Park

Boca Raton
Museum of Art

Boca Raton

International Museum
of Cartoon Art

595

Hillsboro Boulevard

Sawgrass Expresseway

Lyons Boulevard

Dixie Highway

Federal Highway

Atlantic
Ocean

Sawgrass Expresseway

West Atlantic Boulevard

Florida's Turnpike

95

Ocean Boulevard

0          200 kms

0          100 miles

Sawgrass Expresseway

Oakland Park Boulevard

FORT
LAUDERDALE

Hugh Taylor Birch State
Park and Bonnet House

Sunrise Boulevard

Federal Hwy

Las Olas
Blvd

Fort Lauderdale Riverwalk,
Museum of Discovery and Science,
Fort Lauderdale Museum of Art

International Swimming
Museum and Hall of Fame

**Boca Raton Museum of Art $**
*801 Palmetto Park Road; tel: (561) 392-2500. Open Mon–Fri 1000–1600.*

**International Museum of Cartoon Art $** *201 Plaza Real; tel: (561) 391-2200. Open Tue–Sat 1100–1700, Sun 1200–1700.*

**Red Reef Park $** *1400 N Ocean Boulevard; tel: (561) 393-7989. Open daily 0700–2200.*

socialites to his intended city. Excellent guided tours weave through the hotel's cloisters and courtyards revealing many of the features of Mizner's time.

**Boca Raton Museum of Art**, one of Florida's best small art museums and rated highly enough to attract notable travelling exhibitions, grew from the Mayers Collection of late-19th and early 20th-century works, bequeathed in 1989 and including artists such as Braque, Modigliani, Léger, Degas, Matisse and Picasso, the latter remembered here with several interesting charcoal sketches.

With 160,000 drawings from all over the world, anyone who ever smiled at a cartoon will find something to enjoy at the **International Museum of Cartoon Art**, a substantial repository devoted to cartoons and their creators. Featured strips range from *Garfield* and *Dilbert* to *Felix the Cat* and *Flash Gordon*, and related areas such as graphic novels, greeting cards, caricature and computer-generated art are also covered. Changing exhibitions highlight cartoonists' skills in advertising and editorials, and display original artwork and cells from Disney animations and classic TV shows such as *Roadrunner* and *Bugs Bunny*.

With its excellent beach flanked by a boardwalk passing over coarsely vegetated sand dunes, **Red Reef Park** makes the most of its natural setting and is a justifiably popular place for swimming, sunbathing and weekend barbecues. It is also a noted spot for snorkelling, its piers providing access to an artificial reef that attracts myriad species of brightly coloured tropical fish. The park extends across Hwy-A1A to include the **Gumbo Limbo Nature Center**, where an informative visitors' centre provides the inside info on the complexities of Florida's coastal ecosystems. A boardwalk trail plots a course over coastal dunes and mangrove wetlands and through hammocks of hardwood and sable palm. A 40-ft-high observation tower offers a scintillating view of the park.

## Accommodation and food in Boca Raton

**Boca Raton Resort and Club $$$** *501 E Camino Real; tel: (561) 395-3000 or (800) 327-0101.* The most luxurious place to stay along this section of the coast, and a major chapter in local history.

**Ocean Edge Motel $$** *531 N Ocean Boulevard; tel: (561) 395-7772.* Well-furnished rooms just across Hwy-A1A from the beach.

**Maxaluna $$–$$$** *Boca Center, 5050 Town Center Circle; tel: (561) 391-7177.* Exceptionally inventive Tuscan-influenced fare served for lunch and dinner; the food is high class but the mood is relaxed.

**La Vieille Maison $$$** *770 E Palmetto Road; tel: (561) 391-6701.* Top-rated French cuisine served inside a 1924 mansion designed by Addison Mizner. Extremely popular so make a reservation.

# DELRAY BEACH❖❖

**Cason Cottage** $ 5
*NE 1st Street; tel: (561)
274-9578. Open Tue–Fri
1000–1600.*

Quiet and welcoming Delray Beach grew from a struggling agricultural community into a winter resort boasting a very pleasant **beach**. The beach lies at the eastern end of **Atlantic Avenue**, the primary commercial artery lined by art galleries and antiques shops, and illuminated at night by imitation gas lamps. The restored 1910s and 1920s buildings of **Old School Square** provide a centre for cultural events and temporary exhibitions. Close by, the wood-framed **Cason Cottage**, built for a doctor in 1915, brings intriguing insights into pioneer-era Florida living.

## Accommodation and food in Delray Beach

**Bermuda Inn** $$ *64 S Ocean Boulevard; tel: (561) 276-5288.* Friendly staff, good-sized rooms and within a few strides of the beach, as well as being ideally placed for exploring the rest of this enjoyable town.
**Sundy House** $ *106 S Swinton Avenue; tel: (561) 278-2163.* Order a pot of tea or a simple, wholesome lunch inside this 1902 home that also functions as an antiques shop.

# FORT LAUDERDALE❖❖❖

One of the best-known vacation destinations in Florida and for years venue of a riotous Spring Break (the annual pre-exam invasion of American students), Fort Lauderdale is an instantly likeable place. The idyllic beach strip, where the lengthy white sands are shaded by palms, is sufficient allure for many. But since the 1980s the Downtown area, 3 miles inland, has undergone a complete face-lift, gaining two excellent museums, restoring several historic homes and developing the commendable Riverwalk.

The core of Fort Lauderdale's **beach strip** runs for 2 miles along Atlantic Boulevard. Sunbathers and swimmers hit the sands by day and, by night, many of them can be found in adjacent cafés and restaurants cooled by ocean breezes. The 1960 film *Where the Boys Are* cemented Fort Lauderdale's reputation as a Spring Break destination but the annual six weeks of under-age drunkenness and general mayhem ended when Fort Lauderdale set about re-inventing itself as a classy resort town.

Immediately inland from the beach are the slender canals created from mangrove swamps during the 1920s that earned Fort Lauderdale the sobriquet

**❶ Fort Lauderdale Convention & Visitors Bureau** *1850 Eller Drive, Suite 303; tel: (954) 765-4466. Open Mon–Fri 0830–1700.*

**Greater Fort Lauderdale Chamber of Commerce** *512 NE 3rd Avenue; tel: (954) 462-6000. Open Mon–Fri 0830–1700.*

**🏠 Stranahan House $** *335 SE 6th Avenue; tel: (954) 524-4736. Open Sept–June, Wed–Sat 1000–1600, Sun 1300–1600.*

**Fort Lauderdale Historical Museum $** *219 SW 2nd Avenue; tel: (954) 463-4431. Open Tue–Fri 1000–1600.*

**Fort Lauderdale Museum of Art $** *1 E Las Olas Boulevard; tel: (954) 525-5500. Open Wed–Sat 1000–1700, until 2100 on Tue, Sun 1200–1700.*

'Venice of America'. Private yachts tethered in backyards are a common sight in a well-heeled residential area that separates the beach strip from **Downtown Fort Lauderdale**. Local administrative hub and site of the Museum of Discovery and Science (*see page 80*) and Museum of Art (*see below*), Downtown Fort Lauderdale also provides a good impression of the town's history with the 1901 **Stranahan House**, a two-storey wood-framed home built for a settler from Ohio who operated a ferry service across the town's New River.

The 1.5-mile **Riverwalk**, a bricked footpath dotted with seats and picnic stops, meanders along the banks of the New River past a fine group of old buildings, including the 1907 **King-Cromartie House** and the reconstructed 1899 **Schoolhouse**, now under the auspices of the **Fort Lauderdale Historical Museum**, which also displays its own collection of memorabilia.

### Fort Lauderdale Museum of Art✦✦✦

**Above right**
Fort Lauderdale's canals cater to well-heeled boat lovers

In an architecturally splendid 1980s building, designed by the renowned Edward Larrabee Barnes and a significant part of the revitalisation of Downtown Fort Lauderdale, this museum holds a fine collection of mostly modern art including the largest collection of CoBrA work in the Americas. Founded in 1948 by artists from Denmark, Belgium and Holland and named with the initial letters of their capital cities (Copenhagen, Brussels, Amsterdam), CoBrA took inspiration from mythology and children's drawing. The Dane Asger Jorn, Dutchman Karel Appel and Belgian Pierre Alechinski are among the major contributors to the many bold paintings, ceramics, sculpture and graphics on display. With too many works to display as a whole, selections are made to illustrate particular aspects of the movement.

Also strongly represented is William Gluckens, an American realist painter and founder member of The Eight, also known as the Ashcan school for their warts-and-all image of modern society. Relatively minor works by major names such as Andy Warhol, Frank Stella and Larry Rivers are generally less impressive than the displays from Africa and the Pacific region, and Florida's largest collection of Pre-Columbian American art.

### Hugh Taylor Birch State Recreation Area and Bonnet House✥✥

An undeveloped oasis amid the wall-to-wall hotels and restaurants that dominate the coastal section of Fort Lauderdale, the Hugh Taylor Birch State Recreation Area has a long and narrow mangrove-lined freshwater lagoon and is fringed by tall Australian pines. Locals spend many weekend hours boating around this tranquil body of water before enjoying a barbecue at one of the two picnic pavilions. The area was donated to the state in 1942 by the 93-year-old former Chicago attorney Hugh Taylor Birch, who had acquired several hundred acres of oceanside land in 1893.

Directly across Sunrise Boulevard from the park, the Bonnet House is another reminder of times gone by. The house and the 35 acres it occupies was a 1921 wedding present from Hugh Taylor Birch to his son, muralist Frank Clay Bartlett. Touring the 30-room plantation-style dwelling, built in Dade County pine and coral rock, you will come across many of Bartlett's murals, plus the often whimsical art and objects gathered by him and his first and second wives. Bartlett's appreciation of nature is apparent throughout, and the grounds are still inhabited by the swans and monkeys introduced during his time.

### International Swimming Hall of Fame✥

Many diverse facets of watersports are celebrated at the aptly named International Swimming Hall of Fame, where champions from around the world – though most are American – are remembered with displays, video clips and scores of cups, medals, shields and other trophies. Those honoured include Mark Spitz, winner of seven Olympic golds in 1972, and Johnny Weissmuller, the greatest

**Museum of Discovery and Science $$** *401 SW 2nd Street; tel: (954) 467 6637. Open Mon–Sat 1000–1700, Sun 1200–1700.*

swimmer of the 1920s but better known for his Hollywood role as the first on-screen Tarzan.

Also featured are less mainstream aquatic sports such as water polo and synchronised swimming. Other entertaining displays recount the evolution of the swimming costume and future president Ronald Reagan's short career as a life-guard. Outside the main hall, two Olympic-sized pools and sky-high diving boards are regularly used for competition events and training potential champions.

**Museum of Discovery and Science**\*\*
The $30-million Museum of Discovery and Science is among the largest and most entertaining of its kind, providing an introduction to the wonders of the physical world that will keep grown-ups and kids amused for a couple of hours. Innovative and imaginative exhibits cover everything from the ecosystems of Florida, including a coral reef, a cave, and a walk-through beehive, to the workings of the human body.

The Gizmo City section allows access to the internet and the playing of virtual volleyball (less physical but much more cerebrally demanding than the real thing). Visitors can also try their hand at repairing a satellite in orbit and join a simulated space flight to the moon. The adjoining IMAX Theater screens spectacular films, some of them in 3D, on many subjects.

## Accommodation and food in Fort Lauderdale

**Beachcomber Hotel and Villas $$** *1200 S Ocean Boulevard; tel: (954) 941-7830 or (800) 231-2423.* Large rooms, two pools and a patio.

**Riverside Hotel $$$** *620 E Las Olas Boulevard; tel: (954) 467-0671.* Built in the 1920s, this much modernised slice of local history has large rooms and makes an excellent base for Downtown Fort Lauderdale.

**Surf and Sun Hotel & Apartments $** *521 N Atlantic Boulevard; tel: (954) 564-4341 or (800) 248-0463.* One of the best of many small, independently run accommodations adjacent to the beach.

**California Cafe Bar & Grill $$–$$$** *Pier 66, 2301 SE 17th Street Causeway; tel: (954) 728-3500.* Inspired by California cuisine, matching fresh local ingredients to the chef's inspiration to create mouthwatering dishes, served overlooking a marina.

**Ernie's BBQ Lounge $** *1843 S Federal Highway; tel: (954) 523-8636.* Unpretentious hole-in-the-wall spot renowned for its wonderful fresh chowder, served with sherry.

**The Floridian $** *1410 E Las Olas Boulevard; tel: (954) 463-4041.* This simple coffee shop in the trendy heart of Downtown Fort Lauderdale makes a great place to lunch while window-shopping.

# LION COUNTRY SAFARI*

**Lion Country Safari**
**$$** *State Road 80 W,*
*Loxahatchee; tel: (561) 793-*
*1084. Open daily*
*0930–1630.*

**Right**
Tandem zebras at Lion
Country Safari

An 8-mile road loops through the 500-acre Lion Country Safari, split into five areas of replicated wildlife habitats from Asia, Africa and the Americas. Visitors, who must stay inside their cars but can stop as often as they wish, are likely to spot lions, giraffes, rhinos, zebra, bison, elephants, chimpanzees and even Australian emus among the host of inmates who sometimes venture remarkably close, providing a tremendous though somewhat hair-raising photo opportunity. Many of the animals sleep through the hottest parts of the day so early morning is the best time to visit.

# MORIKAMI MUSEUM AND JAPANESE GARDENS***

**Morikami Museum**
**& Japanese**
**Gardens $** *4000 Morikami*
*Park Road; tel: (561) 495-*
*0233. Open Tue–Sun*
*1000–1700.*

Established in the early 1900s, the Yamato Colony consisted of 50 young Japanese settlers who aimed to turn a patch of mosquito-infested wilderness into a thriving pineapple and winter vegetable farm. Eventually, only one settler remained, George Sukeji Morikami, whose success as a grapefruit wholesaler enabled him to become the owner of a sizeable plot of land. On his death this was bequeathed to the local authorities with the proviso that a memorial to the colony, and his home country, be established on it.

The result is the excellent Morikami Museum which explores diverse aspects of Japanese culture with a teahouse (venue of monthly tea ceremonies) and interactive exhibits on traditional arts and

The Gold Coast has several shopping hot spots plus the world's largest shopping mall.

**Las Olas Boulevard** is lined by pricey art galleries, boutiques and specialities stores, the clientele just as chic and up-market as the merchandise. *Los Olas Boulevard, Downtown Fort Lauderdale, mostly around the junction with SE 6th and 7th avenues.*

**Sawgrass Mills** is believably the world's largest discount shopping mall, with some 300 brand-name stores offering new goods at discounted prices. *12801 Sunrise Boulevard, 12 miles west of Downtown Fort Lauderdale.*

**Boca Center** Boca Raton is dotted by stylish shopping centres but none can compete with this conglomeration of clothing, home accessories, books, gifts and much more. *5050 Town Center Circle, off N Military Trail, just west of I-95 (Glades Road exit).*

crafts. Just as the building reflects traditional Japanese architecture with its use of dark wood trim, shoji screens and tatami mats, so the Japanese Gardens outside are designed in formal style. Meditative trails lead through the gardens passing a bonsai display, koi carp- and turtle-filled ponds, and cross narrow bridges to delightful small waterfalls.

Also within the gardens is the villa-like Yamoto-kan where the Yamoto Colony is documented with photographs, grainy monochrome prints giving an impression of the forbidding terrain that the early settlers sought to tame.

# Suggested tour

**Length**: Main tour 25 miles, 60 miles with detours.

**Duration**: Main tour driving time, 2 hours; 4–5 hours with detours. The quick way to tackle this route is to stick largely to I-95, scything north–south through the edge of the coastal communities. The slower and much more scenic alternative is Hwy-A1A, a two-lane route that sticks as close as possible to the ocean. Most of the tour is devised by using a combination of these routes, the two detours making the most of the coastal road.

**Links**: The coastal Hwy-A1A continues south for 23 miles to Miami Beach (*see pages 42–51*). Palm Beach (*see pages 86–93*) is a similar distance north on the same route and 15 miles east of Lion Country Safari on Route 80.

Take any route to **FORT LAUDERDALE ❶**. The heart of **Downtown Fort Lauderdale**, site of the **Riverwalk** and the **Museum of Art** and **Museum of Science and Discovery**, is around the junction of Hwy-1 (Federal Highway) and Las Olas Boulevard. Take the latter for a scenically appealing 3-mile course to the ocean, passing trendy shops and million-dollar homes lining slender canals before crossing New River Sound to reach Hwy-A1A (Atlantic Boulevard) and **beachside Fort Lauderdale**.

From the Hwy-A1A junction, turning right leads into Seabreeze Boulevard and the signposted **International Swimming Hall of Fame**. Turning left takes you through the most popular section of Fort Lauderdale's palm-lined beach. The concentration of restaurants, motels and beach accessory shops suddenly thins as Hwy-A1A passes the undeveloped plot holding the **Bonnet House**, 2 miles ahead and, immediately across Sunrise Boulevard, the **Hugh Taylor Birch State Recreation Area**.

Take Sunrise Boulevard east for 4 miles to reach I-95, and travel north for 16 miles to the junction with Route 808 (Palmetto Park Road) leading into **BOCA RATON ❷**. The route passes the **Boca Raton Museum of Art** on the left, and half a mile later, enters **Downtown**

## Water taxis

An enjoyable way to get around Fort Lauderdale is with the water taxi, which ferries passengers between the beachside area and Downtown using the New River and the town's canal network. Call to have the taxi collect you from the nearest landing stage (*tel: (954) 467-6677*).

## Accommodation

The Gold Coast is one of Florida's most popular vacation areas and accommodation, while plentiful, varies greatly in price according to season. Between December and May, prices may be three times what they are during the summer, and public holiday periods will find some hotels booked months in advance. During these times, reserve well ahead.

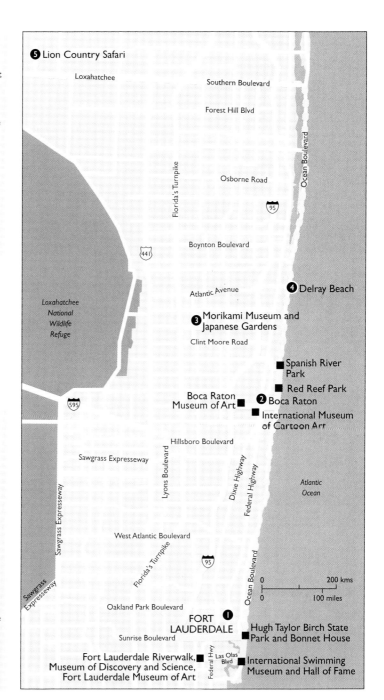

❺ Lion Country Safari

Loxahatchee

Southern Boulevard

Forest Hill Blvd

Ocean Boulevard

Florida's Turnpike

Osborne Road

95

Boynton Boulevard

441

Atlantic Avenue

❹ Delray Beach

Loxahatchee National Wildlife Refuge

❸ Morikami Museum and Japanese Gardens

Clint Moore Road

■ Spanish River Park

■ Red Reef Park

Boca Raton Museum of Art ■ ❷ Boca Raton

■ International Museum of Cartoon Art

Hillsboro Boulevard

Sawgrass Expressway

Lyons Boulevard

Dixie Highway

Federal Highway

*Atlantic Ocean*

Sawgrass Expressway

595

West Atlantic Boulevard

Florida's Turnpike

95

Ocean Boulevard

Sawgrass Expressway

Oakland Park Boulevard

| 0 | | 200 kms |
| 0 | | 100 miles |

FORT ❶
LAUDERDALE

Sunrise Boulevard

Hugh Taylor Birch State Park and Bonnet House ■

Federal Hwy

Las Olas Blvd

Fort Lauderdale Riverwalk, ■
Museum of Discovery and Science,
Fort Lauderdale Museum of Art

■ International Swimming Museum and Hall of Fame

**Spanish River Park**
$ 3001 N Ocean
Boulevard; tel: (561) 393-
7815. Open daily
0800–sunset.

**Boca Raton.** The **Old Town Hall** is to the left on Hwy-1 (Federal Highway), as is the **Mizner Park** shopping mall, site of the **International Museum of Cartoon Art.**

A mile south on Federal Highway, the palm-lined Camino Real is on the left. Take this for the **Boca Raton Resort and Club,** and continue in this direction for Ocean Boulevard, the local section of Hwy-A1A. Turn left, and a mile ahead are **Red Reef Park** and the **Gumbo Limbo Nature Center.** For the next 3 miles, Hwy-A1A skirts the ocean, usually concealed behind rows of Australian pines, before passing **Spanish River Park.**

The north side of the park is bordered by Spanish River Road. Take this for 3 miles west to rejoin I-95. Continue north on I-95, turning west after 4.6 miles on to Linton Boulevard (Route 782). After 3.6 miles, turn south on to Jog Road, following the signs for the **MORIKAMI MUSEUM AND JAPANESE GARDENS ❸.**

**Detour:** An outlook of sea, sun and sand makes it very tempting to stick to Hwy-A1A as it continues north from Fort Lauderdale. After the vibrant beach strip, however, the outlook becomes a fairly dull residential one with a succession of sedate beachside communities such as **Lauderdale-by-the-Sea** and **Pompano Beach,** which claims to be the 'swordfish capital of the world'.

Peppered with seafood restaurants and small motels, Hwy-A1A continues north crossing the **Hillsboro Inlet** into the community of the same name (on the mainland side and holding some very expensive homes at the end of secluded driveways) and an undeveloped beachside strip dominated by the US Coastguard.

Three miles ahead is **Deerfield Beach,** with a peaceful mile-long beach lined by palms and flanked by a zigzagging boardwalk. Snorkelling and diving are popular local pursuits, thanks to two sections of coral reef lying offshore, as is casting a rod from the grandly titled International Fishing Pier. Three miles north is **South Inlet Park,** another invitingly isolated patch of sand and marking the edge of Boca Raton. Just ahead is the junction with Camino Real, part of the main route.

**Detour:** Driving 6 miles north on Hwy-A1A from Spanish River Park leads through the barely developed beach areas of **Highland Beach** and **Atlantic Dunes Park** to the very relaxed **DELRAY BEACH ❹.** Enjoy the beach and explore the shops of Atlantic Avenue, before rejoining the main route and continuing to the Morikami Museum and Japanese Gardens. Alternatively, stick to the coast route which continues for 14 very pleasant miles before reaching Route 80. Head 2.5 miles west to reach I-95 or continue west to **LION COUNTRY SAFARI ❺.** Meanwhile, Palm Beach (*see page 86–93*) is directly ahead.

**Detour:** Leave I-95 by heading west on Route 80 (Southern Boulevard). Residential areas and commercial estates give way to farmland and areas of scrub and swamp as you continue for 16 miles to the signposted access road to Lion Country Safari. It is an unprepossessing route and a good reminder of how much of south Florida's really looks. In comparison, the re-created habitats of the safari park seem luxuriously vegetated.

**Below**
Rollerblading along Fort Lauderdale's seafront promenade

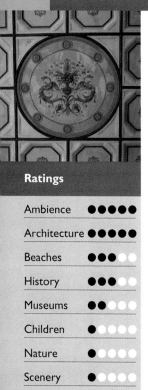

# Palm Beach

## Ratings

| | |
|---|---|
| Ambience | ●●●●● |
| Architecture | ●●●●● |
| Beaches | ●●● |
| History | ●●●○○ |
| Museums | ●●○○○ |
| Children | ●○○○○ |
| Nature | ●○○○○ |
| Scenery | ●○○○○ |

Famous throughout the world as a haunt of the rich and famous, Palm Beach lives up to its reputation with sumptuous homes lining immaculately clean streets scented by the tropical shrubbery that blooms year-round in pampered gardens. Yet just a few hours' exploration reveals the town to be a surprisingly small, friendly and accessible place with a palpable sense of community, even if being a member of that community requires a million-dollar-plus annual income and an ability to be socially at ease with the leading politicians, financiers, film stars, sports champions and other celebrities who make it their winter home.

Henry Flagler's Whitehall mansion, the extremely grand Breakers hotel, and the up-market shops of Worth Avenue provide the cornerstones of a visit, but the town is also laden with the nooks and crannies that reveal curious snippets of local history and some of the best of the Mediterranean style architecture that gives Palm Beach its signature appearance.

## Sights

**ℹ Palm Beach Chamber of Commerce** *45 Cocoanut Row; tel: (561) 655-3282. Open Mon–Fri 0900–1600; from 1000 in summer.*

**ℹ The Breakers** *1 S County Road; tel: (561) 655-6611. Guided tour Wed at 1500.*

### The Beach*

The most unpretentious place in Palm Beach is simply the long and slender beach that runs parallel to the town. Swimming, sunbathing and sandcastle building are all commonly seen here but tanning celebrities are not. Most residents have their own private strand adjacent to their properties.

### The Breakers✦✦✦

Built in 1926, the Breakers hotel casts a commanding presence over Palm Beach. With its palatial size, distinctive twin towers and a golf course which consumes almost the entire width of the island, the Italian Renaissance hotel is Palm Beach's biggest employer and hosts top society occasions.

The current property is the third hotel on the site. The original Breakers was raised in 1896 as oil and transportation magnate Henry Flagler sought to lure the nation's rich and powerful to vacations in

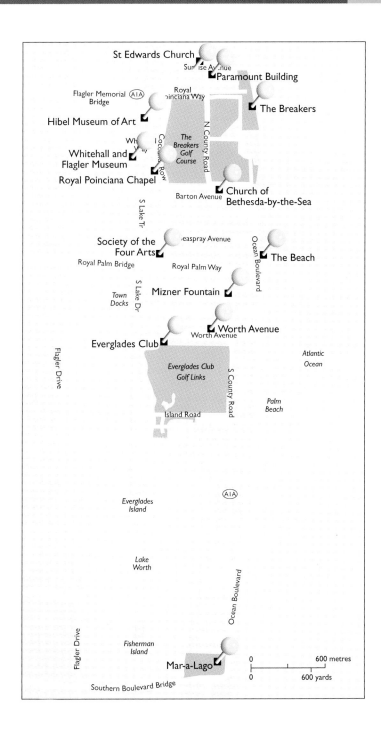

his newly developed town; both it and a 1903 replacement succumbed to fire. Six million dollars was lavished on the present hotel's construction, using 1200 workers and a brigade of artists and craftsmen brought from Europe.

Word has it that the $2000-a-night suites are only slightly smaller than the lobby, which runs the entire length of the hotel. Step inside and pass beneath the vaulted ceiling and its crystal chandeliers, noting the 1920s brass fittings around the concierge's desk and the fireplaces, the frescoes and the 15th- and 16th-century Flemish tapestries along the walls.

Take a peek inside the mind-numbingly opulent Circle Dining Room, where diners are distracted from their food by the scenes of Italian cities etched on to the ceiling, and turn left into the side room which carries exhibits on the hotel's illustrious past. In the grounds are fountain-bearing courtyards and loggias, a croquet lawn and a path that leads to the hotel's private beach to which guests were once ferried by horse-drawn carriage.

**Church of Bethesda-by-the-Sea**

The mere fact that its Gothic Revival looks are completely at odds with Palm Beach's profusion of Mediterranean architectural styles gives the Episcopalian Church of Bethesda-by-the-Sea a certain appeal. Inside, a gorgeous stained-glass window rises above the high altar. Beside the church, the cloistered **Cluett Memorial Gardens** and their stone benches provide a lovely setting for a snack and a meditation on the transient nature of material things.

**Everglades Club**

Self-taught architect Addison Mizner gave Palm Beach its Mediterranean appearance. One of his earliest and best works was the 1918 Everglades Club, complete with fake Moorish bell towers and barrel-tiled roofs. Originally conceived as a convalescent hospital for veterans of World War I, the three-storey building quickly became the base of the most exclusive resort club in the US and remains strictly members only.

**Hibel Museum of Art**

Household name she may not be, but Edna Hibel, who lives in nearby Singer Island, is among the most commercially successful artists in the US. Her finely realised portraits of children and mothers, and other tender scenes, have earned her many admirers and a fortune. A thousand works by the prolific Hibel, who claims to be able to paint 12 hours a day, seven days a week, are held here. Some visitors find them embarrassingly sentimental, others are moved to tears.

**Church of Bethesda-by-the-Sea** *141 S County Road; tel: (561) 655-4554. Open daily 0800–1700.*

**Everglades Club** *356 Worth Avenue; tel: (561) 655-7810. Private club, view from street only.*

**Hibel Museum of Art** *150 Royal Poinciana Plaza; tel: (561) 833-6870. Open Tue–Sat 1000–1700, Sun 1300–1700.*

**Above**
The Breakers Hotel

**Mar-a-Lago** *1100*
*S Ocean Boulevard;*
*private house, no admission.*

**Mizner Fountain**
*S County Road, between*
*Australian and Chilean*
*avenues.*

**Paramount Building**
*139 N County Road.*

**Royal Poinciana Chapel**
*In the grounds of Whitehall;*
*tel: (561) 655-4212. Open*
*by appointment only.*

## Mar-a-Lago**

Not only was breakfast cereal heiress Marjorie Merriweather Post the queen of Palm Beach society for four decades, she also owned what was undoubtedly the island's most extravagant home, Mar-a-Largo. The bright pink building with 118 rooms and sprawling across a 17-acre plot was unveiled to a disbelieving audience in 1927. Some were impressed, some were jealous, others considered the whole thing an $8-million exercise in Mediterranean kitsch.

Even the US government, to whom the house was willed on Post's death in 1973, could not afford its upkeep. In 1985 it was purchased for $15 million by property tycoon Donald Trump with plans to turn it into an exclusive club with $100,000 annual membership fees. A small bronze plaque on Ocean Drive announces the entrance; the overwrought Moorish tower and many other features of the house can be glimpsed over the wall.

## Mizner Fountain*

Marking the heart of Palm Beach as Addison Mizner probably envisaged it, the Mizner Fountain, its three basins held by sculptured horses, sits alongside a narrow palm tree-lined pond opposite Palm Beach's modestly sized Town Hall. The surrounding buildings encapsulate the mish-mash of Mediterranean features that Mizner gave the developing town in the early 1920s. Note the imitation wormholes created in stucco walls with hobnailed boots.

## Paramount Building*

Although a few of the original features can still be spotted amid what is now a routine collection of shops and offices, the 1927 Paramount Building is one of Palm Beach's celebrated structures. It was designed by Joseph Urban, better known as set designer of the *Ziegfeld Follies*, and was a venue for live performances by stars such as Charlie Chaplin and W C Fields, and movie premières attended by the likes of Douglas Fairbanks and Mary Pickford. Season tickets were charged at $1000 a time.

## Royal Poinciana Chapel*

Used by guests staying at Palm Beach's first luxury resort, Henry Flagler's Royal Poinciana Hotel, this clapboard, non-denominational place of worship was raised in 1896 and moved to the grounds of Whitehall (*see page 90*) to make way for the creation of Cocoanut Way. Behind it stands the oldest house in Palm Beach, **Seagull Cottage**, built in 1886 and occupied by Henry Flagler as he awaited the completion of the decidedly grander Whitehall.

### St Edwards Church*

This pretty and ornate Catholic church, completed in 1927, has a cast stone baroque entrance that leads into the nave, over which each segment of the 65-ft-high vaulted ceiling is hand painted. Cast from a

**St Edwards Church**
*144 N County Road; tel:
(561) 832-0400. Open
Mon–Sat 0700–1600, Sun
0700–1300.*

**Society of the Four
Arts** *Four Arts Plaza, of
Royal Palm Way; tel: (561)
655-7226. Galleries open
Dec–Apr, Mon–Sat
1000–1700, Sun
1400–1700; gardens
Nov–Apr, Mon–Fri
1000–1700, Sat
0900–1300; rest of the
year, Mon–Fri 1000–1700.*

**Whitehall and Flagler
Museum $$** *Whitehall
Way, off Cocoanut Row; tel:
(561) 655-2833. Open
Tue–Sat 1000–1700, Sun
1200–1700.*

**Worth Avenue**
*between Cocoanut Row
and Ocean Boulevard.*

**Green's Pharmacy
and Luncheonette**
*$ 151 N S County Road. It
has to be seen to be
believed but this really is a
1937 pharmacy/diner,
dispensing ice-cream sodas
and tasty burgers along
with the medicines.*

single piece of Carrara marble, the enormously imposing main altar occupies a 40-ft-high niche. Among many stained-glass windows is one donated by the Kennedy, regulars at Sunday service when in town and whose presence during the presidency of John Kennedy boosted attendances (*see Lake Trail, page 92*).

## Society of the Four Arts✧✧

Palm Beach is awash with money and a surprising amount of it floats toward the Society of the Four Arts, founded in 1936 to promote art, literature, music and science. The society's offices, lecture halls and exhibition spaces fill several buildings, most attractive of which is the **Four Arts Library**, a gorgeous Italian-influenced construction in coquina rock with an entrance loggia decorated with classical-style murals depicting the Fine Arts. Across the courtyard, the scrupulously well-maintained **gardens** are a sight to behold.

## Whitehall and the Flagler Museum✧✧✧

Oil and transportation magnate Henry Flagler, whose railroad made Florida's east coast accessible, turned Palm Beach into a retreat for the rich from the late 1890s. He built several hotels and lavished $4 million on Whitehall, a home for himself and his third wife for whom it was intended as a wedding present.

Architects Carrère and Hastings, also known for the New York Public Library, created what was eventually labelled 'the Taj Mahal of North America', an extraordinary hotchpotch of ideas and furnishings culled from the aristocratic homes of Europe.

Behind its Doric columns, Whitehall has a marble entrance hall modelled on that of a Roman villa's atrium, a Swiss billiard room, an Italian Renaissance library, an Elizabethan breakfast room, a Louis XIV music room and a 94-ft-long Louis XV ballroom lined by mirrors and illuminated by three vast chandeliers. Upstairs are 14 guest rooms reveaing styles ranging from Colonial American to art nouveau and the Flaglers' own rococo suite with Louis XV-style furniture.

Arched loggias lead into the open courtyard at the centre of the house, a refreshing spot to contemplate the architectural excesses and admire the sculptured Venus rising from the fountain overlooked by four satyrs.

## Worth Avenue✧✧✧

The only street in Florida where top-dollar stores such as Tiffany & Co, Cartier and Lacoste stand side-by-side, Worth Avenue is Palm Beach's main shopping strip and provides clothing, jewellery and household items for the island's many rich residents, most of whom arrive by Jaguar or Rolls Royce and have their chauffeurs wait as the price of new purchases are added to their accounts.

The mock Mediterranean style created by Addison Mizner makes Worth Avenue very enjoyable to explore, even for those who can afford to do no more than window shop. Many of the smaller stores are arranged around cobbled courtyards, reached by alleyways (or *vias*), decorated by wall-fountains and hanging flower baskets, with slender spiral staircases accessing upper levels.

# Accommodation and food

Despite its well-deserved reputation as a playground of the rich and famous, Palm Beach offers accommodation and food at surprisingly affordable prices, particularly in the summer off-season, for those whose funds render the luxury options off-limits.

**Brazilian Court Hotel $$–$$$** *301 Australian Court; tel: (561) 655-7740 or (800) 552-0335.* Pleasant Spanish-style building with a tropical flavour, very comfortable rooms and suites.

**The Breakers $$$** *1 S County Road; tel: (561) 655-6611 or (888) BREAKERS.* The perfect Palm Beach home away from home, this historic hotel (*see page 86*) has lovely rooms, a private beach and faultless service.

**Palm Beach Historic Inn $$–$$$** *365 S County Road; tel (561) 832 4009.* Small and friendly bed-and-breakfast inn occupying a 1921 building facing the Town Hall.

**Bice $$$** *313 1/2 Worth Avenue; tel: (561) 835-1600.* Northern Italian cuisines impeccably prepared and presented in a candle-lit setting.

**Chuck & Harold's $$–$$$** *207 Royal Poinciana Way; tel: (561) 659-1440.* Delicious salads, soups and daily specials, best eaten at the sidewalk tables.

# Suggested tour

**Length**: Main tour, 2 miles; 6 miles with detours.

**Duration**: 3 hours, 6 hours with detours.

**Links**: The northern edge of the Gold Coast route (*see pages 74–85*) is 23 miles south of Palm Beach, separated by an attractive stretch of the coastal Hwy-A1A.

Although you should arrive in Palm Beach by car, the main tour can be undertaken mostly on foot. The Lake Trail detour is a good option by bike but can also be covered by walking.

Enter Palm Beach on Royal Palm Bridge, named for its majestic royal palm trees, and the **SOCIETY OF THE FOUR ARTS ❶** is on the left, adjacent to the commendable **Philip Hulitar Sculpture Garden ❷**. Turn north along Cocoanut Way for **WHITEHALL ❸** the former mansion of Henry

**Lake Trail** *starts off at Royal Poinciana Way close to Flagler Memorial Bridge.*

**Palm Beach Bicycle Trail Shop** *223 Sunrise Avenue; tel: (561) 659-4583.*

Flagler, also known as the **Flagler Museum** ❹. Within the grounds stands the dainty **ROYAL POINCIANA CHAPEL** ❺.

North of Whitehall, secreted amid the shops and offices of Royal Poinciana Plaza, is the **HIBEL MUSEUM OF ART** ❻. Directly ahead across Royal Poinciana Way is the start of the Lake Trail detour.

Turning right along busy Royal Poinciana Way leads to N County Road, the twin-towered **BREAKERS** ❼ hotel and its expansive golf course dominating the view to the right. Turn left on N County Road for the **PARAMOUNT BUILDING** ❽ and, just beyond, **ST EDWARDS CHURCH** ❾. Retrace your steps to the explore the elegant interior and ample public spaces of the Breakers.

Continue south along N County Road for the **CHURCH OF BETHESDA-BY-THE-SEA** ❿, and then turn left along Barton Avenue for a stroll on the sands of Palm Beach's public **BEACH** ⓫. Continuing along Royal Palm Way, turn right into S County Road and look for the entrance on the left into **Phipps Plaza** ⓬, a quiet and rarely visited cul-de-sac with many notable Mediterranean-style buildings.

Walk back along S County Road, crossing Royal Palm Way, reaching the administrative heart of Palm Beach where the **MIZNER FOUNTAIN** ⓭ faces the Town Hall. Three blocks south is the junction with **WORTH AVENUE** ⓮. Stroll this high-class shopping street exploring its many courtyards as you go. At the junction with Cocoanut Way, the **EVERGLADES CLUB** ⓯, one of the first buildings in Palm Beach in the Mediterranean style, can be spotted on the south side.

**Detour:** Palm Beach's almost entirely residential northern reaches are best seen from the 3-mile-long **Lake Trail** ⓰ beginning close to the junction of the Flagler Memorial Bridge and Royal Poinciana Way. Ideally undertaken by bicycle, the meandering route passes local landmarks such as **Duck's Nest** ⓱ (*561 N Lake Trail*), Palm Beach's oldest continuously occupied home in, erected in 1890 from prefabricated material shipped from New York. At that time, boats would bring the faithful to the island's first church, the first **Church of Bethesda-by-the-Sea** ❿, a shingle-fronted building just beyond Duck's Nest.

The trail expires at the northern tip of the island. Returning along North Ocean Boulevard passes the gatehouses of numerous expansive beachfront estates. These include **La Guerida** ⓲ (*No 1095*), bought by Joe Kennedy in 1933, used as a working vacation base in the early 1960s by his son, John F Kennedy, and remaining under Kennedy family ownership until the mid-1990s.

**Detour:** By car or bike, head south along Ocean Boulevard from the eastern end of Worth Avenue. This route has a lovely strip of beach to the left and stupendous mansions to the right, none more spectacular than the partially concealed **MAR-A-LAGO** ⓳, 2 miles ahead.

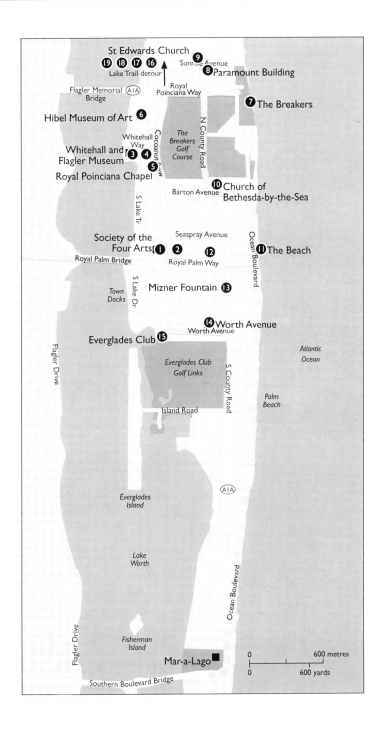

St Edwards Church
19 18 17 16 Sunrise Avenue 9
Lake Trail detour 8 Paramount Building
Flagler Memorial A1A Royal
Bridge Poinciana Way
7 The Breakers
Hibel Museum of Art 6
Whitehall The
Way Breakers
Whitehall and 3 4 Golf
Flagler Museum Course
5
Royal Poinciana Chapel
Coconut Row
N County Road
10 Church of
Barton Avenue Bethesda-by-the-Sea
S Lake Tr
Society of the Seaspray Avenue
Four Arts 1 2 12 11 The Beach
Royal Palm Bridge Royal Palm Way
Ocean Boulevard
Town
Docks Mizner Fountain 13
S Lake Dr
14 Worth Avenue
Worth Avenue
Everglades Club 15
Atlantic
Everglades Club Ocean
Golf Links
S County Road
Flagler Drive
Palm
Beach
Island Road

A1A

Everglades
Island

Lake
Worth
Ocean Boulevard

Flagler Drive
Fisherman
Island

Mar-a-Lago
Southern Boulevard Bridge

0                    600 metres
0                    600 yards

# Florida Keys

## Ratings

| | |
|---|---|
| Fishing | ●●●●● |
| Nature | ●●●●● |
| Snorkelling and diving | ●●●●● |
| Scenery | ●●●◐● |
| Beaches | ●●● |
| Children | ●● |
| History | ●● |
| Museums | ●● |

Few places anywhere in the world have the scenery, history or the romance to match that of the Florida Keys, a chain of islands that spreads from the Florida mainland to Key West. Linked by a single road (Hwy-1, also called the Overseas Highway), each section of the Keys has a personality distinct from its neighbours. One thing they share, however, is a fantastic natural setting: each island like a green speck within a gigantic expanse of sea and sky.

Although the route is packed with visual delights, not least incredible sunsets, many sections are dominated not by nature's handiwork but by the fishing and diving businesses that underpin most local economies. Underwater exploration and numerous types of fishing draw many visitors to the Keys. If these pursuits do not appeal, though, the region's friendly and relaxed mood, epitomised by many the quiet hotels and unpretentious restaurants, certainly will.

## BAHIA HONDA STATE PARK✧✧✧

ⓘ **Bahia Honda State Park** $ *MM36.8, south of Seven Mile Bridge; tel: (305) 872-2353. Open daily 0800–sunset.*

The best beach in the Keys, a strip of fine white sand that separates the ocean from a tranquil lagoon, flanks the 524-acre Bahia Honda State Park. Also in the park are shady picnic tables, swimming areas and a short foot trail weaving through a tropical hardwood hammock and above mangrove entanglements. White-crowned pigeons, great white herons and roseate spoonbills are among the most regularly sighted examples of the local birdlife.

## BIG PINE KEY✧

Several thousand people live on Big Pine Key but the best-known residents are several hundred Key deer, a dwarf species once plentiful throughout the Keys but now found only here. Supplementing the diet of Key West sailors for many years, the deer acquired federal protection in 1954. Though tempting, it is illegal to feed the very tame

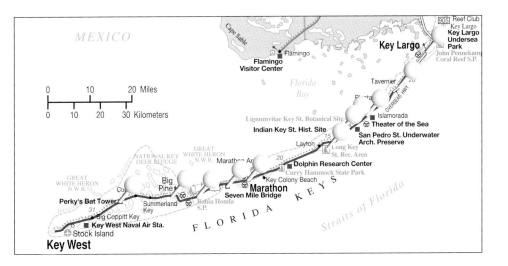

deer which are easily spotted beside Key Deer Boulevard and Watson
Boulevard, and are most numerous in the coolness of early morning
and evening. Another lure for nature lovers is **Blue Hole**, a former
rock quarry now filled with fresh water and home to several alligators
and a multitude of other less formidable creatures.

## Accommodation and food in Big Pine Key

**Barnacle Bed & Breakfast $$** *1557 Long Beach Drive; tel: (305) 872-3298
or (800) 465-9100.* A Caribbean-style house in a peaceful spot, ideal for
exploring this under-visited section of the Keys.

**Mangrove Mama's $$** *MM22; tel (305) 745-3030.* Encapsulates the
unpretentious spirit of the Keys, serving top-notch seafood in a rustic
and convivial setting.

# INDIAN KEY STATE HISTORIC SITE✧✧✧

One of the many eccentrics to become footnotes in Keys' history is
Jacob Housman who, in 1831, bought 11-acre Indian Key intent on
grabbing a share of the Keys' lucrative salvaging business. Housman's
initial success made Indian Key an instant town, with shops, wharves,
warehouses and even a bowling alley. The unscrupulous Housman was
known to deliberately lure vessels to destruction. He lost his salvaging
licence and sold the island to botanist James Perrine in 1839.
Housman and Perrine were both killed a year later when Indians
attacked the island for its stores during the Seminole Wars.

The uninhabited island is overgrown by many of the plant species introduced by Perrine, among them the tea, coffee and sisal that he hoped to exploit commercially. A two-hour guided tour tells the full story of this strange and beguiling island.

# ISLAMORADA*

**Islamorada Chamber of Commerce** *MM82.5, Islamorada; tel: (305) 664-4503 or (800) 322-5397. Open Mon–Fri 0900–1700, Sat–Sun 0900–1400.*

**Theater of the Sea** *$$ MM84.5; tel: (305-664 2431. Open daily 0930–1600.*

Though popular throughout the Keys, fishing is especially big news at Islamorada, a town spreading for 18 miles across four separate islands and holding the region's densest concentration of charter boats and marinas. Photos of satisfied customers holding their catches aloft – usually man-sized tarpon and marlin – encourage many novices to try their hand on a 'party boat', which carries 20 to 30 enthusiastic beginners out to sea and provides the necessary instruction and equipment for a fruitful day's fishing.

For anyone who prefers to watch marine life rather than land it, the **Theater of the Sea** provides a few pleasant low-key hours with sea lion and dolphin shows, and glass-bottomed boat trips.

### Food in Islamorada

**Green Turtle Inn $$** *MM81.3; tel: (305) 664-9031.* Pleasing locals and many others since the 1940s with its excellent seafood; the signature dish is turtle chowder.

**Marker 88 $$$** *MM88; tel: (305) 852-9315.* Given a gourmet twist, Florida fare such as frogs' legs sometimes appears alongside more mainstream items on the menu of this acclaimed restaurant.

# JOHN PENNEKAMP CORAL REEF STATE PARK❖❖❖

**John Pennekamp Coral Reef State Park $** *MM 102.6, Key Largo: tel: (305) 451-1202. Open daily 0800–sunset.*

Protecting a large section of the narrow strip of living coral lying 3 miles offshore and continuing for 200 miles to Key West and beyond, John Pennekamp Coral Reef State Park is the gateway to an underwater world of great complexity and beauty. Some 500 fish species, from 4-ft-long barracuda to the dazzlingly coloured parrotfish, plus an amazing mixture of crabs, sea urchins, starfish, snails, lobsters and shrimps, live around the reef. Many can be viewed on the diving, snorkelling and glass-bottomed boat trips available from the park.

Although its most spectacular sections are underwater, the park's 2300-acre land area provides excellent picnic territory. The visitors' centre has displays on the park's natural history and boardwalk trails around its mangrove forests, which can also be navigated by canoe.

# KEY LARGO❖

**Key Largo Chamber of Commerce** *MM106, Key Largo; tel: (305) 451-1414 or (800) 822-1088. Open daily 0900–1800.*

**Maritime Museum of the Florida Keys** *$ MM102.6, Key Largo; tel: (305) 451-6444. Open Mon–Wed, Fri–Sat 1000–1700, Sun 1200–1700.*

The film of the same name (set around the Keys' 1935 Labor Day hurricane and mostly filmed in Hollywood) has brought Key Largo a fame beyond its due. None the less, further cinematic links are maintained with the *African Queen*, the diminutive vessel that starred in John Houston's 1951 film, now berthed in a local marina. Also meriting a quick look is the **Maritime Museum of the Florida Keys** which displays a modest selection of coins, cannons and other artefacts recovered from wrecked Spanish galleons inside a mock 15th-century castle.

### Food in Key Largo

**Coconuts $$** *MM 101; tel: (305) 453-9794.* Large seafood menu and stunning waterfront location.

**Ganim's Kountry Kitchen $–$$** *MM 100.5; tel: (305) 451-2895.* Small, friendly spot serving wholesome breakfasts and lunches in generous portions.

**Left**
Fishing boat and heron

# LIGNUMVITAE KEY STATE BOTANICAL SITE✦✦✦

**Lignumvitae Key $**
**Boat from MM77.7,**
*south of Islamorada; tel:*
*(305) 664 6196. Departures*
*Thur–Mon at 0830 and*
*1230.*

Much of Lignumvitae Key is covered by a shady hammock containing strangler fig, mahogany, gumbo limbo, mastic, poisonwood, pigeon plum and other exotically named tree types, many of them beginning life in the Keys having arrived as wind- or sea-borne seeds. The trees and their curious idiosyncrasies are entertainingly described on a three-hour guided tour.

The conservation of the island is due largely to W J Matheson, a rich industrialist who bought the island in 1919 and raised the coral rock house which still provides its main sign of human habitation.

# LONG KEY STATE RECREATION AREA✦✦

At the heart of a particularly beautiful segment of the Keys, Long Key State Recreation Area is a mixture of tropical hardwood hammock and mangrove forest interwoven with short nature trails. An observation point brings views of wading birds, especially prevalent here in winter.

# MARATHON✦

**Marathon**
**Chamber of**
**Commerce** *MM53.5; tel:*
*(305) 743-5417 or (800)*
*842-950. Open daily*
*0900–1700.*

**Crane Point**
**Hammock Museum**
*$ MM50; tel: (305) 743-*
*9100. Open Nov–Aug,*
*Mon–Sat 0900–1700, Sun*
*1200–1700; rest of the*
*year, daily 1200–1700.*

Marathon is said to have acquired its name from workers on the Overseas Railroad who, while camped here in the 1910s, would contemplate the 'marathon' nature of their task to continue the tracks south across the forbidding span now straddled by the Seven Mile Bridge (*see page 101*).

Marathon is the venue of several major fishing tournaments, but a year-round local highlight is **Crane Point Hammock Museum**, providing an excellent introduction to Keys' ecology. The museum has a large children's section separated from the main museum by a 15,000-gallon saltwater lagoon, home to creatures such as bonnethead sharks and barracudas.

A number of foot trails have been devised through the 64 acres of tropical hardwood hammock that the museum occupies. Among them, the **Bahama House Trail** reaches the remains of a 1903 Bahamian settlement and explores the tabby-built (a mixture of shells, coral rock and mud) house that belonged to the colony's founder.

## Accommodation in Marathon

**Banana Bay Resort $$** *4590 Hwy-1; tel: (305) 743-3500 or (800) BANANA-1.* Large and tastefully decorated rooms, all within easy reach of the beach. Pool and continental breakfast.

**Hawk's Cay Resort & Marina $$$** *MM61 Duck Key; tel: (305) 743-7000 or (800) 432-2242.* Spread over its own 60-acre island, offering luxury accommodation and a staff trained to pamper.

## Snorkelling and diving

The keys are prized for their snorkelling and scuba-diving opportunities. **John Pennekamp Coral Reef State Park**, **Sombrero Reef**, off Marathon, the **San Pedro Underwater Archaeological Park**, off Islamorada, and **Looe Key Marine Sanctuary** are particularly good areas. The necessary equipment, information, guided trips, and the instruction leading to the certificate essential for the use of scuba equipment, is provided by scores of dive shops along Hwy-1.

**Right**
Diver and turtle wall mural

# PERKY'S BAT TOWER*

**Perky's Bat Tower**
*off Hwy-1 near MM17.*

The rich folklore of the Florida Keys is littered with eccentric schemes but none are more bizarre than that of property spectacular Richter C Perky, who devised what he thought was a foolproof plan to tempt settlers to Sugarloaf Key. Aware that mosquitoes deterred many would-be arrivals, Perky raised a 35-ft wooden tower, now remembered as Perky's Bat Tower, and packed it with a mail-order 'bat bait' (thought to have been bat droppings). Perky believed that bats would take up residence in the tower and rid the area of its mosquitoes. He soon went bust, but the tower remains.

### Henry Flagler's overseas railroad

Hwy-1, the Overseas Highway, follows the route of the Overseas Railroad that was devised by Standard Oil magnate and Florida developer Henry Flagler to link the Keys to the mainland and continue to Key West. Begun in 1904, the line reached Key West eight years later, having claimed the lives of 700 workers and given the Keys a series of multi-arched concrete bridges.

Although the bridges stayed intact, the 200mph winds of the 1935 Labor Day hurricane tore the tracks from the ground. The death toll included 200 people aboard an evacuation train. The loss of the tracks and Americans' growing love affair with the car resulted in the creation of the Overseas Highway, helping the newly accessible Keys become a popular vacation destination. The road crosses many Flagler-era bridges; their environmental impact, not least in changing tidal patterns, is still being assessed.

# SEVEN MILE BRIDGE✢✢

The Seven Mile Bridge, completed in 1982 at a cost of $45 million, was a much-needed replacement for the Flagler-era original, easing traffic congestion on Hwy-1 and tall enough to allow ships to pass beneath. The bridge itself is a jaw-dropping sight and the view from it is every bit as spectacular as you might expect.

# TAVERNIER✢

**Florida Keys Wild Birds Rehabilitation Center** MM93.6; tel: (305) 852-4486. Open daily dawn–dusk.

First settled by Bahamian farmers and later becoming a pineapple and coconut plantation, Tavernier possess a charming **historic district** and the **Florida Keys Wild Birds Rehabilitation Center**, where sick birds are nursed back to health; many can be seen in various stages of convalescence from a boardwalk trail.

## Accommodation in Tavernier

**Bay Breeze Motel $$** *160 Sterling Road, MM92.5 Bayside; tel: (305) 852-5248 or (800) 937 5650.* Good rates beside the bay, with spectacular sunsets and a private beach.

# Suggested tour

**Length**: 95 miles.

**Duration**: Main tour driving time 2.5 hours; detours according to local boat and tour schedules.

**Links**: It would be criminal to travel the length of the Keys without

Left
Florida Keys highway

continuing to Key West (*see pages 104–113*). In the other direction, this route meets the South Miami and the Everglades National Park tour at Florida City (*see pages 64–73*).

As it crosses Florida Bay towards the Keys, the outlook from Hwy-1 is of a vast expanse of ocean dotted with mangrove-fringed islands beneath intensely blue skies. Also known as the Overseas Highway, Hwy-1 runs the length of the Keys (derived from the Spanish word for island, *cayo*) connecting the string of islands between the mainland and Key West.

Two miles after swinging right into **KEY LARGO ❶**, Hwy-1 passes the entrance to **JOHN PENNEKAMP CORAL REEF STATE PARK ❷**, the best place to explore the offshore coral reef. The reef is the reason very few beaches are found along the Keys. From Key Largo, Hwy-1 passes through **TAVERNIER ❸** and on to the first of the four separate islands that comprise **ISLAMORADA ❹**, the route lined by bait-and-tackle shops, petrol stations, dive centres, small supermarkets and side-roads leading to numerous marinas.

Refreshingly, the next 20 miles or so are among the prettiest sections of Hwy-1. This stretch includes **LONG KEY STATE RECREATION**

## Swimming with dolphins

Three places in the Keys allow humans to swim with dolphins, although reservations should be made well in advance and participants must be strong swimmers and adept users of masks and fins: **Dolphins Plus** (*MM 100.5, Key Largo; tel: (305) 451-1993*); **Dolphin Research Center** (*MM 59, Marathon; tel: (305) 289-1121*); and **Theater of the Sea** (*MM 84.5, Islamorada; tel: (305) 664-2431*).

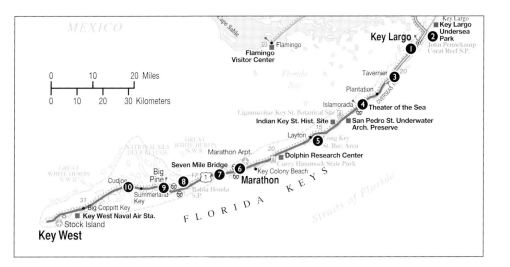

**Left**
Dolphin Research Center

**AREA ⑤** and continues across the 2.3-mile Long Key Bridge into **MARATHON ⑥**. Note the disproportionately large runways of the airport, to the right of Hwy-1, a training strip for B17 bomber pilots during World War II. Immediately south of Marathon is the soaring **SEVEN MILE BRIDGE ⑦** that hits land at **BAHIA HONDA STATE PARK ⑧**, perhaps the most scenic picnic stop in Florida.

Four miles ahead, the route swings right on to **BIG PINE KEY ⑨**. Take a right turn on to Key Deer Boulevard to find the Key Pine deer. Hwy-1 continues on to Sugarloaf Key, turning right just after MM17 leads to **PERKY'S BAT TOWER ⑩**.

**Detour:** Both Lignumvitae Key and Indian Key are accessible only by boat and are best seen on guided tours. Boat departures, which link with the tours, are from a marked point on **Indian Key Fill**, just south of Islamorada near MM78.

## Also worth exploring

Dominated by the enormous Seven Mile Bridge which rises immediately south, **Pigeon Key** provided accommodation for 400 railroad workers from 1908. They were employed in the massive task of erecting the original Seven Mile Bridge, a section of which links Pigeon Key to Hwy-1. Seven wooden cottages on the 5-acre island have been restored and form part of a guided tour starting at the visitors' centre on Knights Key, to the left off Hwy-1 at MM45. No cars are permitted on Pigeon Key, which is reached by tram from the visitors' centre; visitors may also arrive on foot or bicycle.

# Key West

## Ratings

| | |
|---|---|
| Ambience | ●●●●● |
| History | ●●●● |
| Nightlife | ●●●● |
| Architecture | ●●● |
| Children | ●●● |
| Museums | ●●● |
| Scenery | ●●● |
| Beaches | ●● |

Key West is the southernmost city in the continental US and one of the most distinctive. Compact and easily walkable, the city's tree-lined streets are studded with pretty 19th-century homes, many of them open to the public. Some once accommodated luminaries such as Ernest Hemingway, one of many writers with local links, while others now function as small museums displaying mementoes of Key West's seafaring past. The settlement originally grew as a centre for salvaging from ships wrecked on the offshore reefs.

Key West's 30,000-strong permanent population, typically relaxed to the point of catatonia, may be swamped by a million annual visitors but the immense tourist influx fails to lessen the charm or dent the sense of individuality in a community that declared itself an independent republic in 1982. At night the open-sided bars, some of them with deep roots in local history, are at the centre of a famously voracious nightlife.

## Sights

**ⓘ Key West Chamber of Commerce** *402 Wall Street; tel: (305) 294-2587 or (800) LAST-KEY. Open daily 0830–1700.*

**ⓗ Audubon House $** *205 Whitehead Street; tel: (305) 294-4513. Open daily 0930–1700.*

**Audubon House**✢✢
John James Audubon, who visited Key West in 1832 while compiling the wildlife studies that eventually earned him enduring fame as the *Birds of America* series, gives the house its name although links between the artist and the house are tenuous. This attractive, early 19th-century residence was built by a ship's carpenter for a leading Key West citizen, Captain John G Geiger, a salvager and harbour pilot during the days when shipwrecks underpinned the Key West economy.

Re-creating the voices of the Captain and his wife, audio guides (for hire) describe the house and their time in it. An Irish harp, a Chinese tea caddy and Chippendale tables and chairs are among the fixtures and fittings selected to suggest a typical wealthy Key West house of the time. Many Audubon prints line the walls.

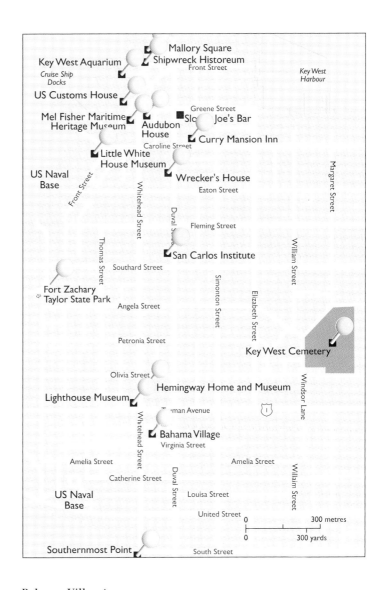

Key West Aquarium
Cruise Ship Docks
US Customs House
Mel Fisher Maritime Heritage Museum
Audubon House
Little White House Museum
US Naval Base
Front Street
Whitehead Street
Thomas Street
Fort Zachary Taylor State Park
Mallory Square
Shipwreck Historeum
Front Street
Key West Harbour
Greene Street
Slo    Joe's Bar
Curry Mansion Inn
Caroline Street
Wrecker's House
Eaton Street
Fleming Street
Duval S
San Carlos Institute
Southard Street
Angela Street
Petronia Street
Simonton Street
Elizabeth Street
William Street
Margaret Street
Key West Cemetery
Olivia Street
Hemingway Home and Museum
Lighthouse Museum
man Avenue
Bahama Village
Virginia Street
Amelia Street
Catherine Street
US Naval Base
Southernmost Point
Whitehead Street
Duval Street
Louisa Street
United Street
South Street
Amelia Street
William Street
Windsor Lane
0        300 metres
0        300 yards

**Bahama Village**
bordered by Virginia, Olivia, Fort and Whitehead streets.

## Bahama Village*

Many of Key West's 19th-century homes were expensively restored through the 1980s and 1990s. One part of town that retains a rustic appearance, however, is the Bahama Village, originally settled by Bahamians and still occupied by many people of Caribbean descent or origin. The atmosphere is informal and redolent of a Caribbean street with few concessions to tourists amid the scurrying chickens and serious domino games.

### Curry Mansion Inn✦✦✦

William Curry, one-time mayor of Key West, made a fortune by supplying salvagers with hardware. In 1855 he began building what grew into the Curry Mansion, greatly expanded by his son in the early 1900s. A plush and rambling affair fronted by an inviting veranda, the mansion's wood-panelled rooms are packed with antiques, including glasswork by Louis Comfort Tiffany, a 1835 piano believed to have belonged to novelist Henry James and Audubon ornithological prints, and is a delight to explore.

Key West folklore suggests that the first Key lime pie (a dessert found throughout the Keys and exciting high passions in devotees) was made here in 1895, when the cook added the newly invented condensed milk to a dish that originated in the Bahamas.

### Fort Zachary Taylor State Historic Site✦✦

Fort Zachary Taylor, its red brick buildings unearthed through the 1970s after decades of neglect, was originally intended as part of the US's coastal defences and helped Key West become the only city south of the Mason-Dixon line to remain in Union hands through the Civil War. The fort's construction, a process lasting 21 years from 1845, was hindered by outbreaks of yellow fever and hurricanes. The story of the fort, now landlocked but originally 1200 feet from shore and linked to Key West by piers, is outlined in a small museum within one of the vaulted rooms.

Another reason to visit is simply the setting: a tranquil site with fabulous ocean views from the walkways along the top of the fort's 8-ft-thick walls. Near by, an alluring white-sand beach makes a perfect picnic venue.

**Above**
Fort Zachary Taylor sculpture

**ⓘ Hemingway Home and Museum** $ *907 Whitehead Street; tel: (305) 294-1575. Open daily 0900–1700.*

**Key West Aquarium** $ *1 Whitehead Street; tel: (305) 296-2051. Open daily 1000–1800.*

**Key West Cemetery** *701 Passover Lane; tel: (305) 292-8177. Open daily sunrise–1800; phone for guided tour details.*

## Hemingway Home and Museum✧✧

This Spanish Colonial house, built for a wealthy Key West merchant in the 1850s, was in a dilapidated condition when it became Ernest Hemingway's first US home after returning from Europe, where he had established his literary reputation in the 1920s. It stayed under the ownership of the Hemingways (Ernest and his second wife, Pauline) for 30 years, although the writer moved out in 1940 when the marriage ended, leaving many of his possessions here but storing his manuscripts in the backroom of a local bar.

Key West was an unlikely setting for a man fast becoming a giant of American literature but Hemingway coveted the deep-sea fishing, the many bars and the easy-going nature of the locals, once describing the town as 'the St Tropez of the poor'. Hemingway wrote about Key West in *To Have And Have Not*, one of two novels (the other was *For Whom The Bell Tolls*) written here in a hunting trophy-lined study accessed from the main house by rope bridge.

Simple furnishings and the writer's knick-knacks are revealed on the guided tours, as is the $20,000 swimming pool, the first in Key West. The tour also recounts a few of the many stories about Hemingway in Key West. Among other achievements, Hemingway's custom helped make Sloppy Joe's bar a legend and his appearance inspired what is now the annual Hemingway lookalike contest, held each July, part of the **Hemingway Days** festival that commemorates the writer and his Key West links.

## Key West Aquarium✧

It may not be state-of-the-art but the Key West Aquarium is an enjoyable place to pass an hour, with sharks, stingrays, turtles, spiny lobsters, angel fish, sea cucumbers, guitar fish and other oddities of the deep in tanks arranged around wooden walkways.

The 50,000-gallon Atlantic Shores exhibit re-creates conditions around a coral reef of the kind found off the Keys, highlighting the delicate and complex reef ecology and showing some of its community including barracuda, tarpon, starfish and the very peculiar reef squid.

The aquarium has shark-feeding sessions (times are posted) and free guided tours throughout the day. It also has a place in local history; opening in 1934 it was one of the first open-air aquariums in the US and part of Key West's attempts to boost tourism and stimulate its economy after the Depression.

## Key West Cemetery✧

A bronze statue commemorating the 266 sailors who perished in the explosion of the USS *Maine* in Havana harbour in 1898, triggering the Spanish-American War, stands at the heart of the 21-acre Key West Cemetery. Many of the tombs, however, are much less solemn and reflect the famously easy-going attitude of the town with dozens of humorous epitaphs, such as 'I told you I was sick' and 'Call me for dinner'. Guided

**Lighthouse Museum $** *938 Whitehead Street; tel: (305) 294-0012. Open daily 0930–1630.*

**Little White House Museum $** *111 Front Street; tel: (305) 294-9911. Open daily 0900–1700.*

tours tell the amusing story of the cemetery, which replaced an earlier one destroyed by a hurricane, and includes a pets section.

### Lighthouse Museum✦

Dating from 1847, the Key West Lighthouse was among the first in Florida, a fact underlining the immense importance of Key West as a salvaging centre. The former lighthouse keeper's cottage, a dainty structure clad in termite-resistant Dade County pine, houses entertaining relics of Key West's maritime past and displays on the trials and tribulations of lighthouse keeping. Climbing 88 steps leads to the balcony just beneath the light itself and an impressive view across the town.

### Little White House Museum✦✦

President Harry S Truman first visited Key West in 1946 and found the climate and the informality much to his liking. He subsequently enjoyed frequent working vacations in this 1890 house, originally built for the commandant of Key West's US naval base and once housing inventor Thomas Edison, employed by the navy during World War I to develop depth charges.

The house is evocatively maintained in the style of Truman's time and packed with small but intriguing mementoes of his stay. They include the modestly sized desk from which the country was sometimes governed during a period that included the Korean War and the rise of McCarthyism. In Key West, however, Truman is best remembered for playing poker into the small hours and his fondness for the coconut cake made by a local woman.

**Below**
Mallory Square Sunset Festival

### Mallory Square✦✦✦

Clowns, jugglers, unicyclists and busking musicians are all likely to be found at Mallory Square for the nightly **Sunset Festival**. What began in Key West's pre-tourist days as a hippie ritual has now evolved into a major celebration that attracts every tourist in town, as well as large number of locals who never tire of the spectacle. Crowds aside, the festival is fun and the sunset is genuinely spectacular.

**Mel Fisher Maritime Heritage Museum $$** *200 Greene Street; tel (305) 294-2633. Open daily 0930–1700.*

**San Carlos Institute** *516 Duval Street; tel: (305) 294-3887. Open Tue–Sun 1100–1800.*

**Shipwreck Historeum** *$$ 1 Whitehead Street; tel: (305) 292-8990. Open daily 0945–1645.*

## Mel Fisher Maritime Heritage Museum**

Among the many vessels to come to grief on the treacherous reef system lying off the coast of Florida were those plying the route between Spain and the Spanish colonies in the Caribbean and Americas. The wrecks and the valuable cargo they carried provide a cue for modern-day treasure seekers to study old maps and make use of the latest technology in the hope of locating a major find. The late Mel Fisher, former California surf shop owner, was more successful than most in this field. In 1985, after years of searching, he located the *Nuestra Señora de Atocha*, a Spanish galleon sunk in 1622. The cargo retrieved from the ship was valued at $400 million.

The museum displays relics from the galleon, an impressive if small stash (much has been sold) of gold and silver jewellery, coins and religious items, and documents the search that lasted 16 years and took the life of Fisher's son. Remnants from the *Henrietta Marie*, the only working slave shipwreck to have been excavated are also displayed. The second floor has temporary exhibitions, focusing on underwater archaeology and other aspects of seafaring.

## San Carlos Institute***

Founded in 1871 by Cuban exiles as a campaigning base for Cuban independence, the San Carlos Institute provided a school and social centre for the Cuban community in Key West (the backbone of a cigar industry flourishing in the late 1800s) and later moved into this pretty, baroque structure completed in 1924. Designed by Francisco Centurión, a leading Cuban architect, the interior of the new building had Cuban-tiled floors, mosaics reflecting Cuba's six regions, and elegant marble staircases. Upkeep was financed by the Cuban government who used its as a consulate until 1961.

The building, restored during the late 1980s, now justifiably claims to have Key West's most beautiful interior. Exhibits on Cuban themes fill three floors, one of them devoted to the life and work of the revered poet and independence fighter José Martí. Other sections illustrate the many links between Cuba, Florida and Key West.

**Conch Train $** *tel: (305) 294-5161. Daily 0930–1600.* This 90-minute guided shunt around Key West orientates and informs. Board at Mallory Square or 3850 N Roosevelt Boulevard. Similar tours are run by **Old Town Trolley** *(tel: (305) 296-6688)*, which can be joined from 14 marked stops around Key West.

## Shipwreck Historeum*

Using actors, lasers, and booty from the *Isaac Allerton*, a ship that sank in 1856 and was excavated in the 1980s, the Historeum re-creates the daily life of Key West in the mid-19th century, a period when it was among the richest cities per capita in the US through the proceeds of salvaging.

Competition to be first to a wreck was intense. Before the advent of radar and radio, salvagers would be alerted of a wreck by the shouts of look-outs posted in elevated points around the shoreline (though in some cases they simply put to sea and hoped for the worst). One such was **Tift Wrecker's Lookout**, re-created on the Historeum's second floor. From it, shipwrecks are unlikely to be spotted but there is a fine view over Key West and beyond.

### Southernmost Point*

At the foot of Whitehead Street, a large red, yellow and black buoy marks the southernmost point in the continental US, just 90 miles from Cuba. Among the most-photographed features of Key West, the buoy weighs several tons to prevent tourists taking it home as a souvenir. Come early to avoid the crowds and enjoy a stroll across the tiny palm-tree-lined **South Beach**.

### US Customs House*

The divinely proportioned US Customs House, raised in 1891 and costing $108,000, has a suitably imposing presence in this town of clapboard homes. Besides its customs role, the redbrick Romanesque Revival structure has served as a federal court, post office, coastguard headquarters and US Navy office. The fact that the interior is as grand as the exterior will be proven when, after years of closure, the building becomes the home of the **Key West Museum of Art and History**.

### Wrecker's House**

Built around 1829, the clapboard Wrecker's House is believed to be the oldest house in Key West. Its first occupant was Captain Francis Watlington, whose salvaging success accounts for the plethora of 19th-century furnishings filling this compact but comfortable dwelling. Many of the architectural features were typical of Key West at the time: the widow's walk, the ship's hatch in the ceiling that provided ventilation, the cistern that collected rainwater from the gutters, and an outdoor kitchen to reduce risk of fire.

## Accommodation and food

**Curry House Inn $$$** *511 Caroline Street; tel: (305) 294-5349 or (800) 253-3466.* Historic mansion (*see page 106*). Several rooms with four-poster beds and more rooms in an adjacent guest wing.

**El Patio Motel $–$$** *800 Washington Street; tel: (305) 296-6531.* Small and reliable with good rates in a useful location.

**Pier House Resort $$$** *1 Duval Street; tel: (305) 296-4600 or (800) 327-8340.* A setting on the Gulf of Mexico ensures sunsets as splendid

**Above**
The southernmost point in the USA

as the service in this luxury resort, a short walk from the main points of interest.

**Southernmost Motel** $$ *1319 Duval Street; tel: (305) 296-6577 or (800) 354-4455.* Comfortable rooms, two poolside bars and a rooftop sundeck.

**Banana Cafe** $–$$ *1211 Duval Street; tel: (305) 296-7227.* Locals' favourite, serving crêpes and other inexpensive fare for breakfast, lunch and dinner.

**Key West Diner** $ *2814 N Roosevelt Boulevard; tel: (305) 292-1968.* In business for years providing buffets meals and staples such as roast beef and meatloaf in big portions.

**South Beach Seafood & Raw Bar** $$ *1405 Duval Street; tel: (305) 294-2830.* Offers breakfast, lunch and dinner but most popular for its large portions of fresh seafood served with ocean views.

**Square One** $$$ *1075 Duval Street; tel: (305) 296-4300.* Scallops on a bed of poached spinach is just one of the chef's special creations; a pianist adds to the soothing ambience.

**Right**
Captain Tony's Saloon

## Key West's bars

Whether to follow in the footsteps of Ernest Hemingway or simply succumb to the relaxed mood, Key West is noted for the open-sided bars where locals and tourists mingle to while away the balmy evenings.

**Captain Tony's Saloon** *428 Greene Street; tel: (305) 294-1838.* The site of Sloppy Joe's during the Hemingway era and very much part of local folklore.

Green Parrot *601 Whitehead Street; tel: (305) 294-6133.* Live music at weekends and always a jukebox with a tremendous stash of blues, zydecko, rockabilly and reggae.

Margaritaville Café *500 Duval Street; tel: (305) 292-1435.* Owned by singer-songwriter and long-time Key West resident Jimmy Buffett and named after one of his biggest hits. Good live music and frozen margaritas.

Sloppy Joe's *201 Duval Street; tel: (305) 294-8585.* Always crowded, Sloppy Joe's dates from 1933 and has become very tourist orientated, partly through its exaggerated Hemingway connection.

# Suggested tour

**Length**: Main tour 1.5 miles, 3 miles with detours.

**Duration**: Main tour 2 hours, 4 hours with detours.

**Links**: The Florida Keys (*see pages 94–103*).

The main route is an easy walk around the historic heart of Key West, beginning on **MALLORY SQUARE ❶**. From here, the **KEY WEST AQUARIUM ❷**, the **SHIPWRECK HISTOREUM ❸**, the **US CUSTOMS HOUSE ❹** and the **MEL FISHER MARITIME HERITAGE MUSEUM ❺** are all within a few strides. Also close by, at the corner of Greene and Whitehead streets, is **AUDUBON HOUSE ❻**.

Two blocks east, Duval Street forms Key West's main commercial artery and is lined by clapboard buildings housing art galleries, boutiques and souvenir shops. Facing you is the legendary **Sloppy Joe's** bar. Walk a block south along Duval Street and turn east on to Caroline Street for the **CURRY MANSION INN ❼**. Go west on Caroline Street for the **LITTLE WHITE HOUSE ❽**.

Return to Duval Street for the **WRECKER'S HOUSE ❾**, between Caroline and Eaton streets. Directly south, on the junction with Eaton Street, Stands **St Paul's Episcopal Church**, its vaulted wooden ceiling resembling an inverted ship's hull.

A block south on Duval Street is the **SAN CARLOS INSTITUTE ❿**. Continue south for three blocks to Olivia Street, then turn right for the **HEMINGWAY HOME AND MUSEUM ⓫** and the neighbouring **LIGHTHOUSE MUSEUM ⓬**. Adjacent are the streets of the **BAHAMIAN VILLAGE ⓭**. Continue south along Whitehead Street for the **SOUTHERNMOST POINT ⓮**.

**Detour**: From the Little White House Museum, walk along Front Street into narrow Emma Street, which meets Southard Street. Turn right

**Boat tours**

Many Key West companies offer deep-sea fishing, snorkelling and diving trips, glass-bottomed trips to coral reefs, nature tours and champagne-fuelled sunset celebration cruises. Among them are:

**Discovery Undersea Tours** *251 Margaret Street; tel: (305) 293-0099 or (800) 262-0099.*

**Lucky Fleet Inc** *Land's End Marina; tel: (800) 292-3096 or (800) 294-7988.*

**Mosquito Coast Wildlife Tours** *1107 Duval Street; tel: (305) 294-7178.*

**The Pride of Key West** *2 Duval Street; tel: (305) 296-GLASS.*

here and follow the signs for the **FORT ZACHARY TAYLOR STATE HISTORIC SITE** ⓰.

**Detour**: To reach **KEY WEST CEMETERY** ⓰ from Duval Street, walk three blocks east on Eaton Street, passing the **Donkey Milk House** (*No 613*), a restored Greek Revival home open for tours, and the **Bahama House** (*No 408*), built in the Bahamas and brought here by its owner in 1846, before turning right along William Street and continuing south.

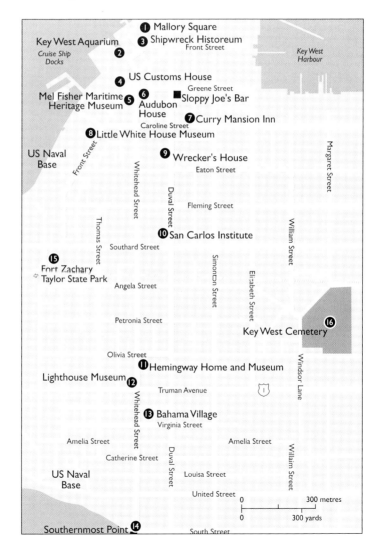

# Coast to coast across the Everglades

The busy and dull I-75 is the main link between south Florida's east and west coasts but the first road to cross the Everglades, gouging a path through swamp and sawgrass prairie stimulating a boom in south Florida's fortunes, was Hwy-41 (the Tamiami Trail), opened in 1928. Today, the two-lane Hwy-41 is a journey through Florida's frontier history, passing thinly populated settlements where fugitives, smugglers and moonshiners once flourished, and where the lack of development brings frontier folklore to life.

Despite being decimated by logging, drainage and human demands for drinking water, the Everglades are very much alive. This route includes everything from steamy swamps to strands of stately royal palm trees, although the view from the road is usually a mind-bogglingly huge expanse of sawgrass. Shark Valley is one highlight; a boat trip from Chokoloskee another. Both will enjoyably initiate newcomers into the complexities of the Everglades.

## BIG CYPRESS NATIONAL PRESERVE❖❖

**ⓘ Gulf Coast Ranger Station** *Route 29, Chokoloskee; tel: (941) 695 3311. Open daily Nov–Apr, 0730–1730; May–Nov, 0830–1630.*

Part of the 2400-square-mile Big Cypress Swamp, the preserve is noted for the slender belts of dwarf and big cypress trees growing along the sides of freshwater channels (or sloughs). Despite the devastation caused by the lumber industry, a few giant cypresses still remain, distinguished by their flared bases. The trees provide a rich and sheltered habitat for many varieties of bird life, including bald eagles and woodstorks, an incentive for the bird-watchers who keenly gather with binoculars and cameras on the short boardwalk trail.

Among other creatures regularly spotted are alligators, turkeys and deer; the very rare Florida panther (secretive big cats that face an uncertain future, although now they are subject to protection and intensive research) and mink are occasionally seen. At the visitors' centre, a short film documents the complex Everglades' ecosystem of which the swamp forms a vital part, and highlights the damage limitation exercise that brought federal protection to this portion of it in 1974.

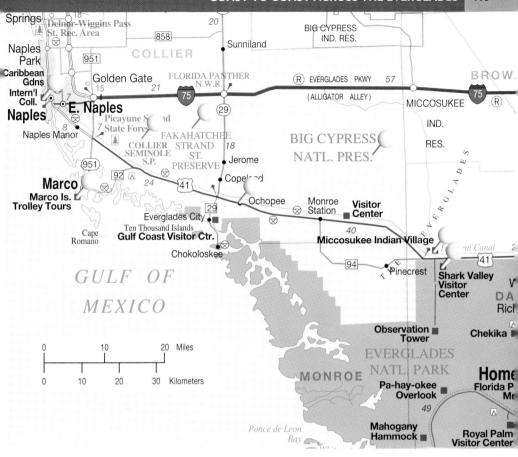

## COLLIER-SEMINOLE STATE PARK✧✧

ⓘ **Collier-Seminole State Park** $ *20200 S Tamiami Trail; tel: (941) 642-8898 or (800) 842-8898. Open daily 0800–sunset; boat trips 0900–1600.*

Cypress swamps, hardwood hammocks, pinelands, mangrove forests and other features typical of the Everglades landscape make up the 6000-acre Collier-Seminole State Park. The most eye-catching element, however, are the rows of Florida royal palms, a species of palm that rises with great elegance and sometimes reaches 120ft high.

Pontoon boat trips on the aptly named Blackwater River which runs through the park are an enjoyable way to experience the varied terrain and, with the guide's commentary, gain insights into local nature (canoes are available for rent). Also in the park, a short foot trail leads to a raised viewing platform from which wood storks, bald eagles, woodpeckers, alligators, mangrove foxes and squirrels might be spotted.

Near the entrance to the park, look out for the weighty slab of metal known as the walking dredge, used to clear a route through the jungle-like foliage for the building of Hwy-41 in the 1920s. The slow progress it made earned it its nickname.

# FAKAHATCHEE STRAND STATE PRESERVE✥

**ⓘ Fakahatchee Strand State Preserve** *Off Hwy-41, 7 miles west of junction with Route 29; tel: (941) 695-4593. Open dawn–dusk.*

Particularly if you missed them at Collier-Seminole State Park, the Florida royal palms that grace Fakahatchee Strand are well worth making the effort to see, as are the enormous number and variety of epiphytic plants, including a wonderful array of orchids that bloom throughout the year. A mile-long boardwalk trail leads to a strand of virgin cypress and into Big Cypress Swamp, one of the few sections of old-growth cypress left intact by the lumber industry. The primordial scene is completed by the steamy atmosphere and a complement of watchful alligators.

# MARCO ISLAND✥✥

**ⓘ Marco Island Chamber of Commerce** *1102 N Collier Boulevard; tel: (941) 394-7549 or (800) 788-MARCO. Open Mon–Fri 0900–1700.*

**🚋 Marco Island trolley tours** $ *tel: (941) 394-1600. Open daily 1000–1645.*

The most northerly link in the Ten Thousand Island chain, Marco Island is studded with up-market resort hotels and expensive homes, and also boasts one of the country's largest bald eagle colonies nesting in its tall pine trees. Remains dating back to the Calusa people of 3500 years ago have been found on the islands and shell mounds, the debris of many generations of prehistoric clam and oyster harvesting, can still be seen.

The island's past and present is outlined on the stress-free **trolley tours**, which last 90-minutes but permit visitors to hop on and off as the mood takes them. One place you might be tempted to do so is **Tigertail Beach Park**. On any sunny weekend, the park is filled with locals flying kites, jogging, or just sunbathing and wildlife-watching: pelicans and ospreys proliferate and dolphins are known to swim close to the shore.

# MICCOSUKEE INDIAN VILLAGE✥

**🏠 Miccosukee Indian Village** $ *On Hwy-41, half-a-mile west of Shark Valley entrance; tel: (305) 223-8380. Open daily 0900–1700.*

**🍴 Miccosukee Restaurant** $ *Miccosukee Indian Village, Hwy-41; tel: (305) 223-8388 or (305) 223-8380. A mixture of standard American diner fare and old-time Florida favourites such as alligator, frogs' legs and catfish, given a Miccosukee treatment.*

Like the Seminoles, with whom they share many cultural traits and history, the Miccosukee are descended from the Creek people of the American Southeast and were driven into the Everglades following the Seminole wars. Speaking a unique language, many Miccosukee now inhabit the 76-square-mile reservation in the Everglades on which the Miccosukee Indian Village stands.

Anyone interested in finding out about Miccosukee lifestyles and beliefs will regard the commercially orientated village as a disappointment. There are demonstrations of alligator wrestling, and handicrafts such as baskets and beadwork are made and offered for sale. Only the small museum provides a slightly more substantial commentary on the tribe.

Miccosukee-operated air-boat rides press deeper into the Everglades, reaching a gathering of traditional open-sided 'chickee' structures surrounded by sawgrass. These are suggestive of everyday Miccosukee life but leave visitors with nothing to do once there other than buy souvenirs.

# NAPLES✤✤

Designer boutiques, high-class restaurants, million-dollar homes and more golf courses per head of population than any other place in Florida help make Naples a byword for wealth and exclusivity. Unlike its glamorous east-coast counterpart, Palm Beach, Naples' residents typically keep a low profile and view celebrity status as rather vulgar.

The half-hour guided tour of the 1887 **Palm Cottage**, its construction financed by Walter S Haldeman, the newspaper proprietor who tried unsuccessfully to develop the area, provides background on Naples' humble origins: it stayed a quiet fishing settlement until the arrival of the railway and the completion of the Tamiami Trail.

**ⓘ** **Naples Area Chamber of Commerce** *3620 N Hwy-41; tel: (941) 262 614. Open Mon–Fri 0830–1700.*

**Previous page**
Fifth Avenue South, Naples

**Above**
Third Street South, Naples

An easy walk from the cottage leads to **Naples Pier**, erected in the 1880s and re-built in 1961 following its third demolition by a hurricane. A haunt of pelicans and fishermen, the pier gives stupendous views across the town's palm-fringed beaches and to the excellent **Lowdermilk Park**, 2 miles north. Stroll from the pier to **Fifth Avenue** and window-shop amid Naples' show-piece stores and art galleries, many of them housed in the former boatyards that serviced the fishing fleet based on Naples Bay, now a departure point for sightseeing cruises.

## Accommodation and food in Naples

**The Olde Naples Inn $$** *801 3rd Street South; tel: (941) 262-5194 or (800) 637-6036.* Within walking distance of the beach and the shopping areas of Old Naples, this elderly building is an atmospheric place to stay.

**The Registry Resort $$$** *475 Seagate Drive; tel: (941) 597-3232.* Despite having 475 fully-equipped rooms and several golf courses, this first-class hotel enjoys a low-key charm. Guests reach the beach via a boardwalk through a mangrove forest.

**Trails End Motel $–$$** *309 S Tamiami Trail; tel: (813) 262-6336 or (800) 247 5307.* Clean and dependable, and one of the few budget-priced lodgings in Naples.

**Bangkok Cuisine $$** *572 North Street North; tel: (941) 261-5900.* Excellent Thai food, particularly good on locally caught seafood, that has been impressing locals for years.

**The Riverwalk Fish & Ale House $$** *Tin City, 1200 5th Avenue; tel: (941) 263-2734.* Seafood, salad and sandwiches served with a view of Naples Bay, plus a long list of beers and exotic cocktails.

# OCHOPEE✧

The tiny white-painted wooden structure that stands in the minuscule settlement of Ochopee, created as a lumber camp in the 1920s, is not a misplaced garden shed but the smallest and most-photographed post office in the US.

# SHARK VALLEY✧✧✧

**Shark Valley $** *Off Hwy-41, 25 miles west of Miami; tel: (305) 221 8455. Entrance open daily 0830–1800; Visitor Center daily 0830–1715.*

At first glance, the Shark Valley section of Everglades National Park seems devoid of life but the two-hour **tram tour**, led and narrated by a park ranger, along a 15-mile paved loop road, reveals a great deal about the unique ecology and wildlife of the area and stops regularly for close-up looks at the multitude of creatures that inhabit this curious terrain. In summer, heavy rains can put much of Shark Valley, including all the trails and roads, under water.

During September and October, a mother alligator tending her young is a common sight, particularly around the artificial lakes known as 'borrow pits' that also attract wading birds and anhingas (snake birds). Midway along the loop road, a 65-ft-high **observation tower** offers views reaching into the distance and downwards to a large pond usually teeming with turtles, otters and alligators.

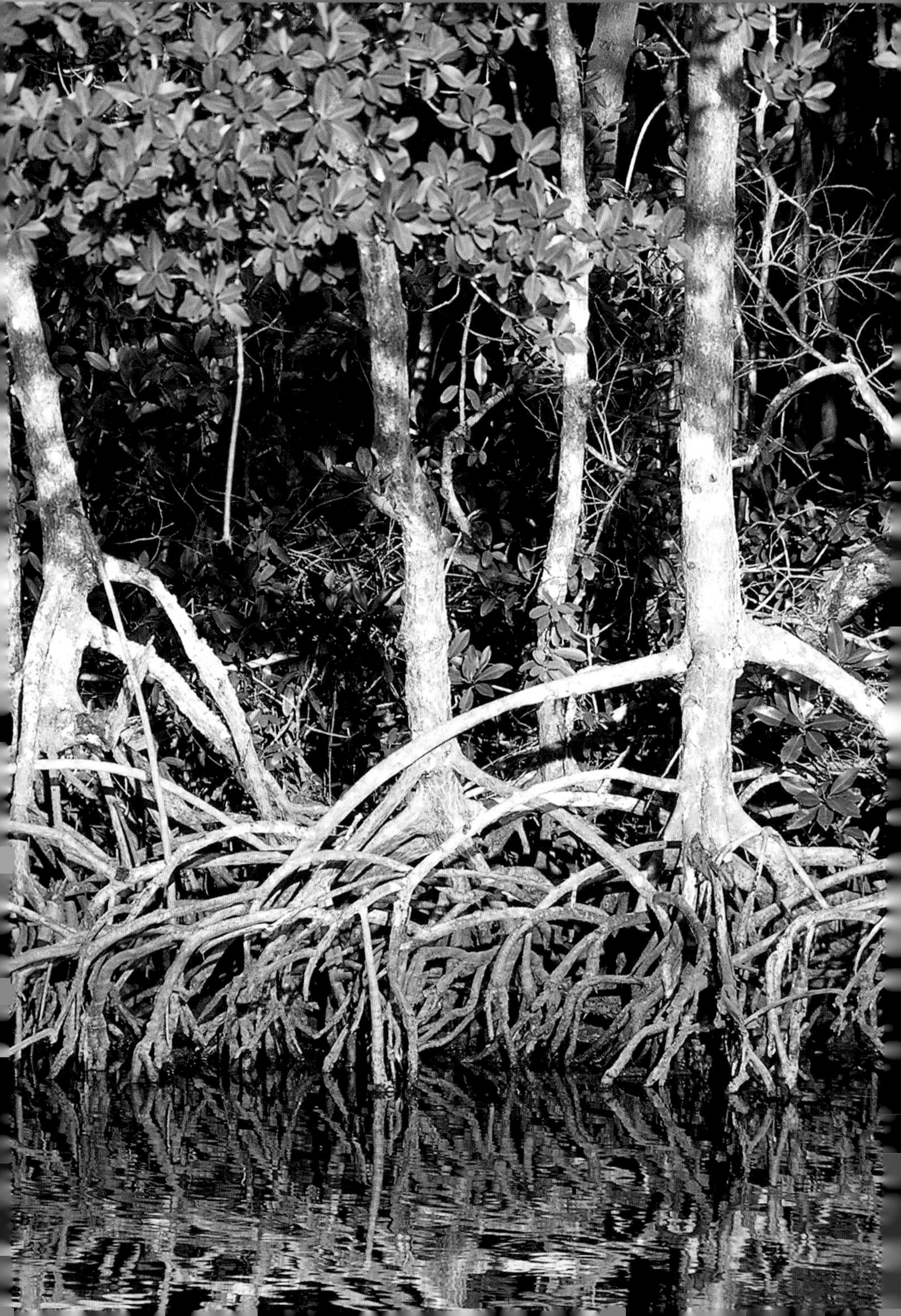

The tram tour provides a welcome initiation into the wonders of Shark Valley, while a bicycle trip along the same road allows further appreciation of the setting and its wildlife. In addition to the usual protection against mosquitoes and the sun, cyclists must carry ample drinking water and heed the safety precautions issued when hiring a bike from the park's rental outlet. Be particularly wary of close encounters with snakes and alligators when moving to the side of the road to allow the tram to pass.

While the loop trail is the main feature of Shark Valley, make time for two short trails close to the visitors' centre: the **Bobcat Boardwalk** and the **Otter Cave Hammock Trail**, both of which penetrate hardwood hammocks.

## Suggested tour

**Length**: Main route, 300 miles; 350 miles with detours.

**Duration**: 6 hours; allow 3–4 extra hours for both detours. With limited time, concentrate on Shark Valley, plus Marco Island and Naples for their beaches and dining, or Collier-Seminole State Park and Big Cypress National Preserve for nature.

**Links**: The eastern part of this route can easily be joined from Miami. Hwy-41 is a continuation of SW 8th Street, the main commercial strip of Miami's Little Havana (*see pages 52–63*). On the west coast, continuing for 36 miles on Hwy-41 north from Naples you reach Fort Myers (*see pages 126–129*).

From Miami, Hwy-41 begins its Everglades crossing west of the Florida Turnpike. The outlook remains similar for much of the route: sawgrass as far as the eye can see; billboards advertising airboat rides; and minuscule settlements that originated as lumber camps and now have a shop and petrol station. **Cooperstown**, which claims a population of just eight, and the evocatively named **Frog City**, are two of the first.

Thirty-six miles from Miami, the entrance for the **SHARK VALLEY** ❶ section of Everglades National Park is to the left; a mile further lies the **MICCOSUKEE INDIAN VILLAGE** ❷, occupying an area of the Everglades designated as a Miccosukee reservation. Three miles on, Hwy-41 deviates from a straight route for the first time at the aptly-named **Fortymile Bend**, also the junction for the **Route 94** detour (*see overleaf*).

**Fiftymile Bend** is 10 miles ahead on Hwy-41 and 7 miles further is the entrance to **BIG CYPRESS NATIONAL PRESERVE** ❸. A further 3 miles on Hwy-41 is **Monroe Station**, a modest settlement that grew in the 1920s as a lumber camp. An annual wild hog barbecue remains the major event here, where the proprietor of the local store will perform 'swamp weddings'.

**Left**
Everglades mangroves

**Right**
Everglades resident

Twelve miles further west, little **OCHOPEE** ❹ is sometimes overwhelmed by tour buses as passengers pause just long enough to photograph its tiny post office. Equally good as souvenir snaps are the Panther Crossing signs which appear for the next few miles, albeit optimistically as the Florida panther is close to extinction. The junction with Route 29 is 4 miles west of Ochopee; turn to the left for Everglades City and Chokolosokee (*see opposite*) or right for **FAKAHATCHEE STRAND STATE PRESERVE** ❺.

From a junction 17 miles further west on Hwy-41, Route 951 covers the 9 miles to **MARCO ISLAND** ❻. On the way, the outlook shifts from sawgrass to mangrove as the distinctions between land and sea become blurred. To reach **NAPLES** ❼, return to Hwy-41 and head west for 7 miles.

**Detour**: A pot-holed road liable to flooding but none the less accessible to two-wheeled vehicles, **Route 94** leaves Hwy-41 at Fortymile Bend and charts a 26-mile single-lane course through a cypress hammock and may bring views through the car windows (if you do step out, be alert for snakes) of deer and alligator, and other creatures that gather around the roadside channels which are the only source of water through the dry winter. On the way is an **Interpretative Center** and the **Tree Snail Hammock Nature Trail**, named for the colourful tree snails that can usually be seen.

**ⓣ E J Hamilton Observation Tower** $ *Adjacent to Route 29 between Everglades City and Chokoloskee. Open 24 hours.*

**Chokoloskee boat trips** $ *usually depart hourly throughout the day 0930–1630; tel: (941) 695-2591 or (800) 445-7724.*

**Smallwood Store Museum** *Chokoloskee; tel: (941) 695-2989. Open Dec–May, daily 1000–1600; May–Nov, Fri–Tue 1000–1600.*

**ⓡ Rod and Gun Club** $$ *200 S Riverside Drive, Everglades City; tel: (941) 695-2101. Hearty portions of seafood, so fresh it was swimming only hours ago.*

**Detour**: Five miles south of Hwy-41 on Route 29, **Everglades City** has a population of just 300 and grew as a base for the building of the Tamiami Trail. Its founder, W S Allen, hoped he would be remembered as the originator of south Florida's biggest city but the lasting landmark of his time is the white-framed building that holds the **Rod and Gun Club**, one of the US's most exclusive sports clubs in the days when the Everglades were synonymous with hunting and fishing rather than appreciation of nature. The club's members included presidents and other national notables. Now open to all, it offers accommodation and food, a lobby filled with stuffed fish and the club crest: an American eagle with fishing rod and rifle.

Continue south on Route 29 passing the **E J Hamilton Observation Tower**, which provides a view from 80-ft high of the area's mangrove forests and countless tiny islands. Immediately beyond, **Chokoloskee**, is even smaller than Everglades City but has a history to call its own documented in the **Smallwood Store**, a trading post established in 1906.

Chokoloskee is a departure point for **boat tours**, some independent, others licensed by the National Parks Service who also operate the **Gulf Coast Ranger Station**, the main source of local information. The boat tour commentary reveals a few of the mysteries of the mangrove, a vital component of the ecosystem, as the boat weaves steadily around the labyrinthine waterways.

Creatures such as mangrove racoons, and bird life such as bald eagles, ospreys and great white herons all find the area to their liking and can often be spotted. Passing the shell mounds left by early Native Americans and recounting tales of the larger-than-life characters who were the area's first white settlers, the tour paints a colourful picture of human settlement in this extreme terrain.

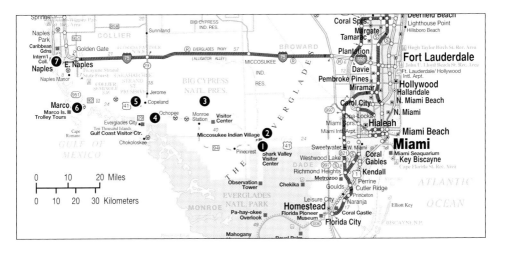

# Fort Myers and the Lee County Islands

**Ratings**

| | |
|---|---|
| Beaches | ●●●●● |
| Nature | ●●●●○ |
| Scenery | ●●●●○ |
| Beachcombing | ●●●○○ |
| Children | ●●●○○ |
| History | ●●●○○ |
| Sunsets | ●●●○○ |
| Museums | ●●○○○ |

The historic city of Fort Myers and the unspoilt islands that flank the mouth of the broad Caloosahatchee River that runs beside it, are among the most appealing yet relatively undiscovered sections of Florida's west coast. Inventor Thomas Edison was one of the first to find the slow pace and the idyllic subtropical scenery to his liking; his winter home is an essential stop. The palm trees Edison planted in the town still grace the route between Fort Myers and the islands.

The islands range from the developed Estero Island, holding vibrant Fort Myers Beach, to Captiva and Sanibel islands, where large tracts provide wildlife refuges and pocket-sized beaches drawing thousands of avid shell collectors. In one of the state's happiest marriages between humans and nature, there are plentiful opportunities to spot dolphins and other marine life surprisingly close to the shore, and on the boat trips that make other even less developed islands accessible.

## CABBAGE KEY✦

An estimated $25,000 worth of dollar bills line the walls of the rustic restaurant on Cabbage Key (accessible only by boat), each signed by the person who left it and part of a tradition established in the 1940s when a customer, worried that he may not have sufficient funds to buy a drink on his return from a fishing trip, left a dollar behind with his name on it. The restaurant occupies the Cabbage Key Inn, which was originally built in 1938 by Mary Roberts Rhinehart, author of mystery stories, as a winter home for her son.

## CAPTIVA ISLAND✦✦✦

**Chapel-by-the-Sea**
*End of Wiles Drive, off Sanibel-Captiva Road.*

Inhabited only by a few hundred privacy-loving souls and largely undeveloped, save for the luxury South Seas Plantation resort (departure point for boat trips to Cabbage Key) that occupies its northern tip, Captiva Island is a must-see even though there is just

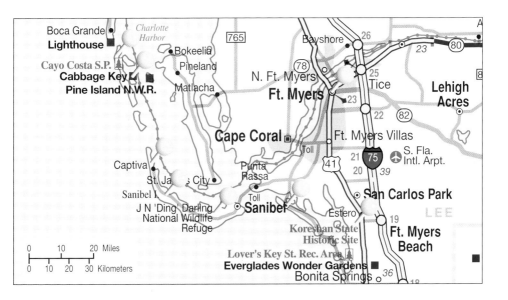

Boca Grande
Lighthouse

*Charlotte Harbor*

765

Bayshore  26
23  80

Cayo Costa S.P.
Cabbage Key
Pine Island N.W.R.

Bokeelia
Pineland
Matlacha

78

N. Ft. Myers
Ft. Myers

25
Tice
23

Lehigh
Acres

22  82

8

Cape Coral

Ft. Myers Villas

Toll

Captiva

Punta
Rassa

41

21  75
20  39

S. Fla.
Intl. Arpt.

St. James City

Sanibel I.

Toll

San Carlos Park

J N 'Ding' Darling
National Wildlife
Refuge

Sanibel

Estero

Koreshan State
Historic Site

19

LEE

Ft. Myers
Beach

0    10    20 Miles
0   10   20   30 Kilometers

Lover's Key St. Rec. Area
Everglades Wonder Gardens
Bonita Springs  36

**Chapel-by-the-Sea**
*End of Wiles Drive, off Sanibel-Captiva Road.*

one place specifically meriting a visit. This is the weather-beaten, white clapboard **Chapel-by-the-Sea**, built in 1901 as the local school and converted to religious use by Methodists before becoming interdenominational.

Now mostly used for weddings, the church has a palm-shaded **cemetery** that provides a resting place for early islanders, including William Howard Binder, whose headstone remembers him as 'First Homesteader Captiva Island, 1888'.

### Accommodation on Captiva Island

**South Seas Plantation $$$** *PO Box 194; tel (941) 472-5111 or (800) 449-1829.* Full-service resort with all imaginable facilities spread across the northern tip of Captiva Island.

**The Bubble Room $$** *15001 Captiva Road; tel: (941) 472-5558.* An effervescent atmosphere and 1940s style décor tend to overshadow the very hearty portions of seafood and steak.

# CAYO COSTA ISLAND STATE PARK❖❖

The only human occupant of Cayo Costa Island, a park ranger, shares the island with abundant bird life and has first pick of the shells that wash ashore on the 9 glorious miles of white-sanded beach lining the western side. The eastern side is composed of mangrove swamps, oak palm hammocks and pinelands. The secluded island can be reached only by boat and can be explored on 5 miles of foot trails. Besides the many shells, look on the beach for the footprints of loggerhead turtles, who come ashore at night to lay their eggs in the sand.

# FORT MYERS*

**ⓘ Lee County Visitor and Convention Bureau**, 2180 W 1st Street; tel: (941) 338-3500 or (800) 237-6444.

**ⓗ Burroughs Home $** 2505 1st Street; tel: (941) 332-6125. Open Tue–Fri 1100–1500.

**Fort Myers Historical Museum $** 2300 Peck Street; tel: (941) 332-5955. Open Tue–Sat 0900–1600.

**Edison Winter Home $$** (includes Ford Winter Home) 2350 McGregor Boulevard; tel: (941) 334-7419. Open Mon–Sat 0900–1600, Sun 1200–1600.

Set beside the broad Caloosahatchee River, Fort Myers has a relaxed air and is enhanced by the many stately royal palms that line its main artery, McGregor Boulevard. Modern Fort Myers sprawls well beyond the sway of the river but this commercially vibrant city keeps much from its first period of growth intact in the small Downtown district centred on 1st Street.

Once the largest and most luxurious house in Fort Myers, the handsome Georgian Revival **Burroughs Home** was built in 1901 for $15,000 and purchased by Midwestern banker and cattle baron Nelson T Burroughs in 1919. A mahogany fireplace, a spiral staircase and detailed reconstruction of the house as it was in the early 1900s add to the appeal, as do tours conducted by costumed guides taking the roles of the Burroughs' daughters, who inherited the house on their father's death in 1932. In character, the guides recount the story of the house and its occupants, and the social life of the time when the Edisons, Fords and tyre-mogul Harvey Firestone were regular visitors.

The **Fort Myers Historical Museum**, housed in a restored former railway depot, arranges local history into neat segments, from the prehistory of the Calusa people – a major native grouping settled throughout southwest Florida with marine skills believed to have taken them as far as Cuba – and relics from Spanish shipwrecks, to notable individuals such as Doctor Franklin Miles, inventor of *Alka Seltzer*. In the grounds, the 84-ft-long *Esperanza*, a private Pullman carriage, gives a taste of the luxury available to well-heeled rail travellers in the 1930s.

Thomas Edison, inventor of the incandescent light bulb, the phonograph, the cine projector and the generating system that brought power to cities, wintered at the 14-acre riverside site now known as the **Edison Winter Home** from 1886 until his death in 1931. Advised to move to Florida from New Jersey for health reasons, Edison relished the local climate for the opportunity to grow tropical plants and trees, utilising their raw material in his experiments (bamboo had provided the filament in Edison's early light bulbs).

The caringly tended and frangipani-scented **gardens** are a highlight of a visit. They include such exotic trees as the African sausage, fried egg and giant tulip, amid a variety of palms, a profusion of wild orchids and many other plants. Also here is the 14-ft-high golden rod tree cultivated for its sap, instrumental in Edison's attempts to develop new forms of natural rubber during the 1920s.

**Above**
Exotic foliage, Edison Winter Home

With its shady porches, Edison's two-storey **house** was designed for the Florida climate but constructed in Maine prior to being shipped south: one of the first pre-fabricated dwellings in the US. Still illuminated by the carbon filament bulbs of Edison's time, the house reveals the elegant yet simple style enjoyed by the inventor and his second wife.

Edison's **laboratory** is evocatively maintained as he left it with rows of test tubes, glass beakers and tripods. Note the small cot to one side of the lab: it was here that Edison would take cat naps during experiments. The colossal impact of Edison's work on the modern world is put in context by the adjoining **museum**, stocking many of his creations and allowing a chronological assessment of his achievements, made all the more remarkable by the fact that his life included just three months of formal education.

Leading car manufacturer and pioneer of the assembly line production system, Henry Ford also enjoyed a long-lasting friendship with Thomas Edison (who had encouraged Ford with his first automobile ideas) and in 1916 bought the winter home next door to the great inventor. For a man who died in 1947 leaving a fortune conservatively estimated at $500 million, the **Ford Winter Home** is a surprisingly unelaborate affair equipped with the 1920s fixtures and fittings of the kind that surrounded the Fords (Henry and his wife) during their occupancy.

**Above**
White ibis, Sanibel Island

The Fords' time in Fort Myers, particularly their close links with the Edisons, is outlined on the guided tours as they pass through the house and across the very pleasant 3-acre gardens of palms, citrus trees and tropical plants.

# FORT MYERS BEACH AND SAN CARLOS ISLAND❖❖

Fort Myers Beach occupies the long and narrow Estero Island and is lined by a fine 7-mile strip of white sand. A homely mood prevails despite the high concentration of motels, seafood restaurants and boat charter services. To the north, **Bodwitch Regional Park** wraps 7 acres of greenery around an attractive beach, with a boardwalk linking it to picnic areas.

To the south are the less developed **San Carlos Island** and **Carl Johnson Park**, where a boardwalk trail to the beach passes rows of Australian pines and crosses a forest of mangrove. The gorgeous **Lover's Key**, also accessible on a small passenger-carrying 'tractor', is at the end of the trail and boasts one of the area's quietest and prettiest beaches.

## Accommodation in Fort Myers Beach

**Island House Motel $$** *701 Estero Boulevard; tel: (941) 463-9282.* Small, but the pick of the area's many motels, with a good position on the northern end of Estero Island.

# J N 'Ding' Darling National Wildlife Refuge❖❖❖

**J N 'Ding' Darling National Wildlife Refuge $** *I Wildlife Drive, Sanibel Island; tel: (941) 472-1100. Open Nov–Apr, Sat–Thur 0900–1700; May–Oct, Sat–Thur 0900–1600.*

Named for the political cartoonist who signed his creations 'Ding' and was also a leading conservationist, this refuge protects a 6000-acre tract on the northern side of Sanibel Island. During springtime, roseate spoonbills can often be sighted at sunset; in summer, night herons, mottled ducks and blue herons may appear and year-round ospreys, racoons, brown pelicans and a very large colony of alligators are frequently seen. The 5-mile Wildlife Drive can be navigated by car but renting a bike from the visitor centre improves the chances of spotting the well-camouflaged creatures.

# Koreshan State Historic Site❖❖

**Koreshan Historic Site $** *off Corkscrew Road, Estero; tel: (941) 992-3311. Open daily 0800–1700.*

The most successful of several utopian-minded communities which sought to establish themselves in Florida over the turn of the 20th century, the Koreshan Unity sect were led by Cyrus Teed (aka 'Koresh'), who claimed that an angelic visitation had convinced him that the world was not a globe but concave, set around the inner edge of a giant sphere.

Some 250 Koreshans lived here during the early 1900s, vowed to celibacy outside marriage, equality between the sexes and shared property ownership as they prepared the 305-acre site for ten million anticipated settlers in the 'New Jerusalem'. Although the last Koreshan lived until 1982, Teed's death in 1908 signalled the sect's decline and its land was donated to the state in 1961. The restored Koreshan homes and communal buildings can be toured and aspects of their curious and intriguing philosophy discovered.

# Sanibel Island❖❖❖

**Sanibel-Captiva Visitors Center** *159 Causeway Road; tel: (941) 472-1080. Open Mon–Sat 0900–2000, Sun 0900–1800.*

A slender, curving island, a third of which is taken up by a wildlife refuge, Sanibel Island attracts shell collectors from near and far, over-eager gatherers sometimes acquiring the bent-back condition known as the 'Sanibel stoop'. The island was linked to the mainland by bridge only as recently as 1963, and retains a distinct and very individual identity, many of its long-time residents tracing their lineage back to the hardy farmers and fishermen who settled here in the 1890s.

**Above**
Sanibel Island beachcombers

The 98-ft-high **Sanibel Lighthouse** was raised in 1884 after man years of campaigning by islanders. The still-operating lighthouse an two adjoining keepers' cottages, raised on stilts to avoid high tides, a the island's oldest buildings. Adjacent to the lighthouse, the south facing **Sanibel Beach** misses the strong tides that deposit shells on th island's other beaches but is popular with sunbathers and swimmer and those who come to watch out in the hope of seeing the dolphin that are regularly sighted at sea.

**Sanibel Historical Village and Museum** $ *950 Dunlop Road; tel (941) 472-4648. Open Dec–Easter, Wed–Sat 1000–1600, Sun 1200–1600; rest of year, closed Sun.*

**Bailey-Matthews Shell Museum** $ *3075 Sanibel-Captiva Road; tel: (941) 395-2233. Open Tue–Sun 1000–1600.*

**Sanibel Captiva Conservation Foundation** $ *3333 Sanibel-Captiva Road; tel: (941) 472-2329. Open late-Nov–Easter, Mon–Sat 0830–1600; rest of year Mon–Sat 0830–1500.*

Sanibel's history may be insignificant in world terms but is very highly regarded and zealously maintained by islanders, and on display in the **Sanibel Historical Village and Museum**. Inside a 1913 'cracker' cottage (the term applied to the simple woodframed dwelling that provided typical living quarters for Florida settlers of the time), are rooms lined with historical artefacts, such as Calusa relics, Spanish shipwreck items, and the paraphernalia of early-1900s island life. The former Sanibel Post Office and Bailey's General Store and Gas Station, dating from the 1920s, are restored in period style and form part of the village complex.

The importance of shells to Sanibel Island should not be underestimated. The east–west orientation of the island and its position at the junction of several currents brings a rich harvest of shells at every low tide. The intriguing **Bailey-Matthews Shell Museum**, which claims to display a third of the 10,000 shell types found in the world, gives some clues as to why people hit the local beaches in the first rays of dawn with hopes of spotting a brown speckled junonia.

Reached by a small foot bridge passing through pinelands and over mangrove swamps, **Bowman's Beach** is the most popular strand on Sanibel Island. It has showers, a shady picnic area and dramatic sunsets.

### Accommodation and food on Sanibel Island

**West Wind Inn** $$ *3345 West Gulf Drive; tel: (941) 472-1541 or (800) 824-0476.* Nicely located for exploring Sanibel Island, with large comfortable rooms and the beach just steps away.

**The Lighthouse Café** $ *Seahorse Shopping Center, 362 Periwinkle Way; tel: (941) 472-0303.* Serving breakfasts and lunches for over 25 years; early risers might tackle the shrimp, crabmeat and scallop sitting on a croissant that forms part of the 'seafood benedict' breakfast special.

## Suggested tour

**Length**: Main route, 50 miles; 73 miles with beach detour; 103 miles with the Koreshan State Historic Site detour.

**Duration**: Main route driving time 2 hours; 3 hours with beach detour; 4–5 hours with Koreshan State Historic Site detour. Allow additional time, and preferably an extra day, for the boat trip to Cayo Costa State Park.

The suggested tour assumes a start in Sanibel and Captiva islands and takes around five hours, focusing on Sanibel and Captiva islands and the main sights of Fort Myers, covering a distance of some 50 miles.

**Above**
Basking alligator

The Fort Myers Beach detour will add an extra two hours or so. The Koreshan State Historic Site and Cayo Costa State Park are much lengthier detours, best undertaken on a separate day.

**Links:** Coast to coast across the Everglades (*see pages 114–23*) and The Culture Coast (*see pages 162–71*). Although the tour can easily be joined from any point on its route, the description begins with Captiva and Sanibel islands, on the assumption that you spend the previous night there.

The Sanibel-Captiva Road passes attractive **Turner Beach** before leaving Sanibel and reaching the ruggedly vegetated **CAPTIVA ISLAND ❶**. Becoming Captiva Drive, the road continues for 3 barely inhabited miles passing Wiles Drive, leading to the **Chapel-by-the Sea**. The main route expires 2 miles further at the South Seas Plantation, where boats continue to **CABBAGE KEY ❷**.

Returning to Sanibel, Bowman's Beach Road branches to the right off the Sanibel-Captiva Road to the excellent **Bowman's Beach**. The main route continues alongside the **J N 'DING' DARLING NATIONAL WILDLIFE REFUGE ❸**, its main entrance 3.5 miles ahead.

Continuing, the route joins Periwinkle Way, which cuts through the residential and commercial heart of **SANIBEL ISLAND ❹**. On the right, the **Sanibel Captiva Conservation Foundation** is a worthwhile stop for its boardwalk trails over mangrove swamps. Also on the right a short distance ahead is the two-storey stucco-fronted building holding the **Bailey-Matthews Shell Museum**.

**Boat trips**

**To Cabbage Key $$**
*Daily from South Seas Plantation, operated by Captiva Cruises; tel: (941) 472-5300; phone for times.*

**To Cayo Costa State Park $$** *from McCarthy's Marina, Bokeelia, Pine Island, operated by Captiva Cruises; tel: (941) 472-5300. Open Nov–May, Tue–Sun; phone for times.*

A further few minutes' drive reaches Dunlop Road on the left, leading to the **Sanibel Historical Village and Museum**. Return to Periwinkle Way and head east for 3.5 miles to the spindly **Sanibel Lighthouse**, adjacent to the welcoming **Sanibel Beach**.

Retrace the route along Periwinkle Way for 1 mile to Causeway Boulevard, which leads to the 3.25-mile **toll bridge** to the mainland. The bridge brings spectacular views of San Carlos Bay and the densely concentrated mangrove forming the Matlacha Pass Wildlife Refuge. As it touches ground, Causeway Boulevard becomes MacGregor Boulevard which continues for 15 miles into the heart of **FORT MYERS ❺** and is the site of the neighbouring **Edison** and **Ford Winter Homes**.

**Detour:** To reach **FORT MYERS BEACH ❻** from the bridge, take Route 869 for 2.2 miles, turning south along San Carlos Boulevard. Estero Island is 3.5 miles ahead. The route continues for 6 miles through the commercialised beach strip before reaching the more peaceful **SAN CARLOS ISLAND ❼**.

**Detour:** Avoid the residential sprawl to the south of Fort Myers by driving 3.5 miles east from the Downtown area on Anderson Avenue (Route 82) to reach I-75, then head south for 14 miles, exiting westbound at the junction with Corkscrew Swamp Road. The **KORESHAN STATE HISTORIC SITE ❽** is 2.4 miles ahead, near the junction with Hwy-41.

**Detour by boat:** Without a vessel of your own, the only way to reach the divinely secluded **CAYO COSTA STATE PARK ❾** is by boat from Bokeelia, on the northern tip of Pine Island (*see below*).

## Also worth exploring

An escape from both the urban development of Fort Myers and the trappings of mainstream tourism around the area's sandy beaches, **Pine Island** is sited between the mainland and the main barrier islands. Reach it from Fort Myers by crossing the Caloosahatchee River on Cleveland Avenue, after 2 miles turning left on Route 78. This continues for 15 miles and crosses the 'fishingest bridge in the USA' on to the island.

Almost entirely fringed by mangrove, the Pine Island economy revolves around fishing. Redfish, spotted seatrout and other species are regularly hooked from the many piers; tarpon and marlin are the main rewards for trips out to sea. Route 767 runs the length of Pine Island. Take it north to reach **Bokeelia**, departure point for boats to Cayo Costa State Park and also the site of a small museum recording local nature and history.

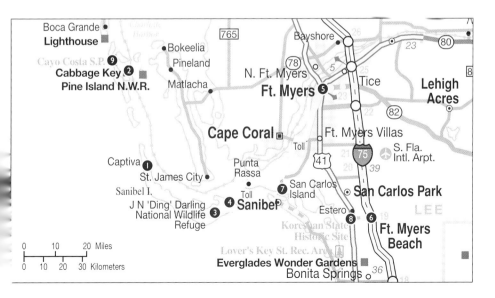

# Tampa

Children ●●●●

Museums ●●●●

Architecture ●●●

Crafts ●●●

Food ●●●

History ●●●

Nature ●●●

Theme parks ●●●

Tampa is the major city of Florida's west coast, and at first sight is large and uninteresting. Yet concealed within its urban sprawl, it has several neighbourhoods of great distinction that repay exploration by foot. Downtown Tampa showcases a fine mixture of old and new architecture and noteworthy attractions from the past, such as the 1890s luxury hotel built by Henry Plant whose railroad put Tampa on the map, and from the present with the splendid Florida Aquarium and an impressive art museum.

A few miles away, Ybor City was for decades a largely Spanish-speaking centre for cigar manufacture; its atmospheric streets are now revitalised with craft shops filling historic redbrick buildings. Further afield, Busch Gardens is a long-running and extremely popular theme park, where state-of-the-art roller-coaster rides vie for attention with elephants and lions. With the Museum of Science and Industry, Tampa has one of Florida's most technologically innovative and child-friendly institutions.

## Sights

**ℹ️ Tampa Bay Visitor Information Center** *3601 E Busch Boulevard; tel: (831) 985-3601. Open daily 1000–1800.*

**Visitor Information Center** *Corner of Ashley and Madison streets, Downtown Tampa; tel: (831) 223-2752. Open Mon–Sat 0900–1700.*

**Ybor City Chamber of Commerce** *1800 E 9th Avenue, Ybor City; tel: (813) 248-3712. Open Mon–Fri 0900–1600.*

**Busch Gardens**✦✦

What began as a bird sanctuary in the grounds of the Anheuser-Busch brewery in the 1950s grew swiftly into the wildlife showcase of Busch Gardens, still among the biggest tourist attractions in Florida. Spread across 300 acres, the park divides into sections that replicate an African country or region with a combination of animals, thrills-and-spills rides and theatrical shows.

Major animal habitats include the 80-acre **Serengeti Plain**, where antelope, rhinos, giraffes, hippos and more can be spotted; **Myombe Reserve**, with gorillas and chimpanzees in a re-created tropical rain forest complete with mist; **Claw Island**, inhabited by white and yellow Bengal tigers; and the **Elephant Habitat**, where Asian elephants dwell beside a water-hole watched by humans from a raised viewing level.

Busch Gardens' reputation among roller-coaster devotees is well deserved. **Kumba** is one of the scariest such rides yet devised, reaching

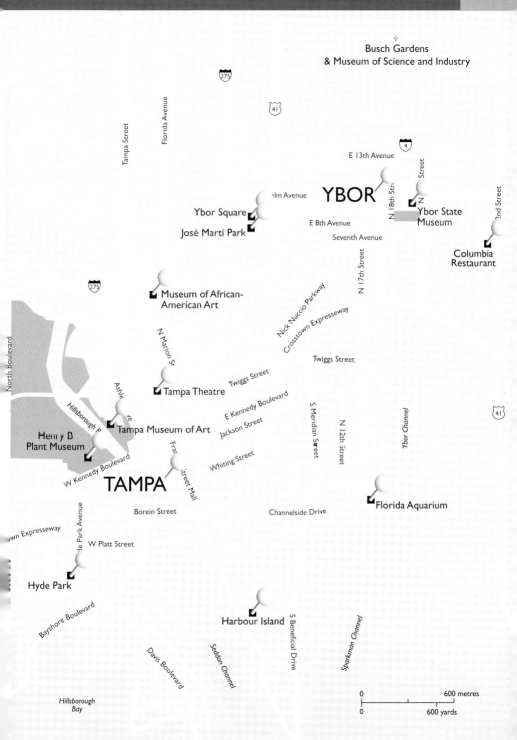

Busch Gardens
& Museum of Science and Industry

275

41

4

E 13th Avenue

Street

YBOR

lm Avenue

Ybor Square

José Martí Park

E 8th Avenue

Seventh Avenue

N 18th Str

N 18th St

Ybor State
Museum

2nd Street

Columbia
Restaurant

Tampa Street

Florida Avenue

275

Museum of African-
American Art

N Marion St

N 17th Street

Nick Nuccio Parkway

Crosstown Expresseway

Twiggs Street

Twiggs Street

Tampa Theatre

Ashle    ve

Hillsborough P

E Kennedy Boulevard

Jackson Street

S Meridian Street

N 12th Street

Ybor Channel

41

Tampa Museum of Art

Henry B
Plant Museum

Frat    treet Mall

Whiting Street

W Kennedy Boulevard

TAMPA

North Boulevard

Florida Aquarium

de Park Avenue

Borein Street

Channelside Drive

wn Expresseway

W Platt Street

Hyde Park

Bayshore Boulevard

Harbour Island

S Beneficial Drive

Davis Boulevard

Seddon Channel

Sparkman Channel

Hillsborough
Bay

0                    600 metres

0                    600 yards

🏛 **Busch Gardens $$$**
3000 E Busch Boulevard;
tel: (813) 987-5082. Open
daily 0900–1800, extended
hours on holidays.

🍴 **Columbia
Restaurant** Corner of
7th Avenue and 21st Street,
Ybor City.

🏛 **City Hall** Corner of
Franklin Street and
Kennedy Boulevard.

**Sacred Heart Church**
Corner of Florida Avenue and
Twiggs Street; tel: (813) 229-
1595.

speeds of 60mph and heights of 140ft. Slightly less terrifying are the double-spiralled **Python** and the **Scorpion**, which includes a 60-ft drop. Similarly exciting are water rides such **Congo River Rapids** and **Tanganyika Tidal Wave**, a jungle adventure culminating in a 55-ft drop over a waterfall. Calmer, infant-geared amusements fill the **Land of the Dragons** area.

### Columbia Restaurant⁕

Originating as a street corner café for Ybor City cigar-makers in 1905, the Colombia Restaurant grew into one of Tampa's most celebrated dining places (as well as the largest, filling an entire block). Note the exterior's exquisite tilework and peek inside for the displays recounting the Columbia's illustrious history. The Spanish cuisine, served by bow-tied waiters, is enlivened by flamenco dancing each evening.

### Downtown Tampa⁕

Dominated by modern high-rise offices and the people who work in them, Downtown Tampa occupies a compact area beside the Hillsborough River. The attractively pedestrianised Franklin Street and prolific public art reflect the successful efforts to enhance the area, while abundant historical markers provide an easily followed guide to Tampa's past. Take a look at the pleasingly *beaux-arts* **City Hall**, dating from 1915 and the powerful Romanesque form of the 1905 **Sacred Heart Church**.

**Below**
Henry B Plant Museum

**Florida Aquarium $**
*701 Channelside Drive;
tel: (813) 273-4000. Open
daily 0900–1800.*

**Harbour Island** *777 S
Harbour Island Boulevard;
tel: (813) 229-5324, events
hotline tel: (813) 229-5000
or (800) 822-4200.*

**Henry B Plant Museum
$** *401 W Kennedy
Boulevard; tel: (831) 254-
1891. Open Jan–Nov,
Tue–Sat 1000–1600, Sun
1200–1600; Dec, daily
1300–2100.*

**Hyde Park** *Centred on
Swann Avenue, between
Bayshore Bouelvard and Platt
Street.*

## Florida Aquarium✷✷

Inside a blue-green glass dome that makes the building resemble a gigantic shell, the $84 million Florida Aquarium showcases the natural wonders of the state's aquatic habitats and ecosystems. From freshwater springs and sawgrass marshes to cypress swamps and beaches, visitors tour the galleries symbolically following the progress of a single drop of water. On the way they encounter some of the 4000 species found in Florida, from tiny molluscs to ever-busy river otters.

The Florida Coral Reefs Gallery includes a simulated 60-ft dive to a piece of living coral, bringing close-up views of darting eels, prowling barracudas and colourful reef denizens such as the rainbow parrot fish. The extraordinary story of the coral's creation is cogently explained and a few of its weird and wonderful shapes displayed.

## Harbour Island✷

One of the many improvements to Downtown Tampa in the 1990s was the transformation of Harbour Island from disused cargo dock to site of luxury condominiums, a smart hotel and a shopping mall. Gift shops and boutiques make for amiable browsing in the mall, which also holds several restaurants and a food court; weekends and holidays bring free waterfront entertainment.

## Henry B Plant Museum✷✷✷

The Henry B Plant Museum, built by transport magnate Plant whose railroad reached Tampa in the 1880s and triggered the city's growth, occupies part of the former Tampa Bay Hotel, its distinctive Moorish minarets rising beside the Hillsborough River.

Opened in 1891, the 500-room hotel was the first building in Tampa with electricity and carried its guests through the grounds and along the quarter-mile-long lobby by rickshaw. In operation for just ten years, the hotel became neglected after Plant's death in 1899 and has been occupied by the University of Tampa since 1933.

One wing houses the museum where a remarkable stash of Wedgwood china, Florentine and Venetian mirrors, and all manner of antiques and statuary – gathered by Plant and his wife on a $500,000 shopping trip to Europe and Asia – indicate the opulence that hotel guests once enjoyed.

## Hyde Park✷✷

Hyde Park provides a welcome contrast to modern Tampa with several blocks of wood-framed and brick-built homes dating from the late 1800s to the 1920s. In styles ranging from Gothic and neo-classical to Mediterranean and Colonial, the homes were mostly built for the well-to-do settlers who arrived in Tampa as the city boomed following the arrival of Henry Plant's railroad and the opening of the Tampa Bay Hotel (*see Henry B Plant Museum, above*).

**José Martí Park**
*Corner of 8th Avenue and 13th Street, Ybor City.*

**Museum of African-American Art** $ *1308 N Marion Street; tel: (813) 272-2466. Open Tue–Sat 1000–1630, Sun 1300–1630.*

**Museum of Science and Industry** $$ *4801 E Fowler Avenue; tel: (813) 987-6300. Open daily 0900–closing hours vary.*

**Tampa Museum of Art** $ *600 N Ashley Drive; tel: (813) 274-8130. Open Mon–Sat 1000–1700, Wed until 2100, Sun 1300–1700.*

**Tampa Theater** *711 Franklin Street; tel: (831) 274-8981. Guided tours ($) twice monthly.*

On tree-lined streets with little traffic, the old homes, now among the most sought-after in the city, make for an enjoyable driving tour. The shops and restaurants of **Old Hyde Park Village** provide a weekend rendezvous for locals with free entertainment outside pricey shops and restaurants. As you leave, drive along **Bayshore Boulevard** which scenically skirts Tampa Bay.

### José Martí Park*

Revered Cuban poet and independence fighter José Martí frequently visited Cubans in the US to raise money for the struggle against Cuba's Spanish rulers. In Ybor City he addressed cigar workers from the steps of what is now Ybor Square. Many donated part of their earnings to buy the arms and ammunition that helped bring about Cuban independence in 1898. This small park bears a statue of Martí, hand outstretched in mid-oration.

### Museum of African-American Art*

A small but important gathering of African-American art frequently bolstered by quality temporary exhibitions, the museum's permanent stock includes works from the 19th century, the Harlem Renaissance (the blossoming of Black American culture in 1920s New York) and the present.

### Museum of Science and Industry**

It may prove hard to tear young and inquisitive minds away from the innovative interactive and multimedia exhibits of this tremendous museum. Be it the workings of the human body, the life cycle of a butterfly, a simulated hurricane or the three-dimensional walk-through Florida postcard, the exhibits never fail to entertain and inform. Adjoining are a planetarium and an IMAX cinema where highly realistic films are projected on to a 10,500-sq-ft screen.

### Tampa Museum of Art**

Dividing its energies and half its gallery space to temporary exhibitions, this highly regarded museum often attracts prestigious travelling shows. Space limits the amount that can be displayed from the permanent stock, which spans classical antiquities – including some treasured painted Greek vases – sculpture, photography, and modern painting from artists such as Jim Dine, Robert Rauschenberg and Frank Stella.

### Tampa Theater**

The Tampa Theater, completed in 1926, was heralded as 'the South's most beautiful theatre' when fashion dictated that cinema interior should be as lavish and as fantastical as the films they screened Inspired by the opera houses of Europe and intending the interior to resemble an outdoor auditorium, architect John Emberson hoped the audience would be enchanted by 'colonnades of graceful arches, romantic balconies, the towers of ancient castles, and the mystical beauty of an old Spanish cathedral window'. Specially designed lighting and smoke machines create the illusion of stars and clouds passing across a night-time sky. The wonderfully restored interior can be admired at a film screening or on twice-monthly guided tours.

**Right**
Ybor City wall mural depicting the area in the 1920s

### Ybor City✦✦✦

Ybor City (which covers just a few blocks despite its name) is a lively and historic corner of Tampa, filled with craft shops and studios. Its main streets are lined by brick buildings with decorative tile work and illuminated by five-globe street lamps.

The city takes its name from Don Vicente Martinez Ybor who in 1886 arrived in what was then a palmetto-covered scrubland and opened what would become the world's largest cigar factory, employing 4000 people. Most of the cigar workers were Cubans, a major component in what soon became a multiethnic community of 20,000 including Spanish, Italian, German and Jewish settlers. Ybor City gave birth to the country's first tri-lingual newspaper, *La Gaceta*, which continues to be published in Spanish, Italian and English.

The decline in the cigar industry led to the splintering of the local community and Ybor City became badly rundown. A revitalisation programme launched in the late 1980s bore great dividends, putting many of the historic buildings to fresh use and encouraging the plethora of new restaurants, bars and clubs that make Ybor City one of Tampa's busiest nightlife areas.

### Ybor State Museum**

This small collection charts the rise of Ybor City and occupies the former Ferlita Bakery, opened here in 1923 when its original premises burnt down. Enormous bread ovens recall the bakery, while expanded photos depict the massed cigar workers in what is now Ybor Square (*see below*) and record the fundraising visits of José Martí (*see page 138*).

Other exhibits highlight the local community's ethnic mix and the decline in hand-rolled cigar consumption that signalled the demise of Ybor City. Next door, the tiny **Cigar Worker's Cottage** dates from 1895 and reveals much about the simple domestic arrangements experienced by Ybor City residents of the time.

**Ybor State Museum $** *1818 9th Avenue, Ybor City; tel: (813) 247-6323. Open Tue–Sat 0900–1200 and 1300–1700; Cigar Workers Cottage Tue–Sat 1000–1200 and 1300–1500.*

**Ybor Square** *1911 N 13th Street, Ybor City; tel: (813) 247-4497. Open Mon–Fri 1000–1800, Sat 1200–1730.*

### Ybor Square*

The cigar factory that provided the focal point of life in Ybor City for 40 years to the 1930s is now Ybor Square, its three storeys occupied by a variety of shops and eateries. Although the building is steeped in history, the only place where the aroma of tobacco lingers is at the small Tampa Rico Cigar Company on the first floor. Here, amid a wealth of smoking accessories and souvenirs, hand-rolled cigars are still made and sold.

## Accommodation and food

Apart from a plethora of chain motels close to Busch Gardens and business-oriented chain hotels in Downtown, Tampa offers little attractively priced or well-located accommodation. It makes sense to visit the city as a day-trip from the St Petersburg area, to which there are good road links (avoid rush hours) and where there are many more overnight options.

**Gram's Place $–$$** *3109 Ola Avenue North; (831) 221-0956.* A plain neighbourhood conceals this friendly bed-and-breakfast spot housed in two adjoining cottages and devoted to the memory and music of country-rock legend Gram Parsons.

**Value Inn $** *2523 E Busch Boulevard; tel: (831) 033-6760.* Among the best priced of the many clean and simple motels close to Busch Gardens.

**Wyndham Lodge Harbour Island Hotel $$$** *725 S Harbour Island Boulevard; tel: (813) 229-5000 or (800) 631-4200.* Up-market option, complete with marina for boat-owning guests, adjacent to the redeveloped Harbour Island and within walking distance of Downtown Tampa. Rates are usually lowest at weekends.

**Atomic Age Café & Lounge $–$$** *1518 E 7th Avenue, Ybor City; tel (813) 247-6547.* Amid décor resembling the set of a 1950s sci-fi film is an eclectic and creative menu of snacks and larger meals.

**Above**
Ybor Square cigar factory

**Café Cohiba $$** *1430 E 7th Avenue, Ybor City; tel: (813) 248-0357.* Stylishly presented Spanish fare, and very tasty pizzas and calzones.

**Café Creole & Oyster Bar $$** *1330 E 9th Avenue, Ybor City; tel: (813) 247-6283.* A popular hang-out for creole and cajun dishes, plus fresh oysters.

**Caffe Firenze $$–$$$** *719 N Franklin Street; tel: (813) 228-9200.* A rare quality eatery in Downtown Tampa, with excellent, predominantly Tuscan-influenced, Italian dinner fare.

**Ho Ho Chinois $–$$** *720 Howard Avenue, Hyde Park; tel: (813) 254-9557.* The inexpensive buffets at this Chinese restaurant make for a very filling lunch when exploring Hyde Park.

# Suggested tour

**Length**: Main route, 8 miles; Florida Aquarium detour 1.5 miles; Museum of Science and Industry 10 miles (from Downtown Tampa); Busch Gardens 10 miles (from Downtown Tampa).

**Duration**: Main route, 45 minutes driving time; Florida Aquarium detour 10 minutes driving time; Museum of Science and Industry and Busch Gardens each 20 minutes driving time from Downtown Tampa.

**Links**: Easily accessed by I-4 and I-275 and with the Tampa Crosstown Expressway connecting the city to I-75, Tampa links easily with St Petersburg and its beaches (*see pages 144–53*), Between Tampa and Orlando (*see pages 172–79*) and The Culture Coast (*see pages 162–71*).

Downtown Tampa and Ybor City, each best explored by foot but requiring a car to travel between them, and Hyde Park, form the main route. The Florida Aquarium is an easy detour from the Downtown route and a good location for kids. An extra day is required to do justice to the Museum of Science and Industry and Busch Gardens.

From the Fort Brooke Parking Garage, the People Mover monorail provides easy access to **HARBOUR ISLAND ❶**. In the other direction, walk along Franklin Street into the heart of **DOWNTOWN TAMPA ❷**. Crossing Kennedy Boulevard reveals the elegant **City Hall ❸** on the right, architecturally holding its own amid glass and steel high-rises. Two blocks ahead, the forceful **Sacred Heart Church ❹** is to the right on Twiggs Street.

Continue on Franklin Street, crossing Zack Street for the **TAMPA THEATER ❺** on the right. Return to Zack Street, turn right and walk two blocks to the Hillsborough River, passing the gleaming **Curtis Hixon Convention Center ❻** to reach the **TAMPA MUSEUM OF ART ❼**. Looming across the river is the unmistakable Moorish profile of the former Tampa Bay Hotel, now holding the **HENRY B PLANT MUSEUM ❽**; reach it by crossing the Kennedy Boulevard bridge.

**Hillsborough River State Park** $ 20 miles northeast of Downtown Tampa, from I-4 take Exit 6 on to Hwy-301; the park entrance is on the left after 14 miles; tel: (813) 986-1020. Open daily 0800–sunset.

Southwest of the museum lies **HYDE PARK ❾**. This can be reached on foot, but if you are planning to continue to Ybor City, retrieve your car and use it to cruise the historic homes of Hyde Park. To reach **YBOR CITY ❿**, take Cass Street which becomes Nuccio Boulevard. After 3 miles, turn right on to 8th Avenue and use the car-park facing **YBOR SQUARE ⓫**. From elsewhere, reach the same destination by taking the Ybor City exit off I-4 on to 21st Street, turning right on Palm Avenue, and after four blocks, left on to 13th Street.

Facing Ybor Square across 8th Avenue is the small **JOSE MARTI PARK ⓬**. Walk east along 8th Avenue, passing numerous one-off shops, many of them outlets for locally based artisans (more line 7th Avenue). Go left on to 18th Street and, passing **Centennial Park ⓭**, right on to 9th Avenue for **YBOR STATE MUSEUM ⓮**. From the museum, walk two blocks south on 19th Street, turning right on to 7th Avenue where the **COLUMBIA RESTAURANT ⓯** fills the block between 21st and 22nd streets, greatly expanded since it opened in 1905 as a cigar workers' café.

**Detour:** On the western edge of Downtown Tampa, the **FLORIDA AQUARIUM ⓰** is a just over half-a-mile from the heart of Downtown Tampa; reach it along Channelside Drive from the southern end of Franklin Street. The route passes the new and expanding **Cruise Ship Terminal ⓱**.

**Detour:** Deep within the characterless urban sprawl that fills much of northern Tampa, **BUSCH GARDENS ⓲** are easily accessed from Downtown Tampa or Ybor City from I-275. Leave at Exit 33, heading east on to Busch Boulevard. The gardens are signposted 2 miles ahead.

**Detour:** A mile northeast of Busch Gardens, the **MUSEUM OF SCIENCE AND INDUSTRY ⓳** is accessed from Exit 34 off I-275, then heading east for 3 miles on Fowler Boulevard.

## Also worth exploring

If the network of freeway interchanges engulfing Tampa make the city seem too much of a metropolis, find a bucolic escape within the 3000-acre **Hillsborough River State Park**. The river from which the park takes its name forms dashing rapids as it passes over limestone outcrops; elsewhere in the park it becomes placid enough for boating. Nature trails pick through the park's swamplands and penetrate its hammocks of magnolia, bald cypress, live oak and sabal palm to reach shady picnic areas.

The park occupies the site of Fort Foster, built in 1837 as a base for US soldiers during the Second Seminole War. At weekends there are guided tours of the fort's reconstructed wooden buildings. A major battle between the soldiers and the Seminoles they came to subdue, is enthusiastically re-enacted during March.

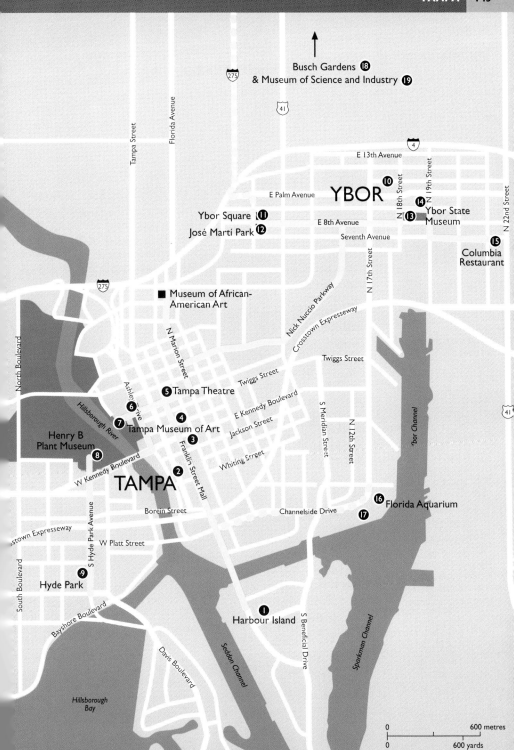

Busch Gardens ⑱
& Museum of Science and Industry ⑲

E 13th Avenue

YBOR ⑩

E Palm Avenue

⑭
Ybor Square ⑪          E 8th Avenue    ⑬ Ybor State
José Martí Park ⑫                              Museum
                         Seventh Avenue
                                                        ⑮
                                                   Columbia
                                                   Restaurant

■ Museum of African-
   American Art

⑤ Tampa Theatre

Twiggs Street

Twiggs Street

⑥

⑦

④

Henry B          Tampa Museum of Art
Plant Museum

⑧                                        E Kennedy Boulevard

                Jackson Street

W Kennedy Boulevard

                ②
TAMPA

Whiting Street

Borein Street

                                    Channelside Drive       ⑯
                                                         Florida Aquarium
W Platt Street                                    ⑰

⑨
Hyde Park

                    ①
            Harbour Island

Hillsborough
Bay

Florida Avenue

Tampa Street

N 18th Street
N 19th Street
N 22nd Street

Nick Nuccio Parkway
Crosstown Expresseway

N 17th Street

N Marion Street
Ashley Drive
Hillsborough River

Franklin Street Mall

S Meridian Street
N 12th Street

Ybor Channel

Sparkman Channel

S Hyde Park Avenue
stown Expresseway
South Boulevard
North Boulevard

Bayshore Boulevard

Davis Boulevard

Seddon Channel

S Beneficial Drive

0 ————————— 600 metres
0 ————————— 600 yards

# St Petersburg and its beaches

## Ratings

| | |
|---|---|
| Beaches | ●●●●● |
| Scenery | ●●●●○ |
| Arts and crafts | ●●● |
| Boat trips | ●●●○○ |
| Children | ●●●○○ |
| History | ●●●○○ |
| Nature | ●●●○○ |
| Museums | ●●○○○ |

Along the western edge of the Pinellas Peninsula, which divides Tampa Bay from the Gulf of Mexico, nature has sculptured a 25-mile string of barrier islands with idyllic beaches, soul-stirring sunsets and some of Florida's most benevolent weather with barely a cloud seen all year. Predictably the area is a major hit with international travellers and much is an unbroken line of hotels, motels, beachside bars and seafood restaurants.

Amid the commercialism, however, this route reveals sights to savour, ranging from a wild bird sanctuary to a luxury pink hotel of the 1920s. And with the seductively pristine Caladesi Island comes a glimpse of the area as it looked before the advent of package tourism. Across the peninsula from the beaches, St Petersburg is a town in the throes of upward mobility, evolving as a major centre for arts and culture as well as sheltering oddities in its midsts such as an ex-Soviet submarine.

## CALADESI ISLAND STATE PARK✦✦✦

🏛 **Caladesi Island State Park $** *Open daily 0800–sunset; accessible by boat only, see below.*

🚢 **Ferries to Caladesi Island via Honeymoon Island $** *Clearwater Ferry Service, from City Beach Marina, Clearwater Beach; tel: (813) 442-7433.*

Beautifully unspoilt Caladesi Island, accessible only by boat, is a welcome reminder of how all of Florida's barrier islands looked before the dawn of mass tourism. From the mangrove-enshrouded landing stage, where a snack bar is a rare sign of human habitation, a short boardwalk trail runs to a usually deserted 2-mile-long white sand beach. If shell collecting, sunbathing and swimming are not sufficient to pass the time, take the 2.5-mile nature trail cutting through the pine flatlands and oak hammocks amid the tall grasses of the island's interior.

## CLEARWATER BEACH✦✦

Anchoring the northern end of an 18-mile string of holiday islands, Clearwater Beach has a friendly atmosphere, enjoyable restaurants and a cluster of nightspots. Small motels fill the side-streets while more expensive accommodation boasts enviable locations overlooking

**ⓘ Clearwater Beach Welcome Center**
*40 Memorial Causeway; tel: (813) 446-2424. Open Mon–Fri 0900–1700.*

**🐟 Clearwater Marine Aquarium $** *249 Windward Passage; tel: (813) 441-1790. Open Mon–Fri 0900–1700, Sat 0900–1600, Sun 1100–1600.*

**Captain Memo's Pirate Cruise $$** *from Clearwater Beach Marina; tel: (813) 446-2587.* Board a mock pirate vessel for swashbuckling treasure hunts and dolphin discovery trips.

the Gulf. Although the main attraction is a very broad white-sand beach, Clearwater Beach is also a major departure point for short boat trips, such as sunset cruises and riotous excursions aboard 'pirate' ships.

The commendable **Clear-water Marine Aquarium** rescues and rehabilitates injured marine mammals, sea turtles and river otters; it also has exhibits on Florida's coastal ecology, and tanks of stingrays and sharks.

## Accommodation and food in Clearwater Beach

**Clearwater Beach Hotel $$–$$$** *500 Mandalay Avenue; tel: (813) 441-2425.* On the beach and a short walk from the heart of the town, one of the area's nicest and oldest, though fully modernised, places to stay.

**EbbTide Suites $$** *621 Bay Esplanade; tel: (813) 441-4121 or (800) 635-0620.* Ideal for a stay of several nights; smallish suites equipped with kitchens.

**Tropical Breeze Motel $–$$** *333 Hamden Drive; tel: (813) 442-6865.* Clean and simple rooms in a good location. The motel also has its own fishing dock and a barbecue and picnic area.

**Frenchy's Saltwater Café $** *416 E Shore Drive; tel: (813) 461-6295.* Deservedly popular for its great-value seafood such as conch chowder and grilled grouper sandwiches, served inside or at outside benches. Success has spawned several local branches.

# Don Cesar Resort✧✧

**Don Cesar Resort**
*3400 Gulf Boulevard, St Pete Beach; tel: (813) 360-1881 or (800) 247-9810.*

The unmistakable Don Cesar Resort, a large and intensely pink creation in concrete and stucco, looms beside Gulf Boulevard and occupies 7 beachfront acres. Raised in the 1920s for $1.5 million, this luxury hotel (known simply as 'the Don') attracted high-calibre guests such as Franklin Roosevelt and F Scott Fitzgerald in its short-lived heyday. The Depression heralded decades of neglect until the property was restored and re-opened in the 1970s.

Despite the marble fountains, Italian crystal chandeliers, French candelabra and Cuban tiles, the interior does not quite match the pizzazz of the Moorish-Mediterranean exterior. None the less, take a look inside this piece of local history and, if possible, join the illuminating guided tour for the full story on this remarkable edifice and Thomas Rawle, the Boston-born man who built it.

# Fort de Soto Park✧✧

**Fort de Soto Park**
*Mullet Key; tel: (813) 866-2484. Open daily dawn–dusk.*

In 1849, Robert E Lee, then an army engineer but later to find lasting fame as leader of the Confederate Army in the Civil War, recommended that Mullet Key, one of five small islands south of St Pete Beach, be fortified as part of Florida's coastal defences. Not until 50 years later during the Spanish-American War did Fort de Soto come into being. Used as a training base in the two world wars, the curious if rather paltry remains of the fort can be explored on a history trail, described in a free leaflet.

Today, the park is better known for its fabulous stretch of beach and plentiful palm-shaded picnic tables. The view across the mouth of Tampa Bay is a stunning one with passing freighters and the shimmering profile of the soaring Sunshine Skyway Bridge (*see The Culture Coast, pages 162–71*).

# John's Pass Village✧

**John's Pass Village**
*Madeira Beach; tel: (813) 393-7679*

**Right**
Great blue heron

John's Pass Village is a group of art galleries, clothing, jewellery and souvenir shops in intentionally ramshackle structures, loosely based on the fishing village established here from the 1870s. The unusual merchandise of many of the stores makes for amiable browsing. A fleet of pleasure boats and fishing charter vessels, and numerous restaurants, add to the appeal. One of the area's major events is the seafood festival held here each November.

# PASS-A-GRILLE*

**Gulf Beaches
Historical Museum**
115 10th Avenue; tel: (813)
360-2491. Call for hours.

**Hurricane Seafood
Restaurant $$** 807
Gulf Way, Pass-a-Grille; tel:
(813) 360-9558.
Delectable fish sandwiches
are among the most
ordered dishes in this
enjoyable eatery.

At the southern tip of the barrier island chain, Pass-a-Grille is the only
local beach community not dominated by tourists, motels and high-
rise condominiums. The village began as a fishing settlement in the
1910s and still holds some of the dainty cottages of that time, along
with the seafood eateries and bars that have been serving locals for
years. The **Gulf Beaches Historical Museum** captures the homely
mood with a modest but engaging run-down on local history. The
quiet beach is a fine place to enjoy the sunset.

# ST PETERSBURG**

**St Petersburg
Chamber of
Commerce** 100 2nd
Avenue N, St Petersburg; tel:
(813) 821-4715. Open
Mon–Fri 0830–1700.

**St Pete Beach
Chamber of
Commerce** 6990 Gulf
Boulevard, St Pete Beach; tel:
(813) 360-6957. Open
Mon–Fri 0900–1700.

**Florida
International
Museum $$** 100 2nd
Street; tel: (813) 821-1448
or (800) 777-9882. Open
daily 0900–1800.

St Petersburg was once best known as one of the US's sunniest
retirement communities, but during the last few years has beome an
increasingly respected centre for the arts and has gained a younger
population. Several new museums have joined the already established
and well regarded Fine Arts and Salvador Dali museums.

Many new arrivals, employed in the area's expanding financial and
service sector industries, are attracted to St Petersburg for its successful
blend of old and new architecture, and the several miles of landscaped
parks beside Tampa Bay.

Also overlooking the bay is the **Renaissance Vinoy Resort**,
originally the Vinoy Park Hotel; for two decades following its 1925
opening it encouraged the rich and famous to winter in St Petersburg.
President Calvin Cooleridge and baseball superstar Babe Ruth were just
two early guests. Given a $93 million face-lift after years of neglect,
the hotel re-opened in 1992.

Almost two million people attended the first four exhibitions staged
at the **Florida International Museum**, which opened in 1995 to show
large-scale exhibitions from around the globe across 20,000ft of

ⓘ **The Pier** *Eastern foot of 2nd Avenu; tel: (813) 821-6164. Open Mon–Thur 1000–2100, Fri–Sat 1000–2200, Sun 1100–1900.*

**St Petersburg Museum of History** $ *335 2nd Avenue NE; tel: (813) 894-1052. Open Mon–Sat 1000–1700, Sun 1300–1700.*

**Russian Submarine** $ *The Pier; tel: (813) 821-6164. Tours open daily 1000–1900.*

display space in a former department store. The first exhibition displayed Romanov treasures borrowed from Moscow's Kremlin museums; later ones have focused on the *Titanic*, Ancient Egypt, Alexander the Great and the lost civilisations of Peru. To prevent overcrowding, visitors must usually make a reservation ahead of arrival.

Resembling an upside-down pyramid, the **Pier**, actually the name given to the building on the end of the half-mile-long pier itself, is the most eye-catching object on the St Petersburg waterfront. The five-storey-high structure is popular for its restaurants and small aquarium and each evening makes a pleasant base to enjoy free entertainment and the cool breezes crossing the bay.

Lined by jet-ski and boat rental stands, the approach to the Pier also passes the **St Petersburg Museum of History** with its entertaining accounts of local history from Native Americans finds to the story of the world's first commercial airline flight, which took place here in 1914 when the mayor was flown to Tampa by airboat.

The Pier makes an unlikely setting for two contrasting sea-going craft. A Juliette class **Russian Submarine**, built during the 1960s to

**The Bounty** $ *The Pier;*
*tel: (813) 821-6443.*
*Open Nov–May, Mon–Sat*
*1000–1800, Sun 1100–1800.*

**Museum of Fine Art** *255*
*Beach Drive NE; tel: (813)*
*896-2667. Open Tue–Sat*
*1000–1700, Sun 1300–1700.*

launch guided missiles, was purchased from the Russian Ministry of
Defence in 1994 and is now open for tours. Also beside the pier
through the winter is **HMS *Bounty***, a detailed replica of the British
navy's original and built for the 1962 re-make of *Mutiny on the Bounty*.
The vessel can be toured and occasionally puts out to sea.

With its collections arranged in small galleries spread through the
ground floor of a Palladian-style villa, the **Museum of Fine Arts**
creates an air of intimacy ideally suited for viewing the displayed art.
The permanent collections include pre-Columbian, Native American
and Asian artefacts but wins most acclaim for its 19th- and 20th-
century French and American paintings. The French art includes
striking canvases by Cézanne, Gauguin, Daumier, Renoir, and Monet,
whose *Houses of Parliament*, a shimmering depiction of a fogbound
London, is the gem. The American art ranges from Whistler to
Lichtenstein and includes several of Georgia O'Keeffe's close-up flower
paintings, notably the powerful and vibrant *Poppy*.

The last thing most people expect to find in Florida is one of the
world's most complete chronicles of the career of Spanish surrealist

**Salvador Dali Museum** $ *1000 3rd Street; tel: (813) 823-3767. Open Mon–Sat 0930–1730, Sun 1200–1730*

Salvador Dali, but with more than a thousand of the artist's works from 1914 to 1980, the **Salvador Dali Museum** justifies such a description and opened in 1982 to house the collection amassed by a Cleveland industrialist who befriended Dali. The rotating permanent collection includes works such as *Daddy Longlegs of the Evening... Hope!* and *Slave Market with the Disappearing Bust of Voltaire*, featuring Dali's strange imagery and vividly coloured dream-like landscapes, rich in Freudian symbolism, that helped define surrealism from the 1940s for a mass audience (while purists dismissed Dali for his commercialism).

Intriguingly, the museum also shows some of Dali's early canvases, revealing his orthodox artistic skills while mimicking Impressionist and Cubist styles. By contrast, the culmination of Dali's career might be the monumental canvases, mostly created during the 1950s and 1960s and each at least a year in the making, such as *The Hallucinogenic Toreador* and *The Discovery of America by Christopher Columbus*, in which he grapples with major themes of history and religion, and lets his penchant for double images run wild.

## Accommodation and food in St Petersburg

Although the bulk of the area's accommodation is concentrated at the beaches, St Petersburg has a growing number of viable options, usually less busy than its Gulf-side counterparts.

**Dolphin Beach Resort** $$ *4900 Gulf Boulevard, St Pete Beach; tel: (813) 360-7011 or (800) 237-8916*. A giant among the many small motels in the vicinity with 174 rooms and nightly entertainment in the cocktail lounge.

**Mansion House** $$ *105 5th Avenue NE, St Petersburg; tel: (813) 821-9391*. Believed to have been the home of St Petersburg's first mayor, this offers six guest rooms – one with beamed ceiling and four-poster bed – and a full English breakfast served by the Welsh owners.

**Woody's Waterfront Café & Beach Bar** $–$$ *738 Sunset Way, St Pete Beach; tel: (813) 360-9165*. Begun as a bait hut serving hot dogs to local fisherman and now offering seafood, burgers and steaks in an informal atmosphere. Live music most evenings.

# SAND KEY PARK**

**Sand Key Park** *10600 Gulf Boulevard; tel: (813) 595 7611. Open daily 0700–sunset.*

Among the scores of beachfront parks intended to prettify the Florida coast, few come bigger or better than Sand Key Park, 65 acres of dazzlingly white-sand beach fringed by greenery. Ranked among the best in the US, the beach stretches for 12 miles, its popular northernmost section evocatively flanked by tall palm trees.

# SUNCOAST SEABIRD SANCTUARY❖

**Suncoast Seabird Sanctuary** *18328 Gulf Boulevard, Indian Shores; tel: (813) 391-6211. Open daily 0900–sunset; guided tours Wed and Sun at 1400.*

The Suncoast Seabird Sanctuary began when a local zoologist found a broken-winged cormorant on Gulf Boulevard in 1971, and has grown into the US's largest wild-bird hospital. In various stages of recuperation, some 600 birds commonly injured by fishing lines or environmental pollution can be seen. Many are large brown pelicans, ubiquitous along the Gulf beaches, although herons and egrets are also plentiful. More exotic patients have included Arctic loons and peregrine falcons.

**Opposite**
Renaissance Vinoy Hotel,
St Petersburg

# Suggested tour

**The Lobster Pot**
$$$ 17814 Gulf Boulevard, Redington Shores; tel: (813) 391-8592. Although serving many varieties of seafood, lobster cooked in a multitude of styles draws the crowds.

**Length**: Main tour, 20 miles. Add 8 miles to reach Downtown St Petersburg and 23 miles to tour Pass-a-Grille and Fort de Soto and return.

**Duration**: Main tour driving time, 1 hour. Allow a day to cover the main route and one detour; another half-day is necessary to cover all the detours. The Caladesi ferry runs twice-daily, allowing a maximum of four hours on the island.

**Links**: Tampa (*see pages 134–43*), The Nature Coast (*see pages 154–61*), The Culture Coast (*see pages 162–71*).

The main tour is a simple drive through the adjoining barrier island beach communities following the single road that links them. The remainder of the day should be spent on one or more of the coastal detours, venturing inland to St Petersburg, and exploring this bayside town on foot, or enjoying the seclusion of Caladesi Island.

Take any route to **CLEARWATER BEACH ❶**. With its beckoning beach and abundance of hotels and motels, this provides a good introduction to the beach communities. Head south along Coronado Drive, which sweeps eastwards to cross the bridge on to the palm-lined **SAND KEY PARK ❷**. Becoming Gulf Boulevard, the road continues for 3 miles, passing the tall condominiums of **Belleair Shores** and, 5 miles further, reaching **Indian Shores** where the **SUNCOAST SEABIRD SANCTUARY ❸** is on the right, shortly after the junction with Park Boulevard.

For the next 5 miles the outlook is one of hotels, restaurants and slender pathways providing beach access as the route moves through undistinguished **Redington Beach** and into **Madeira Beach**, at the southern end of which is **JOHN'S PASS VILLAGE ❹**. From Madeira Beach, a large concrete bridge carries Gulf Boulevard on to **Treasure Island**, boasting one of the area's nicest strands.

Ten miles on, the route passes through the highly developed centre of **St Pete Beach** (formerly called St Petersburg Beach, the name some signs continue to use) before encountering the **DON CESAR RESORT ❺**, rising mirage-like beside the beach.

**Boat trips**

**Dolphin Landings $$**
4737 Gulf Boulevard, St Pete Beach; tel: (813) 360-7411. Sunset cruises and dolphin-watching excursions.

**Detour**: City Beach Marina, on the south side of Route 60 on the bay side of Clearwater Beach, is the local departure point for the ferry to **CALADESI ISLAND STATE PARK ❻**. Take a picnic lunch and spend several blissful hours at this pristine spot.

**Detour**: From the Don Cesar Resort, Pass-a-Grille Road continues south into the largely residential **PASS-A-GRILLE ❼**, a contrast to the more touristed beach areas. The **Gulf Beaches Historical Museum** is found by turning right along 10th Avenue. From the museum, return to the Don

**Great Explorations**
*1120 4th Street; (813)
821-8885. Open Mon–Sat
1000–1700, Sun
1200–1700*

Cesar Resort and turn right on to Pinellas Bay South (toll), continuing for 1.5 miles before swinging right across a series of slender islands and, after 6.6 miles, reaching the junction with Anderson Boulevard. Turn right here and continue for 1.5 miles to **FORT DE SOTO PARK ❽** and a winning outlook across Tampa Bay.

**Detour:** The most direct route to St Petersburg from the beaches is Route 150, which leaves Gulf Boulevard at Treasure Island, becoming Central Avenue as it crosses the heavily populated Pinellas Peninsula and, after 8 miles, reaching Downtown St Petersburg.

The Downtown area is best seen on foot. At the end of an extended causeway running from 2nd Avenue is **The Pier** and beside it are **HMS *Bounty*** (winter only) and the **Russian Submarine**. At the pier's foot is the **St Petersburg Museum of History**. A few steps north is the **Museum of Fine Arts**, while the extravagant **Renaissance Vinoy Resort** can be spotted on the north side of the yacht marina.

Walking inland along 2nd Avenue for three blocks you reach the **Florida International Museum**. A mile south along Fourth Street N is **Great Explorations**, an enjoyable museum of hands-on exhibits aimed at kids. A block east is the outstanding **Salvador Dali Museum**.

# The Nature Coast and rural Florida

Freshwater springs, sinkholes, nature refuges and thoroughbred horse farms all feature in the Nature Coast, where sandy beaches and hi-tech theme parks are conspicuous by their absence. Instead, the land meets the sea in a vast expanse of mangrove and marshlands, and quiet coastal roads terminate at pocket-sized communities that seldom see a visitor. The region also holds two of Florida's oldest tourist attractions: the dancing mermaids of Weeki Wachee and the glass-bottomed boat trips at Silver Springs.

Linking the larger coastal towns, the tour takes in Tarpon Springs, evolved from a community of Greek sponge divers, Crystal River, renowned for its frequently seen manatees, and Cedar Key, a secluded island settlement and one of Florida's most attractive off-the-beaten-track communities. Inland, the route explores rural central Florida, including the university town of Gainesville, and Ocala, set amid the pastoral surrounds that have raised some of the nation's champion racehorses.

## CEDAR KEY✧✧✧

**Cedar Key Historical Society Museum $** 609 2nd Street; tel: (904) 543-6007.

**Cedar Key State Museum $** 1710 Museum Drive; tel: (904) 543-5350.

**The Captain's Table** $–$$ Dock Street; tel: (352) 543-5441. On stilts above the water, this unpretentious spot is ideal for sampling local favourites such as smoked mullet and deep-fried trout.

With timber-framed, tin-roofed buildings and sidewalks overhung by wooden balconies, Cedar Key is a picture of a bygone Florida. A century ago it was a thriving port with an important railway line and regular boat connections to New Orleans, Key West and Cuba. By contrast, the local pace today is slow and relaxed. Among a population of several hundred attracted to live here by the easy-going atmosphere and laid-back pace are numerous artists whose work is displayed in local craft shops and art galleries. Others here earn a living from the sea, harvesting crabs and oysters or running boat trips to the **Cedar Key Wildlife Refuge**, a group of tiny islands providing nesting grounds for ospreys, pelicans and other species.

To emphasise its past importance, Cedar Key has two historical collections: the **Cedar Key Historical Society Museum** and the smaller **Cedar Key State Museum**, both tracing the 19th-century heyday of the town. The latter boasts an immense shell collection, illustrating the huge variety of exotic shells to be found in the region.

# CRYSTAL RIVER NATIONAL WILDLIFE REFUGE*

**🐟 Crystal River National Wildlife Refuge** *tel: (904) 563-208. Open Mon–Fri 0730–16.00.*

Almost transparent warm spring water makes this offshore refuge a good place to see manatees, which congregate here during the winter. The bulbous, 10-ft-long creatures, one of Florida's most loved but endangered creatures, can be admired from a boat, though it is permitted to swim, snorkel and scuba dive. Boat trips and guided dives are readily available in the area.

# CRYSTAL RIVER STATE ARCHAEOLOGICAL SITE**

**ℹ Nature Coast Chamber of Commerce** *28 NW Highway 19, Crystal River; tel: (352) 795-3149. Open Mon–Thur 0830–1700, Fri 0830–1600.*

**🐟 Crystal River State Archaeological Site $** *3400 N Museum Point Road, Crystal River; tel: (904) 795-3817.*

Native Americans are believed to have occupied islands in the Crystal River area from 200 BC and to have buried their dead at this 14-acre site where burial mounds, temple mounds and midden mounds (built from the discarded shells of the seafood that underpinned the native diet) remain.

The story of the mounds, the largest 235ft long, and finds such as arrowheads and tools, are documented at the visitors' centre. Curiously, much less is known about the site's two ceremonial stones believed to have been used in solar rituals. Their similarity to stones found in Central America has prompted speculation on local links with the ancient people of Mexico's Yucatan Peninsula and on native skills in long-distance boat travel.

# GAINESVILLE*

**ℹ Alachua County Visitors & Convention Bureau** *30 E University Avenue; tel: (352) 374 5231. Open Mon–Fri 0830–1700.*

The University of Florida and its 40,000 students bring a youthful and energetic air to the rural town of Gainesville. The university is the oldest in the state, dating from 1853, and its 2000-acre campus holds several museums including the **Florida Museum of Natural History** (*University of Florida; tel: (352) 392-1721. Open Mon–Sat 1000–1700, Sun 1300–1700*) with a plethora of fossils, mounted butterflies and insects, and displays on Florida ecosystems. Gainesville itself has many streets lined by graceful live oaks and a well-tended **historic area** with elegant homes from the late 1800s.

# MANATEE SPRINGS STATE PARK*

**🐟 Manatee Springs State Park** *near Chiefland; tel: (352) 493-6072. Open daily 0800–sunset.*

The first-magnitude natural spring that gives this park its name is among the most powerful of Florida's 320 springs, daily issuing 117 millions gallons of crystal-clear water. The result is a fascinating ecosystem, which can be studied at close hand as a boardwalk weaves through the park's cypress and maple tree-lined swamps bringing occasional views of wading birds, alligators and bald eagles.

# OCALA❖

**Ocala-Marion Chamber of Commerce** *110 E Silver Springs Boulevard; tel: (352) 629-8051. Open Mon–Fri 0830–1700.*

**Appleton Museum of Art** *$ 4333 NE Silver Springs Boulevard; tel: (352) 236-7100. Open Tue–Sat 1000–1630, Sun 1300–1700.*

**Don Garlits Museum of Drag Racing** *$ 13700 SW 16th Avenue; tel: (352) 245-8661. Open daily 0900–1730.*

**Seven Sisters Inn** *$$–$$$ 820 SE King Street; tel: (352) 867-1170.* Handsome bed-and-breakfast inn with beautifully furnished rooms in an 1888 house.

**Horse Farm Tours: Florida Thoroughbred Breeder's Association** *1727 NW 80th Avenue; tel: (352) 629-2160.* Many of the horse farms in the Ocala area open their doors for free tours at a particular time each week. Details can be checked with the above, as well as with the local Chamber of Commerce.

Ocala's thoroughbred horse industry became established in the 1950s following the success of the locally bred Needles in the Kentucky Derby and Belmont Stakes. The undulating pastures on the northwestern outskirts of Ocala hold 600 breeding and training farms employing 25,000 people on plots from 10 to 5000 acres; many of them welcome visitors.

Ocala itself is a place of quiet streets and quieter lifestyles. In this unlikely setting is the $8.5 million **Appleton Museum of Art**, a repository of cultural treasures that would not be misplaced in a major city. The marble-clad museum's stash spans classical antiquities, pre-Columbian art, Asian arts and crafts, and has a floor devoted to 18th- and 19th-century European art.

By contrast, Ocala's other major historical collection is the **Don Garlits Museum of Drag Racing**, where trophies, posters, press cuttings and the ultra-sleek drag cars themselves chart the rise of drag racing from humble origins in 1930s California to one of the US's most popular forms of motor sport.

# PAYNES PRAIRIE STATE PRESERVE✦✦

**Paynes Prairie State Preserve $**
*Near Micanopy; tel: (352) 466-3397. Open daily 0800–sunset.*

Anyone who thinks the Everglades are Florida's wildest place should reserve judgement until they have seen Paynes Prairie State Preserve, a 20,000-acre expanse of swamp, hammocks, pinelands, ponds, sinkholes and prairie that is simultaneously forbidding and compelling. Sandhill cranes, eagles and hawks, wading birds, alligators and otters are among the creatures that thrive in these varied habitats. Follow a short trail to an observation tower for the best viewing point.

# SILVER SPRINGS✦✦

**Silver Springs $$**
*5656 E Silver Springs Road; Ocala; tel: (352) 236-2121.*

Silver Springs was one of Florida's earliest tourist attractions, drawing northerners in the late 1800s to view the natural springs, palms and live oaks hung with Spanish moss. Much of the town looks just as good today, even though the original park has expanded a themed complex with animal shows and various jeep and boat 'safaris', and 'jungle cruises' venturing into the 350-acre site to view an imported population of zebra, deer, emu, ostrich, giraffe and gibbon, as well as many native alligators. There are excellent narrated glass-bottomed boat trips to several of the springs.

# TARPON SPRINGS✦✦✦

**Spongerama $** *510 Dodecanese Boulevard; tel: (813) 942-3771. Open daily 1000–1700.*

**St Nicolas Greek Orthodox Cathedral** *36 N Pinellas Avenue; tel: (813) 937-3540. Open daily 0800–1600.*

Settled by Greek sponge divers in the early 1900s, Tarpon Springs became and remains a predominantly Greek community even though the sponge-diving trade was effectively ended by increased production of synthetic sponges. Greek food, music and souvenirs are sold at the tourist-orientated shops lining Dodecanese Boulevard, adjacent to the **sponge docks** where boats carry visitors to re-created sponge dives. The techniques and history of the local sponge trade are documented in the **Spongerama Exhibition Center**.

The rest of Tarpon Springs is much less crowded and boasts the resplendent Byzantine Revival **St Nicolas Greek Orthodox Cathedral**, starting point of the US's biggest Epiphany procession and holding an allegedly weeping icon of St Nicolas.

# WEEKI WACHEE SPRINGS✦

**Weeki Wachee Springs $$** *Hwy-19, Weeki Wachee; tel: (352) 596-206. Open daily 0930–1730.*

At Weeki Wachee Springs, built around a freshwater spring, mermaids perform choreographed underwater dances. The Wilderness River Cruise passes through a typically Floridian landscape populated by otters, racoons and wood storks, to a pelican reserve where injured seabirds are brought back to health.

# YULEE SUGAR MILL RUINS STATE HISTORIC PARK*

**ⓘ Yulee Sugar Mill Ruins State Historic Park** $ *Route 490, near Homosassa; tel: (352) 795-3817. Open daily 0800–sunset.*

Ruined limestone buildings are all that remain of the 5100-acre sugar plantation that thrived here in the 1850s. Worked by a thousand slaves, the plantation belonged to David Yulee, Florida's first member of Congress and a founder of the trans-Florida railway which carried goods between the Atlantic and Gulf coasts.

## Suggested tour

**ⓘ Buccaneer Bay** $$ *Hwy-19 near Weeki Wachee; tel: (352) 596-2062. Open late-Mar–Labor Day, daily 1000–1700 or later.*

**Length:** 168 miles, 258 miles with detours.

**Duration:** The main tour can be covered in 6–8 hours, but allow two days to take in the detours and spend time in deserving small towns.

**Links:** Tarpon Springs is 16 miles north of Clearwater Beach, making for a simple connection via Alt Hwy-19 with St Petersburg and its beaches (*see pages 144–53*).

Alt Hwy-19 provides a main route through **TARPON SPRINGS** ❶; the sponge docks are a short distance west on Dodecanese Boulevard. Continuing north, Alt Hwy-19 joins Hwy-19 3.6 miles from Tarpon Springs and passes several condominium communities before the high-rises give way to the forests that dominate the view on both sides of a very straight road.

### Manatees

One of the delights of natural Florida is the West Indian manatee (also known as the sea cow on account of its fondness for aquatic grasses and plants), found in the state's warm and shallow coastal waters, rivers and springs. Despite resembling a bloated seal, the manatee, which can reach 14ft in length and typically weighs around 1000lb, has a gentle manner and moves gracefully through the water. Florida manatees, though protected since colonial times, are facing extinction largely due to human impact on the environment.

Twenty-six miles from Tarpon Springs, the junction with Route 50 finds the neighbouring attractions of **WEEKI WACHEE SPRINGS** ❷ and Buccaneer Bay, a water park built around one of the area's freshwater springs.

Continuing north on Hwy-19 for 24 miles, Route 490 branches to the left. This route reaches the entry point for **Homosassa Springs State Wildlife Park** and passes the **YULEE SUGAR MILL RUINS STATE HISTORIC PARK** ❸ before continuing into the small town of **Homosassa**. Sugar mill owner David Yulee brought short-lived prosperity to the tiny but attractive Homosassa in the 1800s, extending his cross-Florida railway here from Cedar Key.

Returning to Hwy-19, **Crystal River** is 9 miles north. Turn left along Route 44 and wind around Kings Bay, departure point for trips to **CRYSTAL RIVER NATIONAL WILDLIFE REFUGE** ❹. Returning to Hwy-19, the signposted turning for **CRYSTAL RIVER STATE ARCHAEOLOGICAL SITE** ❺ is 4 miles north, the site enjoying a tranquil setting on the north bank of the Crystal River.

Hwy-19 continues for 8.5 miles before crossing the **Florida Barge Canal**, a relic of an ill-fated attempt to provide a coast-to-coast transport route, and bends to the right at **Inglis**, marking the junction with Route 40.

**Devil's Millhopper State Geological Site** $ *4732 NW 53rd Avenue, Gainesville; tel: (352) 336-2008. Open daily 0800–sunset.*

**Magnolia Plantation Bed and Breakfast Inn** $$ *309 SE 7th Street; tel: (352) 375-6653.* Every room is named for a tree in this quiet, antique-filled house dating from 1885.

**The Grady House** $$ *420 NW 1st Avenue, High Springs; tel: (904) 454-2206.* It's well worth continuing 20 miles north from Gainesville for this excellent bed-and-breakfast inn, where the rooms are cosy and the owners are a great source of local knowledge.

**The Sovereign** $$$ *12 SE 2nd Avenue; tel: (352) 378-6307.* Eclectic but always outstanding American cuisine made more enjoyable by the setting, a converted barn.

Venture along Route 40 on any weekend and the marinas around the small town of **Yankeetown** will be lined by the pick-up trucks of local fisherman.

Twenty-one miles north of Inglis, Hwy-19 meets Route 24. Turn right and head east for 36 miles to reach **GAINESVILLE ❻**. A few miles west of Gainesville, I-75 provides a speedy link to **OCALA ❼**, 30 miles south. Eight miles west of Ocala on Silver Springs Boulevard is **SILVER SPRINGS ❽**.

**Detour:** Turning left off Hwy-19 on to Route 24 leads for 21 miles through the marshlands of **Waccasassa State Preserve** before reaching the coast and crossing on to the island holding **CEDAR KEY ❾**. The only route out of Cedar Key is the one you arrived on, but after 9 miles turn left on to Route 345 to **Chiefland**, 19.5 miles ahead. Briefly re-join Hwy-19 before taking Route 320 west for 7 miles to **MANATEE SPRINGS STATE PARK ❿**.

**Detour:** With time in hand, travel south from Gainesville toward Ocala on the slower but more scenic Hwy-441. This passes through the moody landscapes of **PAYNES PRAIRIE STATE PRESERVE ⓫**, its main entrance on the left, 7.5 miles from Gainesville. About 4.5 miles ahead, Route 25A leads to **MICANOPY ⓬**. Like **McIntosh**, 5 miles further south on Hwy-441, Micanopy is a small town with several 19th-century buildings now holding antique shops. Continuing south for 17 miles, the route passes through the calcium-enriched pastures of the thoroughbred horse farms north of OCALA.

**Detour:** This detour from a detour can be joined from Hwy-441, close to Micanopy. Travel 10 miles east on Route 346 and turn right at the junction with Route 325, reaching **Cross Creek** after 3.5 miles. The home of Marjorie Kinnan Rawlings is signposted. Leave Cross Creek heading south on Route 325, after 4.8 miles turning right on to Hwy-301 and re-joining Hwy-441 9.2 miles further.

## Also worth exploring

Jumping into one of the many natural springs is one way to cool off in this part of Florida, another is by descending into the **Devil's Millhopper**, a 120-ft-deep sinkhole 7 miles north of Gainesville. Formed by rainwater eroding underground limestone deposits, forming a cavern and eventually causing the roof to fall in, sinkholes are common in Florida – around 400 new ones appear annually – but this is among the largest, its story detailed by a short video shown at the visitors' centre. A wooden walkway and staircase provides access to the sinkhole's depths, where the temperatures are markedly lower than at the surface and the vegetation resembles that commonly seen in cooler, northerly regions.

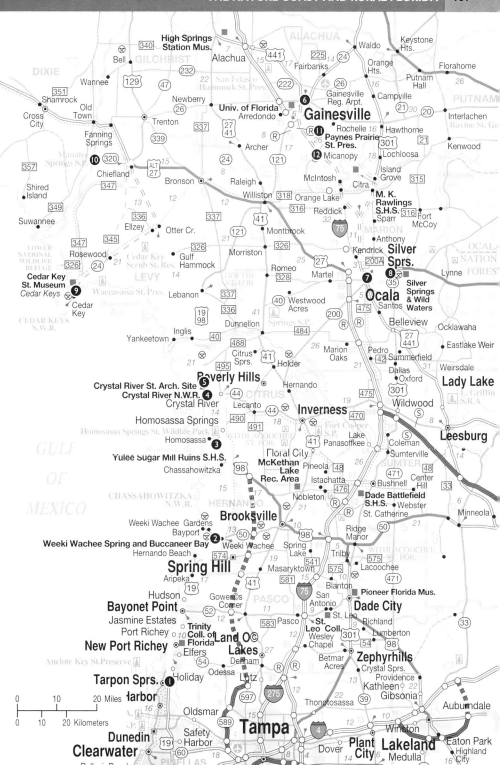

# The Culture Coast

**Ratings**

| | |
|---|---|
| Beaches | ●●●●● |
| Nature | ●●●●● |
| Art | ●●●○○ |
| Children | ●●●○○ |
| History | ●●●○○ |
| Scenery | ●●●○○ |
| Museums | ●●○○○ |
| Shopping | ○○○○○ |

A wealthy circus owner with a passion for European art gave this section of Florida's west coast a reputation as a cultural hotspot from the 1920s. The legacy is most strongly felt in Sarasota where galleries, performing arts venues and a major collection of baroque art contribute to the appeal of one of the state's most enjoyable small cities. Sarasota is the only mainland area featured as part of this route, which otherwise sticks to the coast.

Long and slender barrier islands form a 35-mile frame to the Culture Coast, linked for the most part by a continuous road lined on one side by Australian pines and on the other by some of the state's finest white-sand beaches. The islands hold insular, affluent communities each concerned to protect the environment – ospreys and egrets are still more common visitors to parts of this region than tourists – from the rampant development seen elsewhere along the coast.

## ANNA MARIA ISLAND❖❖

**❶ Anna Maria Island Chamber of Commerce** *502 Manatee Avenue; tel: (941) 778 1541. Open Mon–Fri 0900–1700.*

Anna Maria Island stretches for 7.5 miles and is the northernmost of the barrier islands that separate the Gulf of Mexico from the Intracoastal Waterway. The pick of its many white-sand beaches are **Coquina Beach** and **Bayfront Park**. To discover more about the island, browse the entertaining **Anna Maria Historical Society Museum**.

## DE SOTO NATIONAL MEMORIAL❖❖

**🏛 De Soto National Memorial** *North end of 75th Street NE, Bradenton; tel: (941) 792-0458. Open daily 0900–1700.*

Spaniard Hernando de Soto and a force of 600 soldiers are believed to have landed hereabouts in 1539, the start of a four-year, 4000-mile trek that would bring the first European sighting of the Mississippi River and the first celebration of Christmas in what became the US. Failing to find the gold believed to be buried in Florida or establish the colonies that De Soto had promised the Spanish king, the expedition also claimed the lives of De Soto and half his men.

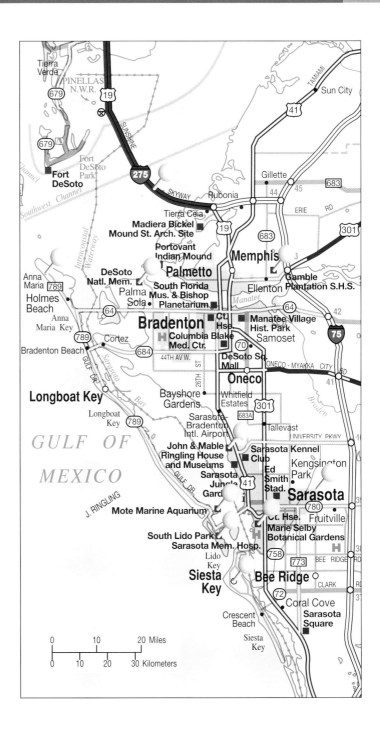

Tierra
Verde
PINELLAS
N.W.R.
(679)
(19)
Sun City
(41)
(679)
Fort
DeSoto
Park
Fort
DeSoto
(275)
Gillette
(683)
SKYWAY
Rubonia
44
45
ERIE
RD
Tierra Ceia
Madiera Bickel
Mound St. Arch. Site
(19)
(683)
(301)
Portovant
Indian Mound
Memphis
3
Anna
Maria (789)
DeSoto
Natl. Mem.
Palmetto
Gamble
Plantation S.H.S.
South Florida
Ellenton
Holmes
Beach
Palma
Sola
Mus. & Bishop
Planetarium
Manatee
(64)
42
(64)
Anna
Maria Key
Bradenton
Ct.
Hse.
Manatee Village
Hist. Park
(789)
Cortez
Columbia Blake
Med. Ctr.
Samoset
(75)
Bradenton Beach
(684)
44TH AV W.
(70)
DeSoto Sq.
Mall
ONECO - MYAKKA CITY RD
41
Oneco
26TH ST
Longboat Key
Bayshore
Gardens
Whitfield
Estates
(301)
Braden
Longboat
Key (789)
Sarasota-
Bradenton
Intl. Airport
(683A)
Tallevast
UNIVERSITY PKWY
GULF OF
John & Mable
Ringling House
and Museums
Sarasota Kennel
Club
Kengsington
Park
MEXICO
Sarasota
Jungle
Gard
Ed
Smith
Stad.
(41)
J. RINGLING
Mote Marine Aquarium
Ct. Hse.
Fruitville
Sarasota
(780)
South Lido Park
Sarasota Mem. Hosp.
Marie Selby
Botanical Gardens
Lido
Key
(758)
(773)
BEE RIDGE RD
Siesta
Key
Bee Ridge
CLARK
RD
(72)
Coral Cove
Crescent
Beach
Sarasota
Square
Siesta
Key

0        10        20 Miles
0    10    20    30 Kilometers

An explanatory video at the visitors' centre describes the expedition and its small museum displays a few related artefacts. Outside, a boardwalk trail through the mangrove swamps suggests the type of terrain through which De Soto and his band of men would have hacked their first steps.

# GAMBLE PLANTATION STATE HISTORIC SITE❖❖

**Gamble Plantation**
$ *3708 Patten Avenue, Ellenton; tel: (941) 723-4536. Open Thur–Mon 0800–1700; guided tours, 0930, 1030, 1300, 1400, 1500, 1600.*

This excellently maintained ten-room antebellum mansion was built in the mid-1800s for Major Robert Gamble who oversaw a 3500-acre sugar plantation from it. A small museum documents Gamble's life and decline as falling sugar prices forced him to sell the house and grounds. Other exhibits record the arrival here in 1865 of Judah P Benjamin, Secretary of State in the Confederate government, fleeing Union troops. An accomplished lawyer, Benjamin escaped by boat to England where he became a leading member of the British bar.

# MARIE SELBY BOTANICAL GARDENS❖❖

These fragrant and colourful 11 acres, which evolved from the garden of Marie Selby who moved with her oil magnate husband to a bayfront home here in the 1920s, should delight even the least horticulturally minded visitor. The gardens also enjoy a magnificent setting overlooking Sarasota Bay (*811 S Palm Avenue, Sarasota; tel: (941) 366-5730. Open daily 1000–1700*).

Walkways wind between the individually planted sections revealing cacti, cycads, native Florida plants, herbs and the Tropical Food Garden with oddities such as the giant-leaf edible hibiscus and the liquorice-flavoured black sapote among pineapple, papaya and banana trees. The path continues through groves of banyan and pine and a remarkable forest of bamboo.

# MOTE MARINE AQUARIUM✧

**Mote Marine Aquarium $** *1600 Ken Thompson Parkway, Lido Key; tel: (941) 388-4441. Open daily 1000–1700.*

Primarily a research facility specialising in the study of sharks and environmental pollution, this aquarium blends science and entertainment to good effect. The displays and exhibitions highlight the many problems faced by Florida's marine life while allowing close-up views of creatures as diverse as sea horses and sharks. Another large tank holds two male manatees: try to see them when they chomp through some of the lettuce, cabbage and carrots that forms part of their vegetarian diet.

# RINGLING HOUSE AND MUSEUMS✧✧✧

**Ringling House and Museums $$** *5401 Bayshore Drive, Sarasota; tel: (941) 359 5700. Open daily 1030–1730.*

The Ringling House, known as Ca'd'Zan ('House of John' in Venetian dialect) is among the most beautiful homes in Florida. It was built as a winter residence for circus owner John Ringling and his wife Mable. Set beside Sarasota Bay and completed in 1926, the house is modelled on a Venetian Gothic palace but incorporates many other Mediterranean features.

Ringling's intention was for guests to arrive by gondola and cross a 200-ft-wide terrace, decorated with exquisite tile work, before entering the house. Present-day visitors pass a palm-lined driveway to reach the house and continue into the marble-floored court, the main living area and venue for large dinner parties. The $50,000 Aeolian organ that Mable sometimes played stands on one side, while columns of Mexican onyx rise toward a 30-ft-high ceiling.

Other ground-floor rooms include the Ballroom, with ceiling panels by the *Ziegfeld Follies'* set designer; the Taproom, with its stained-glass panels; and the French Renaissance-style Dining Room. Upstairs, John Ringling's bedroom holds an eight-piece French Empire-style suite; the adjoining bathroom has a Siena marble bathtub. Mable, meanwhile, slept amid a nine-piece suite in Louis XV-style on pillows of Venetian, Belgian and Irish lace.

Restored to its 1920s appearance, the house gives a warm impression of the Ringlings. Unfortunately, their enjoyment of the house did not last long. Mable died in 1929 and the Depression eroded much of the $200 million Ringling fortune; John himself died in 1936.

John Ringling began buying art while touring Europe looking for new talent for his circus. He took a particular shine to baroque art, then financially and critically undervalued, and amassed what is now one of the finest private collections in the world.

Surrounded by replica Greek and Roman statuary, the **Ringling Art Museum** has some 10,000 pieces, none more impressive than the four large-scale canvases by Rubens, painted around 1625 and commissioned by a Hapsburg archduchess as tapestry cartoons. Other excellent baroque works, such as Piero di Cosimo's absorbing *Building*

**Below**
Marie Selby Botanical Gardens

*of a Palace*, feature among the selections from the permanent collections, expanded considerably since Ringling's time. Temporary shows often focus on contemporary art.

Opened after John Ringling's death, the **Circus Gallery** sits rather oddly amid the estate's art and architectural treasures but records the great years of the Ringing Brothers circus, at its peak through the 1920s and 1930s before transport costs and changing tastes led to its demise. A fine collection of circus posters and interesting accounts of dwarf acts, such as Tom Thumb and Emmet Lee Kelly, are among the exhibits.

**Below**
Ringling Museum complex

Also in the grounds is the 18th-century **Asolo Theater**, a 300-seat horseshoe-shaped auditorium built in Italy and transported here brick by brick in 1950, now used for educational programmes and other events.

# SARASOTA❖❖❖

**Sarasota Convention & Visitors Bureau** *665 N Hwy-41; tel: (941) 957-1877 or (800) 522-9799. Open Mon–Sat 0900–1700.*

Sarasota, one of the few places in Florida where locals might be more familiar with Italian opera than Mickey Mouse, is a small and cultured city in a splendid setting. Given a taste for the fine arts by circus-owner John Ringling (*see opposite*) in the 1920s and set beside a gorgeous bay, Downtown Sarasota occupies an easily walked area. Intimate cafés and restaurants are grouped on and around Main Street, as are a number of antiques shops, art galleries and book stores ideal for browsing.

## Food in Sarasota

**Kevin's Country Café & Deli** $ *1578 Main Street; tel: (941) 951-2483.* Omelettes, salads, sandwiches, burgers and tasty soups served for breakfast and lunch.

**Sugar & Spice** $–$$ *1850 Tamiami Trail; tel: (941) 953-3340.* Traditional Amish cooking which includes turkey dinners, large sandwiches and delicious cakes and tarts.

**Tropical Thai** $–$$ *1420 Main Street; tel: (941) 364-5775.* Wide choice of Thai cuisine and excellent-value lunches.

# SIESTA KEY❖

**Siesta Key Chamber of Commerce** *5100 Ocean Boulevard; tel: (941) 349-3800. Open Mon–Fri 0900–1700.*

Siesta Key is prized for the powdery texture of its white-sand beaches, composed of almost pure quartz with little shell or other debris to get trapped between the toes of sunbathers and swimmers. The appeal of its beaches is slightly lessened by the soulless high-rise condos that loom beside them but both crowds and condos thin towards the southern end of the island

## Accommodation in Siesta Key

**Crescent View Beach Club** $$–$$$ *6512 Midnight Pass Road; tel: (941) 349-2000 or (800) 344-7171.* One- and two-bedroom apartments, and a heated pool, a shell's throw from the beach.

**Turtles** $$ *8875 Midnight Pass Road; tel: (941) 346-2207.* Waterfront dining; the daily seafood specials are unbeatable.

# SOUTH LIDO PARK✣✣

**South Lido Beach Park** *Open daily 0900–sunset.*

**Lido Beach Inn** *$$–$$$ 1234 Ben Franklin Drive, Lido Key; tel: (941) 388-1293 or (800) 444-9233.* Fully-equipped, apartment-like rooms within easy reach of St Armands Key and South Lido Park. The inn has two bars and nightly entertainment.

On weekdays, comparatively few people take advantage of this excellent 100-acre beach park fringed by tall rows of Australian pine. The peaceful landscapes range from the Gulf-side beaches to the north side's mangrove-lined bay, which can be explored on a boardwalk trail and by rented canoe. Directly south are views across Big Pass to Siesta Key; east across Sarasota Bay is the Downtown Sarasota skyline.

**Right**
South Lido Park sunset

# SUNSHINE SKYWAY BRIDGE✧✧

**ⓘ Longboat Key Chamber of Commerce** *6854 Gulf of Mexico Drive, Longboat Key; tel: (941) 383-2466. Open Mon–Fri 0900–1700.*

**ⓗ Pelican Man's Bird Sanctuary** *1708 Ken Thompson Parkway, Lido Key; tel: (941) 388-4444. Open daily 1000–1700.*

**ⓒ Silver Sands $$** *5841 Gulf of Mexico Drive, Longboat Key; tel: (941) 383-3731 or (800) 245-3731. Well-priced motel rooms with bay or beach views; also offers one- or two-bedroom kitchen-equipped apartments and a three-bedroomed house.*

**Starfish Motel $–$$** *2929 Gulf of Mexico Drive, Longboat Key; tel: (941) 383-3117 or (800) 333-7335. Good-priced rooms with kitchens and Gulf views; picnic and barbecue areas for guests' use.*

**ⓜ Lynches Landing $–$$** *4000 Gulf of Mexico Drive, Longboat Key; tel: (941) 383-0792. Irish-style pub offering Cork cottage pie and Irish stew alongside more common seafood and meat dishes.*

This vital traffic link and accomplished piece of engineering carries I-275 for 15 miles the across the mouth of Tampa Bay, reaching 250ft at its highest point. It cost $215 million and replaced an earlier bridge, struck by a tanker during a storm in 1980. The collision caused the deaths of 35 people as vehicles fell from the collapsed central span. The southern section of the old bridge now serves as an over-long fishing pier; the submerged span has become an artificial reef.

## Suggested tour

**Length**: Main tour 48 miles, 70 miles with detours.

**Duration**: Driving time 2 hours, 3 hours with detours.

**Links**: To the north, the Sunshine Skyway Bridge links this tour with St Petersburg and its beaches (*see pages 144–53*). Heading south, Hwy-41 or I-75 provide access to Fort Myers and the Lee County Islands (*see pages 124–33*).

After crossing Tampa Bay with the **SUNSHINE SKYWAY BRIDGE ❶**, I-275 continues over the mangrove-skirted **Tierra Ceia Island**, dotted by prehistoric shell mounds. Join Route 55 which, after 2.5 miles, connects with Hwy-41 to head south through **Palmetto** on the north bank of the broad Manatee River. Hwy-41 continues across the river into **Bradenton**, more given to commerce and industry than its Culture Coast neighbours.

Half-a-mile after the river crossing, turn right on to Route 64 (Manatee Avenue). This charts an uninspiring course with numerous traffic-lights but is the main route to the rewarding barrier island beach communities. The first of these is **Holmes Beach**, 9 miles ahead and one of three separately-governed communities of **ANNA MARIA ISLAND ❷**.

Turn left on to E Bay Drive which quickly joins Gulf Boulevard, the main artery linking the barrier island chain. After 1.75 miles, the route passes **Bradenton Beach**, an unpretentious community where most visitor interest focuses on the excellent **Coquina Beach** occupying Anna Maria Island's southern tip.

Crossing from Anna Maria Island on to **Longboat Key**, the route becomes Gulf of Mexico Drive and for the next 11 miles passes condominiums, beachfront resorts, golf courses and a few small motels. A fine, unbroken strip of sand lines the Gulf. Just before reaching Lido Key, a left turn on to Ken Thompson Parkway leads to the **MOTE MARINE AQUARIUM ❸**. Adjacent to the aquaruim is **Pelican Man's Bird Sanctuary**, a volunteer-run organisation that cares for several thousand injured birds annually; pelicans, owls and cormorants can be viewed from a boardwalk.

🏛 **Anna Maria
Historical Society
Museum** 402 Pine Avenue;
tel: (941) 778-0492. Open
Jun–Aug, Tue–Thur and Sat
1000–1300; Sept–May,
Tue–Thur and Sat
1000–1600.

🌙 **Harrington House**
**$$$** 5625 Gulf Drive,
Holmes Beach, Anna Maria
Island; tel: (941) 778-5444.
Extremely charming
beachside bed-and-
breakfast inn with 13
antique-filled rooms.

**Accommodation and
food**

Beachside hotels and
resorts are found all
along the coast, while
scores of inexpensive
motels line the
approach roads into
mainland cities,
particularly on Hwy-41
as it approaches
Sarasota. Food is no
less readily available,
whether you want to
grab a wholesome
snack while sightseeing
or indulge in a leisurely
seafood dinner while
watching the sunset.

Reaching Lido Key, the route becomes John Ringling Parkway, named after the circus owner who made these barrier islands accessible from the mainland and who bought much of the replica neo-classical statuary that decorates **St Armands Circle**, directly ahead and ringed by boutiques and speciality shops.

Running east from St Armands Circle, John Ringling Boulevard passes the Sarasota Yacht Club and the small island of Bird Key as it crosses Sarasota Bay, reaching **SARASOTA** 2.25 miles ahead. Follow signs for Main Street to explore Downtown Sarasota, directly ahead. Turn left along Hwy-41 for the **RINGLING HOUSE AND MUSEUMS** ❹, 3.75 miles north. Turn right along Bayfront Drive to pass the pleasantly landscaped Bayfront Park and reach the **MARIE SELBY BOTANICAL GARDENS** ❺.

Stay on Bayfront Drive (the local section of Hwy-41) as it swings left and ascends a hill to reach the junction with Hwy-319 (Washington Boulevard). Turn right and continue south. After 1.8 miles, turn right on to Siesta Drive and the most populated section of **SIESTA KEY** ❻ is a mile ahead. On Siesta Key, Siesta Drive becomes Higel Avenue. After 0.75 miles, Midnight Pass Road forks to the left. Take this for 1.8 miles to reach the junction with Beach Drive where **Siesta Public Beach** occupies 2400ft of shoreline.

Continuing south on Midnight Pass Road penetrates the less developed portions of Siesta Key, reaching the rarely crowded **Crescent Beach** and **Turtle Beach**. After 5 miles, the road expires facing Midnight Pass.

**Detour:** From Palmetto, turn left on to Hwy-331 towards Ellenton. After 2.7 miles of this busy route, watch for the signposted turning for **GAMBLE PLANTATION STATE HISTORIC SITE** ❼, located on the north side of the route off Ellenton Gillete Road.

**Detour:** Between Bradenton and Anna Maria Island, 4.6 miles from the junction with Hwy-41, turn right along 75th Street NE. Although little on this tree-lined residential street suggests it, 2.4 miles ahead is the **DE SOTO NATIONAL MONUMENT** ❽, remembering a 16th-century Spanish landing.

**Detour:** To see more of **Anna Maria Island** continue on Manatee Avenue from Holmes Beach and turn right on to Gulf Boulevard. After 3 miles, turn right on Pine Avenue for the **Anna Maria Historical Society Museum**. Directly ahead is the engagingly ramshackle **Anna Maria Pier**. To the left is **Bayfront Park**, the heart of this relaxed coastal community.

**Detour:** From St Armands Circle, take Benjamin Franklin Drive, which for half-a-mile swings along the edge of **Lido Beach**, a favourite spot for sunset strolls on the sand. The edge of the beach marks the start of a tree-lined hotel strip running for less than a mile until the route reaches the entrance to **SOUTH LIDO PARK** ❾.

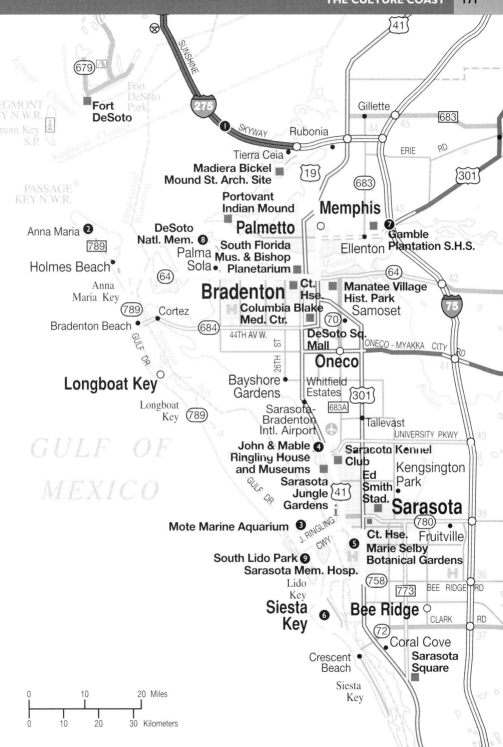

Fort DeSoto

679

EGMONT
EY N.W.R.
mont Key
S.P.

Fort DeSoto Park

41

275

SKYWAY

SUNSHINE

Gillette

683

Rubonia

ERIE        RD

Tierra Ceia

Madiera Bickel
Mound St. Arch. Site

19

683

301

PASSAGE
KEY N.W.R.

Portovant
Indian Mound

Memphis

Anna Maria ❷

789

DeSoto
Natl. Mem. ❽

Palmetto

Gamble
Plantation S.H.S. ❼

Ellenton

Holmes Beach

Palma
Sola

South Florida
Mus. & Bishop
Planetarium

Anna
Maria  Key

64

Bradenton

Ct.
Hse.

Manatee Village
Hist. Park

64

75

789    Cortez

Columbia Blake
Med. Ctr.

Samoset

Bradenton Beach

GULF DR

684

44TH AV W.

70

DeSoto Sq.
Mall

ONECO - MYAKKA   CITY   RD

Longboat Key

Bayshore
Gardens

Whitfield
Estates

Oneco

301

Longboat
Key    789

Sarasota-
Bradenton
Intl. Airport

683A

Tallevast

UNIVERSITY PKWY

GULF   OF

John & Mable ❹
Ringling House
and Museums

GULF DR

Sarasota Kennel
Club

Ed
Smith
Stad.

Kengsington
Park

MEXICO

Sarasota
Jungle
Gardens

41

Sarasota

780

Mote Marine Aquarium ❸

J. RINGLING

CWY

Ct. Hse.  Fruitville

South Lido Park ❾
Sarasota Mem. Hosp.

❺

Marie Selby
Botanical Gardens

Lido
Key

758

773

BEE RIDGE   RD

Siesta
Key

❻

Bee Ridge

CLARK    RD

Crescent
Beach

72

Coral Cove

Sarasota
Square

Siesta
Key

0      10      20  Miles

0    10    20    30 Kilometers

# Between Tampa and Orlando

**Ratings**

| | |
|---|---|
| Gardens | ●●●●● |
| Architecture | ●●●● |
| Lakes | ●●●● |
| Nature | ●●●● |
| Scenery | ●●●● |
| History | ●●● |
| Children | ●● |
| Museums | ●● |

Theme parks and tourism may be the mainstays of central Florida's economy today but once it was citrus that underpinned the region's prosperity, as it kept the rest of the nation supplied with orange juice through winter snows. Small towns set amid the world's largest concentration of citrus groves form the core of this tour. Often pleasantly removed from major traffic routes and reached by specially designated scenic highways, the growth of such towns has been stunted by distance from major urban centres allowing the preservation of their early-1900s Downtown areas.

Countless lakes also improve the outlook. Beside one of them is Cypress Gardens, the area's only fully blown tourist attraction. By contrast, most local sights are one-of-a-kind affairs such as the whimsically designed Chalet Suzanne, whose home-made soups have been eaten in space, and the beautiful Bok Tower Gardens, its immense carillon one of the few things to disturb the peace of this lovely and under-visited part of Florida.

## AVON PARK*

Set amid rolling hills and citrus groves, Avon Park could well be the sunkissed Florida retirement community on which all others are based. Golf courses and shuffleboard courts predominate in and around a community that labels itself 'city of charm'. The town was founded in 1881 by an English settler from Stratford-Upon-Avon, and its past is ably chronicled by the **Avon Park Museum**.

## BLACK HILLS PASSION PLAY*

**Black Hills Passion Play** Hwy-27A near Lake Wales; tel: (941) 676-1495 or (800) 622-8383.

This passion play – a dramatic reconstruction of Christ's last seven days and his subsequent resurrection – is believed to have originated in Germany in 1242 and been carried to the Black Hills of Dakota by German settlers in 1932. It has been staged at this specially constructed amphitheatre since 1952, taking place around Easter. The play is a well-attended event advertised by enormous billboards all around Lake Wales.

# Bok Tower Gardens✧✧✧

**Bok Tower Gardens $ 1151**
Tower Boulevard, Lake Wales; tel: (941) 676-1408. Open daily 0800–1700. Carillon recitals 1500 daily. Pinewood, visit by guided tour only; telephone number as for gardens, separate fee $.

Bok Tower Gardens reveal a side of Florida that few first-time visitors believe exists – 130 acres of bucolic serenity spread over the highest point (295ft above sea-level) in the Florida peninsula. Shady trails lined by palms, pines and live oaks draped with Spanish moss chart a meandering course through the gardens passing colourful seasonal displays of azaleas, camellias and magnolias, and a host of other plant life.

Inquisitive squirrels and a colony of wood ducks are often sighted in the gardens; the resident racoons, bobcats and foxes tend to be more secretive. More wildlife can be surreptitiously viewed at the **window-by-the-pond**, a concealed overlook revealing the egrets, herons and other birds that nest in pond-side vegetation.

Built of pink and grey Georgia marble and coquina, Bok Tower rises 205ft and houses a carillon of 57 bronze bells. The bells, some weighing 12 tons, resound through the gardens as they mark each half hour, and are heard to best effect in the afternoon recital.

Intended as a sanctuary for birds, animals and people, the gardens provide a fitting reminder of the ideals of their founder, Dutch-born publisher, editor, writer and philanthropist Edward Bok, who donated this land to the people of his adopted country. Much of the landscaping was the work of Frederick Law Olmsted, best known for New York's Central Park.

The garden's history is detailed in the visitors' centre, occupying a pioneer-era cracker cottage. By contrast, the grounds also hold **Pinewood**, a Mediterranean Revival mansion built in 1931 for steel magnate Charles Austin Beck. The luxury home cleverly blends into its natural setting displaying some of Beck's extensive antique collection.

# CYPRESS GARDENS❖❖

**ⓘ Cypress Gardens $$**
*2641 S Lake Summit Drive, Winter Haven; tel: (941) 324-2111. Open daily 0930–1730 or later.*

**Ⓒ Ranch House Inn $–$$** *1911 Cypress Gardens Boulevard, Winter Haven; tel: (941) 324-5994.* Perfectly located for Cypress Gardens and also a good general touring base, offering well-priced motel rooms and kitchen-equipped efficiencies. The attached restaurant serves inexpensive and generously sized breakfasts, lunches and dinners.

It was not Walt Disney but the much less celebrated Dick Pope, an Iowa property dealer, who gave Florida its first theme park in 1936. Pope transformed a 16-acre cypress swamp into Cypress Gardens, vowing to get visitors 'punch drunk on floral beauty'.

The gardens now fill 233 acres with 8000 plant species from 90 countries; among the sweetly scented mass are bougainvillaea, hibiscus, roses, bromeliads, magnolias, gardenias and Chinese bauhinia. The garden's natural microclimates and species diversity results in something blooming throughout the year: the mid-November chrysanthemum festival is one of the garden's best-attended events.

The gardens can be explored on foot and by the boats that wind around the network of canals off Lake Eloise, around whose cypress-lined banks the gardens are arranged. The lake is a venue for water-ski shows, often featuring daredevil stunts such as human pyramid formations. Also on the lake, the Island-in-the-Sky provides a bird's-eye view of the gardens from a 153-ft-high revolving platform.

Some of the garden's most photographed attractions are not plants but the Southern Belles, hoop-skirted young ladies originally introduced to divert attention from the vines withered by freezing weather in the 1940s. The Belles appear in three particularly photogenic areas at a set time daily.

# FLORIDA SOUTHERN COLLEGE❖❖

The Florida Southern College is a Methodist academic institution founded in 1885, of note for its Frank Lloyd Wright buildings – the

**Florida Southern College** *111 Lake Hollingsworth Drive, Lakeland; tel: (941) 680-4597. Open Tue–Fri 1100–1600, Sat 1000–1400, Sun 1400–1600; visitors' centre closed during college holidays.*

1930s campus forms the largest single grouping of the celebrated architect's work. Calling the project his 'Child of the Sun', Wright envisaged the campus growing in harmony with the citrus grove that occupied the site. He used local stone and employed the geometric forms that had become trademarks of the 'organic architecture' that made his reputation.

The campus fell short of Wright's vision, however, with only eight of the intended 18 buildings completed. None the less, the campus is well worth a visit; the architectural details are described by free leaflets distributed in boxes along the covered walkways linking the buildings. A visitors' centre displays some of Wright's original campus drawings and other items.

# HIGHLANDS HAMMOCK STATE PARK✤✤

**Highlands Hammock State Park** *$ off Hwy-27 near Sebring; tel: (941) 386-6094. Open daily 0800–sunset.*

One of Florida's oldest, biggest and best state parks, Highlands Hammock fills 4700 acres. A series of paved and boardwalk trails access damp and shady fern pockets, orange groves, pine flatwoods, scrubland and a cypress swamp. Florida scrub jays are among the frequently sighted birds; at ground level, white-tailed deer and alligators are abundant. A ranger-led tram tour visits the remoter reaches of the park.

The park was constructed in the 1930s by the Civil Conservation Corp, created during the Depression to provide work for unemployed young men. They are remembered, alongside natural history exhibits, in the park's museum.

# LAKE WALES✤✤

**Lake Wales Chamber of Commerce** *340 W Central Avenue; tel: (941) 676-3445. Open Mon–Fri 0830–1700.*

**Spook Hill** *on North Avenue near junction with Burns Avenue (Hwy-17A), Lake Wales.*

**The Depot** *$ 325 S Scenic Highway; tel: (941) 678-4209. Open Mon–Fri 0900–1700, Sat 1000–1600.*

**Right**
Chalet Suzanne

Little Lake Wales has a surprising number of unusual sights in and around it. Strangest is **Spook Hill**, an optical illusion (though some offer spiritual and scientific explanations) making cars appear to roll uphill. To experience this slightly unnerving phenomena, park at the signposted spot, take the vehicle out of gear and await the results.

A more orthodox place is **The Depot**, where a 1927 railroad station has been turned into a historical museum and cultural centre, forming part of an attractively restored Downtown area. Among an extensive array chronicling the town's growth is a mesmerising display of citrus crates and labels. Railroad links are maintained with an elegant 1920s Pullman carriage and a 1944 locomotive.

Founded by a gourmet cook seeking to make ends meet during the Depression, **Chalet Suzanne** acquired its present form – the pink walls, turrets and towers conceal an insane conglomeration of rooms spread across 14 different levels – when a stable, rabbit hutches and chicken houses were knocked together in the 1940s. The chalet is now a Florida landmark and famed for its fine cuisine, including soup, which is available in tins and was carried to the moon by Apollo 15 astronauts in 1973. It makes an entertaining visit – there's an excellent gift shop and the chance to peep into the luxurious room.

## Accommodation and food in Lake Wales

**Chalet Suzanne** $$$ *3800 Chalet Suzanne Drive; tel: (941) 676-6011.* Noted local landmark (*see page 175*) that offers some of Florida's best cuisine in a lovely setting. Stay overnight in whimsically furnished rooms beneath turrets and spires.

**Black Forest Buffet Restaurant** $ *Hwy-27 south of Lake Wales; tel: (941) 638-3036.* Large portions of filling food but primarily worth a call for the kitsch Bavarian décor and cuckoo clocks.

**Christy's Sundown** $–$$ *Junction of Avenue K and Hwy-17-S; tel: (941) 293-0069.* Prime rib, fresh seafood and assorted pasta dishes are mainstays of this dependable and popular restaurant. Closed on Sun.

**Vinton's New Orleans Restaurant** $$$ *229 E Stuart Avenu; tel: (941) 676-8242.* Faultless cajun cuisine in a refined setting as New Orleans jazz bubbles in the background; reservations recommended for dinner.

# LAKELAND*

Lakeland's appearance is greatly enhanced by the 13 lakes within its borders, including Lake Mirror which flanks the tastefully landscaped **Munn Historic District** where many 1910s and 1920s commercial buildings now house antiques shops. A few blocks away, the **Polk**

**ℹ Lakeland Chamber of Commerce** 35 Lake Morton Drive; tel: (941) 688-8551. Open Mon–Fri 0830–1700.

**🏛 Polk Museum of Art** 800 E Palmetto Street; tel: (941) 688-7743. Open Tue–Fri 0900–1600, Sat 1000–1600, Sun 1200–1600.

**🍴 Wellesley Inn Lakeland $$** 3520 N Hwy-98; tel: (941) 859-3399 or (800) 444-8888. Up-market motel on the edge of town; rooms have coffee-makers and there is a coin-operated laundry.

**Museum of Art** has small but strong permanent collections, mostly of American painting, photography and sculpture, and regularly brings good-quality travelling exhibitions to the town.

# SEBRING✣

The main streets of Sebring follow an unusual circular pattern, spreading outwards from the oak tree planted in 1912 by the town's founder, a ceramics manufacturer from Ohio called George Sebring. Much of the once-commercially important old centre has been pleasantly restored and provides a setting for **Roaring Twenties Day**, which finds merchants donning 1920s attire and many related events taking place.

In total contrast, the **International Grand Prix Sports Car 12-hour Endurance Race** brings nationwide attention to Sebring each March.

# Suggested tour

**Length**: Main tour 40 miles, 95 miles with detours.

**Duration**: Main tour, 4 hours; add 2–3 hours for the Bok Tower Gardens or Avon Park detours, and 4 hours minimum for Cypress Gardens.

**Links**: This tour is accessed from I-4 and Hwy-27 and links easily with Tampa (*see pages 134–43*) and Orlando and its theme parks (*see pages 180–91*).

Exit I-4 heading south on Hwy-98, which becomes Florida Avenue and continues for 3.2 miles into the historic centre of **LAKELAND** ❶. After exploring the immediate area, continue south on Florida Avenue, turning left on to McDonald Street after half-a-mile and immediately right on to Johnson Street, where the **FLORIDA SOUTHERN COLLEGE** ❷ sits prettily on the north bank of Lake Hollingsworth.

Leave Lakeland on Hwy-92 and travel 9.5 miles east before turning right on to Route 544. After 3.2 miles, turn right on to Hwy-17, where you will quickly be passing the rows of motels and restaurants that dominate the small town of **Winter Haven**, serving visitors to Cypress Gardens (*see detour*).

Turn left on to Route 542, which after 6.2 miles crosses the busy Hwy-27 to reach the hamlet of **Dundee**. Turn right here for Hwy-27A (Route 17), a quieter, scenic alternative to Hwy-27. **LAKE WALES** ❸ is 9 miles ahead on a route that passes **Chalet Suzanne**. The amphitheatre staging the **BLACK HILLS PASSION PLAY** ❹ is signposted 1.5 miles south of Lake Wales on Hwy-27A. To rejoin I-4, take Hwy-27 north from Lake Wales and continue for 24 miles.

Detour: CYPRESS GARDENS ❺ is the area's major tourist attraction and very well signposted. Pass through Winter Haven on Hwy-17 and turn left on to Route 540, where the entrance is 5 miles ahead.

Detour: Far less commercialised than Cypress Gardens, **BOK TOWER GARDENS** ❻ occupies one of the highest section of the Florida Ridge (a limestone bulge forming the 'spine' of the Florida peninsula). Two miles north of Lake Wales on Hwy-27A, turn right on to Burns Avenue (Hwy-17A) where the gardens lie at the end of a signposted 5-mile route.

Detour: Continue south from Lake Wales on Hwy-27A, after 14 miles passing through **Frostproof**, a little settlement whose name signalled the ability of the local citrus crop to survive the winter. Six miles ahead, Hwy-27A joins Hwy-27; continue south for 6.5 miles, turning left for **Avon Park** on Route 64 (Main Street). Look for the right turn on to Hwy-17, which charts a scenic 10-mile course passing the lakes, citrus groves and golf courses that characterise the area, before reaching **SEBRING** ❼. Leave Sebring on Lakeview Drive, skirting the

edge of Lake Jackson before briefly joining Hwy-27 and making a left turn on to Route 634 (Hammock Road). This continues for 5.5 miles to **HIGHLANDS HAMMOCK STATE PARK** ❽.

## Also worth exploring

Between Lake Wales and I-4, Hwy-27 is crossed by Hwy-92. Travel 5 miles west on Hwy-92 to **Lake Alfred**, a village filled with an impossibly large number of antiques shops and self-consciously quaint tea rooms. The shops deal in everything from vintage neon signs and moose heads to fine china, jewellery and silver. A slightly smaller number of similar shops can be found in **Haines City**, 2.5 miles east on Hwy-92. Another small town, **Auburndale**, 5 miles west of Lake Alfred may be unable to match its neighbours for antiques shops but can boast one of Florida's best inland beaches on the banks of Lake Ariana.

# Orlando and its theme parks

**Ratings**

| | |
|---|---|
| Children | ●●●●● |
| Nightlife | ●●●●● |
| Theme parks | ●●●●● |
| Nature | ●●● |
| Shopping | ●●● |
| Museums | ●● |
| History | ● |
| Scenery | ● |

**M**uch of the Orlando area is Florida as first-time visitors usually imagine the whole state to be: a mass of freeway interchanges, gigantic billboards, chain hotels and the theme parks that provide the world's most technologically advanced entertainment. Filling an area twice the size of Manhattan, Walt Disney World opened its first park here in 1971 and made Florida a pacesetter in international tourism. Disney continues to develop new parks, as does Universal Studios, and both vie fiercely for visitor attention along with other major draws such as SeaWorld.

Be it in accommodation, dining or daytime activities, competition for the tourist dollar is fierce and Orlando, while not always cheap, offers excellent value for money. Away from the razzle-dazzle of theme parks, Orlando has several intriguing neighbourhoods and engaging minor museums, ranging from a centre for injured birds to displays of Tiffany glasswork and the proof that Orlando really did exist long before the arrival of Mickey Mouse.

## DISNEY'S ANIMAL KINGDOM✢✢

**ⓘ Tourist Information
Centre** *Mercado
Shopping Mall, 8445
International Drive; tel: (407)
363-5871. Open daily
0800–2000.*

**Kissimmee/St Cloud
Convention & Visitors
Bureau** *1925 E Hwy-192,
Kissimmee; tel: (407) 847-
5000. Open daily
0800–1700.*

Turning a flat and featureless chunk of central Florida five times the size of the Magic Kingdom into a landscape of vine-covered crags and waterfalls, Animal Kingdom opened in 1998, promising a 'new species of theme park'. The animals that roam the varied sections include gorillas, hippos, zebra, rhinos, giraffes, miniature deer and tree kangaroos; they are joined by Disney-created dinosaurs. Animal Kingdom radiates outwards from the 14-storey-high **Tree of Life**, intended to symbolise the connectedness of all life with animal forms carved into its gnarled trunk. The park will certainly thrill young children and probably please all who visit, although the mixture of ecology, zoo and theme park, complete with the usual parades and fireworks, sometimes seems an uneasy combination.

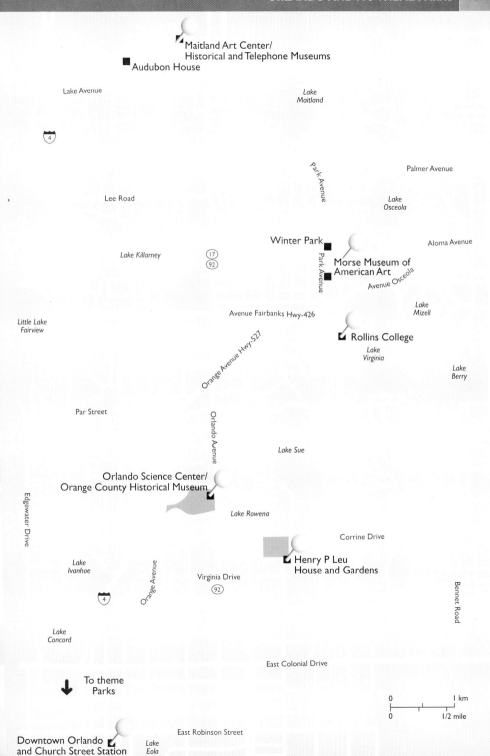

Maitland Art Center/
Historical and Telephone Museums

Audubon House

Lake Avenue

Lake
Maitland

4

Park Avenue

Palmer Avenue

Lee Road

Lake
Osceola

Winter Park

Aloma Avenue

Lake Killarney

17
92

Park Avenue

Morse Museum of
American Art

Avenue Osceola

Lake
Mizell

Avenue Fairbanks Hwy-426

Little Lake
Fairview

Rollins College

Lake
Virginia

Orange Avenue Hwy-527

Lake
Berry

Par Street

Orlando Avenue

Lake Sue

Orlando Science Center/
Orange County Historical Museum

Lake Rowena

Edgewater Drive

Corrine Drive

Lake
Ivanhoe

Orange Avenue

Virginia Drive

92

Henry P Leu
House and Gardens

Bennet Road

4

Lake
Concord

East Colonial Drive

To theme
Parks

0                1 km

0                1/2 mile

Downtown Orlando
and Church Street Station

Lake
Eola

East Robinson Street

# DISNEY-MGM STUDIOS✦✦✦

**Disney-MGM Studios $$$** *Walt Disney World, Exit 26B from I-4; tel: (407) 824-4321. Open daily 0900–1900, until 2200 or 2400 from mid-Jun–mid-Aug.*

Smallest of the main Disney Parks, Disney-MGM Studios combines top-notch rides and shows based on American film and TV, with informative behind-the-scenes tours of the company's film and TV production facilities. The special effects and stunt shows are excellent, and if you have ever wondered how a Disney animation evolves, this is the place to find out.

This is the best Disney park for visitor involvement in shows. Participation ranges from being an extra on the Indiana Jones Epic Stunt Spectacular to appearing – through the magic of video editing – alongside Lucille Ball or the cast of *Cheers* at SuperStar Television. To become involved, be at the head of the queue outside the particular show when volunteers are requested. Be ready to spend time being made up and rehearsed before facing an audience or going on air, and do not volunteer if you are easily embarrassed.

Throughout the day along **Hollywood Boulevard**, a cast of Disney actors create 'Streetmosphere', adding to the illusion of being in Hollywood during its heyday. On **Sunset Boulevard**, Mickey Mouse and other Disney characters can often be spotted, ready to pose for photos and sign autographs. Save for the **Honey, I Shrunk The Kids Movie Set Adventure**, a play area with oversized objects and creatures, and some shows based on recent Disney film releases, there is little in the park specifically to appeal to small children.

The park has some of Disney's best rides. Combining film, sound and plenty of heart-stopping swerves and bumps, **Star Tours** takes visitors on a flight-simulator trip to the Moon of Endor with the characters of the Star Wars films. Equally effective, **The Twilight Zone Tower of Ter**ror traps participants in a spooky Hollywood hotel on an elevator that makes a dizzying 13-floor plunge in two seconds. The less frenetic **Great Movie Ride** takes place inside a re-creation of Hollywood's Mann's Chinese Theatre and passes a series of classic movie scenes with AudioAnimatronic robots taking the parts of celebrated actors.

Of the shows, the **Indiana Jones Epic Stunt Spectacular** demonstrates stage explosions, fights, and general stunt work; the riotous **Jim Henson's Muppet 4D Vision** has great 3D effects; and **SuperStar Television** pitches audience volunteers into classic TV shows with hilarious results. Audience participation also features at **Monster Sound Show and SoundWorks**, entertaining and informative looks at the making of sound effects.

The nuts and bolts of film-making are revealed on the **Backlot Tour**, taking visitors through genuine Disney sound stages, sometimes with filming in progress, to **Catastrophe Canyon** which brings first-hand experience of simulated floods, explosions and other dramatic movie effects. The calmer **Magic of Disney Animation** describes the processes involved in cartoon creation and peeks at Disney's own animators working on new productions.

# DOWNTOWN ORLANDO✣

The surprisingly few square blocks that comprise Downtown Orlando are studded with the architecture that recalls the city's slow but steady pre-Disney growth as a citrus and cattle centre. The expansion seen across the area since the major theme parks opened has had relatively little impact here, as a daytime walk around the park-lined **Lake Eola** will prove. Downtown Orlando is an important nightlife area (*see page 190*).

**Right**
Downtown Orlando

# EPCOT✣✣

**EPCOT $$$** *Walt Disney World, Exit 26B from I-4; tel: (407) 824-4321. Open daily 0900–2100, until 2200 or 2400 from mid-Jun–mid-Aug.*

EPCOT, the most ambitious Disney park, was intended to present a vision of tomorrow's world today and to celebrate the cultures of the world's nations. It is the toughest Disney park to explore within a day and the least interesting for children. The park divides into two sections, Future World and World Showcase, each housing a series of pavilions.

**Future World** explores the wonders of science and the natural world with a few rides and numerous exhibits. **Wonders of Life** includes EPCOT's best special-effects ride, *Body Wars*, replicating a bloodcell's journey through the human body. Less nerve jangling is the amusing *Cranium Command*, exploring the workings of the brain of a 12-year-old schoolboy through a typical day. *The Making of Me* is a child-aimed explanation of the human reproductive process.

**Right**
EPCOT's Moroccan Pavilion

Another Future World highlight, **Journey Into Imagination** has a 3D film, *Honey, I Shrunk The Audience*, with innovative effects making visitors feel they have been reduced to a fraction of their normal size. *The Image Works*, likely to occupy young teens for long periods, is a large collection of user-friendly, interactive creative games including the Electronic Philharmonic, an entire orchestra ready to play to your command.

The most impressive section of Future World is **The Living Seas**, which begins with a simulated descent to Sea Base Alpha, a deep-sea research centre. A range of exhibits and displays inform on the mysteries of ocean life, many examples of which inhabit the gigantic tank holding six million gallons of sea water and 6000 creatures.

Beside a large lagoon, World Showcase features the cultures of 11 nations with a film or ride focusing on the particular country, and a supposedly typical collection of its shops and restaurants. Highlights are **China**, with its *Wonders of China* film displayed across nine screens showing historic sites and landscapes. The China Pavilion is one of the most architecturally distinctive in World Showcase, not least for its half-size replica of Beijing's Temple of Heaven.

The **Norway** pavilion has a stave church, fishermen's cottages and a medieval castle, and World Showcase's best ride, *Maelstrom*, a longboat journey in the company of Viking raiders. A more restful voyage, along *El Rio del Tiempo* in the **Mexico** pavilion, finds events in Mexican history re-enacted life by AudioAnimatronic characters. The

**United Kingdom** has a collection of façades in British architectural styles and a re-created traditional pub, the *Rose & Crown*, selling imported beer and Cornish pasties.

# FLORIDA AUDUBON SOCIETY✣

**Florida Audubon Society** *1101 Audubon Way, near Maitland; tel: (407) 539-5700. Open Tue–Sat 1000–1600.*

A down side to the great expansion of Orlando has been the injuries to ospreys, bald eagles, owls, vultures and other birds of prey caused by increased human settlement. Several hundred are brought here annually, receiving treatment at one of the state's longest-running conservation centres. The aviary provides a glimpse of many feathered creatures usually only fleetingly spotted in the wild.

# HARRY P LEU HOUSE AND GARDENS✣✣

**Harry P Leu House and Gardens** $ *1920 N Forest Avenue, Orlando; tel: (407) 246-2620. Open daily 0900–1700.*

Green-fingered visitors will relish a trip to this gorgeous 50-acre array of roses, azaleas, camellias and other plants, that began with the botanical collection of a local businessman, Henry P Leu, in the 1930s. Should your visit coincide with the start of a guided tour of the Leu House, take the opportunity to see inside the 19th-century farmhouse that Leu and his wife made into a comfortable home

# MAITLAND✣

**Maitland Art Center** *231 W Packwood Avenue, tel. (407) 539-2181. Open Mon–Fri 1000–1630, Sat–Sun 1200–1630.*

**Maitland Historical & Telephone museums** *221 W Packwood Avenue; tel: (407) 644-1364. Open Thur–Sun 1200–1600.*

Maitland became an unlikely artists' colony during the 1930s when André Smith bought six lakeside acres and raised the striking stucco and concrete complex of **Maitland Art Center**, arranged around a central courtyard and decorated with Aztec and Mayan motifs. Although changing art exhibits fill the small galleries, it is the centre's striking design that steals the show. Next door, the adjoined **historical** and **telephone museums** display a rich clutter relating to the early days of Maitland, including the bulky switchboards and wind-up devices through which its residents once communicated.

# MORSE MUSEUM OF AMERICAN ART✣✣✣

**Morse Museum of American Art** $ *445 Park Avenue N, Winter Park; tel: (407) 645-5311. Open Tue–Sat 0930–1600, Sun 1300–1600.*

This small but excellent collection displays many examples of the decorative glasswork of Louis Comfort Tiffany. Pioneering the use of coloured glass, Tiffany became a legend for his lamps, vases and stained-glass windows that decorated the homes of the rich and famous as well as many public buildings. A highlight among many striking works is the *Four Seasons Window*, made in 1900 for a Paris exposition which established Tiffany's reputation at the forefront of art nouveau design.

# ORANGE COUNTY HISTORICAL MUSEUM❖

**Orange County Historical Museum**
$ Loch Haven Park, Orlando; tel: (407) 897-6350. Open daily 0900–1700.

It is easy to forget that Orlando existed before the arrival of Walt Disney World and easier still to forget that before even Orlando existed the area was inhabited by the Timucua, a people remembered here by a dugout canoe, tooled animal bones and other items. Subsequent periods are recorded with farming implements, a re-created Victorian parlour, old newspaper presses and a restored 1926 fire station.

# ORLANDO SCIENCE CENTER❖❖

**Orlando Science Center** $$ Loch Haven Park, Orlando; tel: (407) 896-7151. Open Mon–Sat 0900–1700, Sun 1200–1700.

Informing and entertaining young minds on the natural world through interactive exhibits spread across 42,000sq-ft, the Orlando Science Center is an ideal place for children on rainy days. The adjoining planetarium reveals some of the mysteries of the star-filled sky.

# ROLLINS COLLEGE❖

**Rollins College** 1000 Holt Avenue, Winter Park.

Founded in 1885, Rollins College was the first officially recognised college in Florida. The 67-acre campus is studded with Mediterranean Revival buildings set along palm-lined walkways in a lakeside setting. The architecturally accomplished **Knowles Memorial Chapel** is the venue of a springtime Bach Festival.

# SEAWORLD❖❖❖

**SeaWorld** $$$ 707 SeaWorld Drive, south of Orlando off I-4; tel: (407) 351-3600. Open daily 0900–1900, until 2200 mid-May–Sept.

With its dolphin and whale shows, and state-of-the-art exhibits on marine life, SeaWorld educates and entertains as well as carries out research and conservation work. Recently, it has broadened its appeal by introducing theme park-style thrill rides.

A simulated helicopter trip through an arctic blizzard begins **Wild Arctic**; the journey concludes at a re-created, 150-year-old exploration ship from which visitors can admire polar bears, walruses, beluga whales and other creatures who enjoy the very low temperatures on the other side of the glass. The other major ride, **Journey to Atlantis**, takes passengers on a high-speed water ride in the company of mythical sirens to the lost city of Atlantis, created with lasers and holographic imagery.

Of SeaWorld's marine shows, the most popular are those featuring the five killer whales, each called Shamu, of **Shamu – World Focus**. More marine skills are demonstrated by the dolphins participating in **Key West Dolphin Fest**.

Exhibits include **Manatees: The Last Generation?** with interactive displays on and underwater views of manatees as they swim in a

300,000 gallon tank; **Pacific Point Preserve**, a re-creation of the rocky coast of the US's northwest, with South American seals and California sea lions gliding in and out of the water; **Penguin Encounter** where 200 penguins inhabit a replicated Antarctica; and **Terrors of the Deep**, a rogues gallery of dangerous sea dwellers including sharks, barracudas and some very ugly green moray eels.

# SPLENDID CHINA✦✦✦

**Splendid China $$$**
*3000 Splendid China Boulevard, west of Kissimmee off Hwy-192; tel: (407) 397-8825. Open daily 0930–1900 or later.*

Spread across a 76-acre site, this re-creation of China emphasises the country's long history and culture with scale models of its most famous landmarks, such as the Great Wall, the Temple of Heaven and the Imperial Palace. Everything is produced with mind-boggling attention to detail, no single portion more impressive than the Terra Cotta Warriors. Texts unravel the complexities of 3000 years of Chinese history. Come after dark to see the park beautifully illuminated. Park shops specialise in Chinese handicrafts.

# UNIVERSAL STUDIOS✦✦✦

**Universal Studios $$$** *1001 Universal Studios Plaza, Exit 29 from I-4; tel: (407) 363-8000. Open Mon–Fri 0900–1800, Sat–Sun 0900–1900, later during summer and holidays.*

**Below**
Face to face with 'Jaws', Universal Studios

Universal Studios is a combined theme park and TV and film production facility with the emphasis very much on fun. Universal has the best special-effect rides of any Orlando theme park and appeals chiefly to adults and older children, although several areas are intended for the very young.

The park divides into **Hollywood, San Francisco/Amity** and **New York**, each with replicated streets and buildings; **Production**, where most of the film-technique shows are located; and **Expo Center**, a mixture of kids' entertainments and rides. Throughout the day, speedboats and jet-skiers perform daredevil manoeuvres on the lagoon, also the setting for the **Dynamite Nights Stuntacular**, performed just before closing time.

For thrills and spills, nothing beats **Back To the Future**, a four-minute trip through time with such incredible special effects the ride carries a health warning. Almost as good are **Twister**, a five-storey-high tornado complete with driving wind and rain, and **Terminator 2 3D**, with 3D effects, live actors and impressive stunts. Older rides include **Earthquake – the Big One**, putting visitors into a San Francisco underground train when a major earthquake strikes, and King Kong's assault on New York in **Kongfrontation**.

Tricks of the film director's trade are the subject of **Alfred Hitchcock's The Art of Making Movies**, which includes a 3D scene from *The Birds* prompting the audience to dive for cover. In The **FUNtastic World of Hanna-Barbera** the techniques of

animation are demonstrated in a white-knuckle cartoon chase. The **Gory, Gruesome and Grotesque Horror Make-Up Show** reveals some of the secrets of the blood and guts of horror films; try not to be the volunteer who has their throat cut. **Hercules & Zena: Wizards of the Screen**, describes the creation of two TV heroes with audience participation in battles against evil fiends.

Of the major rides, only **ET's Adventure**, taking visitors to ET's home planet aboard intergalactic bicycles, is calm enough for small children. Youngsters may also enjoy **Fieval's Playland**, with the oversized props of the animated mouse, and **A Day In The Park With Barney**, based on TV's *Barney & Friends*, a dinosaur-hosted musical show. Likely to appeal to adults as well as children are **Animals Actors Stage**, describing the training of animal actors, and the tour of the Nickelodeon TV studios, the children-orientated TV channel.

# UNIVERSAL'S ISLANDS OF ADVENTURE✧✧

**Universal Islands of Adventure $$$** As *Universal Studios.*

Promising to push the boundaries of theme park special effects further than ever, Islands of Adventure occupies 110 acres beside Universal Studios. The still-evolving park features five main areas: **Seuss Landing; Toon Lagoon; Marvel Super Hero Island**, where helping Spiderman fight evil includes a stomach-churning 400-ft 'sensory descent' and the Incredible Hulk Coaster features a 'weightless inversion' 110 ft up; the fog-shrouded **Lost Continent**; and **Jurassic Park**, with breathing, blinking dinosaurs and the steepest water drop ever devised.

# WALT DISNEY WORLD: THE MAGIC KINGDOM✧✧✧

Based on Disneyland in Los Angeles, the Magic Kingdom is the Disney park that everyone expects. Mickey and Minnie Mouse really do live here, and complementing the sense of fun and fantasy based around Disney films and creations are some genuinely thrilling rides.

The Magic Kingdom's 100 acres divide into four major areas: **Adventureland, Tomorrowland, Frontierland** and **Fantasyland**; and three minor ones: **Liberty Square, Mickey's Toontown Fair** and **Main Street USA**, which is where you will enter the park after being given a map and list of the day's special events. The latter includes the parades that find Disney characters marching through the park alongside floats and music from old-time bands. On late-opening nights, the park's closure is marked by Fantasy in the Sky, an elaborate firework display.

Although many of the entertainments are aimed at adults, this is the best Disney park for young children for whom **Mr Toad's Wild Ride, Peter Pan's Flight**, and **Snow White's Adventures** have tremendous appeal. Also relished by infants are **Mickey's Country House**, home of Mr Mouse, and **The Barnstormer at Goofy's Wiseacre Farm**, a gentle roller-coaster.

**Magic Kingdom $$$**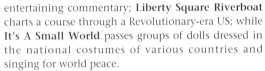
*Walt Disney World, Exit 25B from I-4; tel: (407) 824-4321. Open daily 0900–1900, until 2200 or 2400 from mid-June–mid-Aug.*

Of the cleverly conceived and occasionally genuinely frightening adult-aimed rides, **ExtraTERRORestial Alien Encounter** reveals the downside of inter-galactic teleportation, **Space Mountain** offers a warp-speed trip through space, **Splash Mountain** boat ride climaxes with a hair-raising drop, **Big Thunder Mountain Railroad** is a runaway train ride of white-knuckle jumps and bumps, and the **Haunted Mansion** conceals a selection of ghoulish special effects.

Three water-borne rides make for a relaxing interlude. The **Jungle Cruise** passes through a replicated jungle as the boatman provides an entertaining commentary; **Liberty Square Riverboat** charts a course through a Revolutionary-era US; while **It's A Small World** passes groups of dolls dressed in the national costumes of various countries and singing for world peace.

Best of the Magic Kingdom's shows are **The Time Keeper**, a sweep through world history from the dinosaur-era using a 360-degree screen, and the **Country Bear Jamboree**, a song-and-dance show performed by remarkably life-like AudioAnimatronic bears. Very popular, despite its sentimentality, the **Hall of Presidents** finds more AudioAnimatronic creations, this time replicating US presidents, and a 20-minute tour through US history in the company of Abraham Lincoln.

## Accommodation and food

Every hotel and motel chain worth its salt is represented in and around Orlando, particularly on International Drive and along Hwy-192 in Kissimmee. Within Walt Disney World are several hotels, every bit as imaginatively themed as the parks themselves. Each theme park also offers a choice of dining, from cafeteria lunches to semi-formal dinners; the area also holds several 'show restaurants'.

**Café Tu Tu Tango** $$ *8625 International Drive; tel: (407) 248-2222.* Florida delights such as conch fritters and bite-sized chunks of alligator are offered along with brick-oven pizzas, Cajun-style chicken and lots more.

**Cattleman's Steakhouse** $$ *2948 Vineland Road; Kissimmee; tel: (407) 397-1888.* T-bone, sirloin and ribs served in 16oz portions to test the mettle of meat eaters.

**Cracker Barrel** $–$$ *5859 Caravan Court, Kissimmee; tel: (407) 248-2460.* Meatloaf and catfish fillets are among the homely delights served in generous portions.

**Ming Court** $$–$$$ *9188 International Drive; tel: (407) 351-9988.* Not the cheapest but probably the best Chinese food for miles, served in a serene setting.

**Rain Forest Café** $$ *Downtown Disney, 1670 Buena Vista Drive; tel: (407) 827-8500.* A replicated rain forest with talking banyan trees is the setting for this usually crowded Disney-owned eatery. The food is regular American fare given strange names.

## Nightlife

**Church Street Station** $$ *129 W Church Street, Downtown Orlando; tel: (407) 422-2434.* This nightlife and shopping complex was created in the 1970s from rundown warehouses and hotels. The themed bars and venues include Rosie O'Grady's Goodtime Emporium, with a Dixieland band and can-can girls; the Cheyenne Saloon and Opera House, a pseudo-Wild West bar staffed by stetson-wearing barmen; and Phineas Fogg's Balloon Works, a disco decorated with aviation paraphernalia. A single admission charge allows entry to all sections and there is free entertainment on the pedestrianised street outside.

**Disney West Side** *Walt Disney World, signposted from I-4; tel: (407) 824-4321.* A complex of first-run cinemas, restaurants and music venues; adjacent to Pleasure Island.

**Pleasure Island** $$ *Walt Disney World, signposted from I-4; tel: (407) 824-4321.* New Year's Eve is celebrated nightly in variously themed music and comedy clubs; one admission fee provides entrance to all and there are free shows from an open-air stage; adjacent to Disney West Side.

**Show Restaurants** The Orlando area has several show restaurants offering a multi-course dinner, usually with unlimited drinks, for a set fee, plus spectacular entertainment:

**Arabian Knights** $$ *6225 W Hwy-192; Kissimmee; tel:(407) 239-9223.* Thoroughbred horses and their riders perform in the world's latest indoor equestrian arena.

**King Henry's Feast** $$ *8984 International Drive; tel: (407) 351-5151.* King Henry VIII leads the mead-drinking and feasting as sword swallowers and jesters entertain.

**Medieval Times** $$ *4510 Hwy-192, Kissimmee; tel: (800) 299-8300.* Knights joust and sword fight as dinner is served in a mock 11th-century castle.

**Pirate's Dinner Adventure** $$ *6400 Carrier Drive; near International Drive; tel: (407) 248-0590.* After being sworn-in as a pirate, guests board a ship floating in a 300,000-gallon lagoon; swashbuckling adventures ensue.

**Sleuth's Mystery Dinner Show** *7508 Republic Drive; near International Drive; tel: (407) 363-1985.* Diners meet and cross-examine the cast to find out whodunnit in an Agatha Christie-like setting.

# Orientation

Filling a vast tract of central Florida well beyond the city whose name it bears, the Orlando area is an often unprepossessing mixture of road junctions and petrol stations, with the 43 square miles of Walt Disney World (WDW) making a bucolic contrast to the west.

The 8-mile long **International Drive**, a purpose-built tourist base, lies close to Universal Studios and SeaWorld, 9 miles southwest of Downtown Orlando and 12 miles northeast of WDW. The other major tourist area is **Kissimmee**, spread along Hwy-192 with a seemingly endless line of motels, restaurants and souvenir shops, 20 miles south of Downtown Orlando and 10 miles east of WDW.

Initially confusing, the area soon becomes familiar and easy to travel around, though always carry one of the free maps, readily distributed by hotels and TICs.

## Also worth exploring

Along with its four major theme parks, Walt Disney World also has several smaller parks. There are few better places to cool down on a hot Florida day than **Typhoon Lagoon**, a water park with a wave pool, river and replicated coral reef, where snorkellers can meet real but non-dangerous sharks. The relaxing **River Country** re-creates a water hole surrounded by a wood; visitors can river raft and tackle white-water rapids. **Discovery Island** has flamingos, toucans, tortoises, swans, pelicans and alligators lurking amid 11 acres of exotic foliage. Ski fanatics who chose the wrong holiday can seek solace at **Blizzard Beach**, where the slopes of a replica Alpine mountain are covered by fake snow and the buildings are hung with icicles.

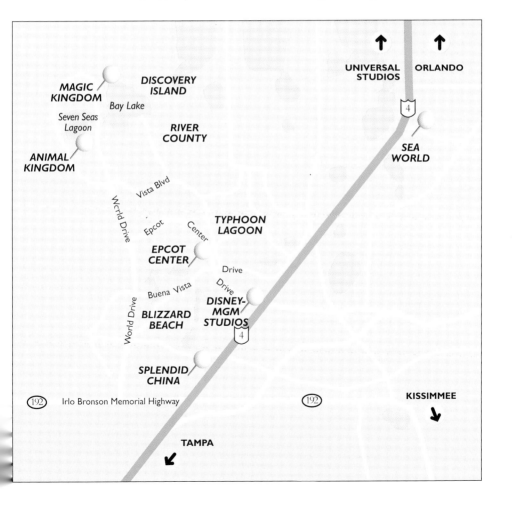

# From Orlando to Daytona Beach

**Ratings**

| | |
|---|---|
| Beaches | ●●●● |
| Motorsports | ●●●● |
| Nature | ●●●● |
| Children | ●●● |
| Food | ●●● |
| Museums | ●●● |
| Scenery | ●●● |
| History | ●● |

Only 54 miles separate Orlando from the world-famous sands of Daytona Beach, making one of Florida's most popular coastal destinations an easy day-trip from the world's theme park capital on the swift I-4. Revealing the best of Daytona Beach, including the racetrack that has done as much as the beach to give the town an international reputation and the lesser-known reaches of the coastal strip, this drive also uncovers some of the less-visited attractions that lie amid the citrus groves, scrubland and golf courses that dominate the view from the Interstate.

Two of the area's natural springs are protected as state parks, one of them as popular with manatees as it is with people, and both allow ample opportunity to enjoy natural Florida at its best. Also within easy reach of I-4 is DeLand, where the creator of the stetson hat funded the university whose campus fills half the town, and the other-worldly community of Cassadaga.

## BLUE SPRING STATE PARK*

**Blue Springs State Park** $ *2100 W French Avenue, off Hwy-92; tel: (904) 775-3663. Open daily 0800–sunset.*

The crystal-clear waters of a natural spring make this park popular for swimming, scuba diving and canoeing. Humans are not permitted to swim with the manatees who frequent the park in winter, but the creatures can be observed from the park's boardwalks as they enjoy the warmth of the 72°F waters. In prehistoric times, sandbanks here held the snails that provided food for native people. The discarded shells formed a mound that subsequently provided a foundation for the 1872 **Thursby House**, inside which are mementoes of the paddle-steamers that once travelled on the St John's River, fed by the spring.

## CASSADAGA*

Inhabited almost entirely by spiritualists who offer half-hour consultations, Cassadaga was founded by George Colby, a New York-born travelling medium who chose the 35-acre site in 1875 with the

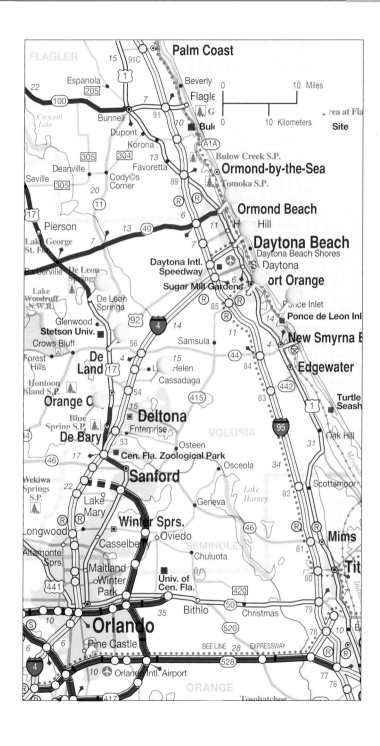

**Cassadaga Information Center**, Andrew Jackson Davies Building, Stevens Street; tel: (904) 228-2880. Open Mon–Thur 0930–1730, Fri–Sat 0930–1800, Sun 1200–1800.

help of a Native American spirit guide. A large number of the simple wood-framed cottages of the 1920s, built when many believers settled here, remain and create a slightly spooky first impression. This is quickly dispelled by the helpful staff of the information centre inside the Andrew Jackson Davies Building and the realisation that all who practice here are sincere in what they do.

## DAYTONA BEACH✦✦✦

**Daytona Beach Area Convention & Visitors Bureau** 126 E Orange Avenue; tel: (904) 255-0415 or (800) 854-1234. Open Mon–Fri 0900–1700.

**Daytona International Speedway** $ 1801 W International Speedway Boulevard; tel: (904) 254-2700. Open daily 0930–1600.

**Halifax Historical Society Museum** $ 252 S Beach Street; tel: (904) 255-6976. Open Tue–Sat 1000–1600.

**Museum of Arts and Science** $ 1040 Museum Boulevard; tel: (904) 255-0285. Open Tue–Sun 0900–1600, first Tue of month 0900–2100.

Daytona Beach, probably the most famous and certainly one of Florida's biggest expanses of sand, is 18 miles long and 500ft wide at low tide. This is one of the few Florida beaches where driving on the sand is possible and permitted, from marked access points and with a strictly enforced speed limit of 10mph.

Cars have been driven on Daytona Beach since 1902, a period when the firm sands offered a better and straighter surface than most roads for auto designers such as Henry Ford, Ransom Eli Olds and Louis Chevrolet to put their latest vehicles to the test. Speed records were frequently set, the last in 1935 by Malcolm Campbell who achieved 276mph.

Away from the endless motels and souvenir shops lining the beach strip, Daytona is a surprisingly small city with a nicely restored Downtown area and two commendable museums (see below) occupying the mainland area, divided by the Halifax River from the beach.

When motor racing on the beach was deemed unsafe, the completion of **Daytona International Speedway** in 1959 enabled the city to retain its money-spinning links with speed. The stadium, which holds 150,000 people, hosts eight major race meetings annually, the biggest being the Daytona 500. The track can be toured aboard a minibus which makes an informative if disappointingly slow navigation of the circuit, allowing close-up views of the 30-degree bank beds and some of the burn marks produced by champion racers as they brushed the wall at 190mph.

The tours begin from **Daytona USA** which also holds a multimedia exhibition charting the history of auto racing at Daytona Beach. Other computer-aided displays allow visitors to design their own racing car, participate in a timed pit stop and add their own commentary to a race.

Proof that there has been life in and around Daytona even before its beach brought the area international renown is provided by the well-stocked **Halifax Historical Society Museum** inside the ornate beaux arts-style Merchants Bank building. Native American relics include a 800-year-old dugout canoe; other items document Florida's Spanish and British periods when sugar and cotton plantations were established locally, and entertaining photographs and exhibits chart Daytona Beach's motor-racing legacy.

The natural history section of Daytona Beach's **Museum of Art and Science** has plenty to appeal to children, not least the skeleton of

**Above**
Daytona USA

a locally found 13-ft-high giant ground sloth, 130,000 years old and striking an angry pose. Adjacent exhibits are designed to provide an introduction to the delights of fossils and Florida ecosystems. A planetarium adjoins the museum, whose arts section includes a major collection of pre-revolution Cuban painting, much of it from the collection donated by the country's one-time dictator General Batista who was ousted in 1959 and spent his exile near Daytona Beach. The works explore the rise of Cuban art from the colonial-era through independence to the modernism that blossomed in 1950s Havana.

The Arts in America Wing documents the US's artistic heritage from the Pilgrim Fathers to Victorian times. The cache includes Philadelphia cabinets, Chippendale chairs, decorative glass and silverware, and art from influential figures such as portraitist Gilbert Stuart and landscape painter George Inness.

## Accommodation in Daytona Beach

**Atlantic Dunes $–$$** *1993 S Atlantic Avenue; tel: (904) 255-7501 or (800) 292-7501.* Choice of regular rooms and cottages sleeping up to eight people.

**Capri Motel $–$$** *832 N Atlantic Avenue; tel: (904) 252-2555 or (800) 225-3691.* Small, friendly beachside motel with a games room and coin-operated laundry.

**Coquina Inn $$** *544 S Palmetto Avenue; tel: (904) 254-4969 or (800) 727-0678.* This beautifully furnished 1912 home with just four guest rooms makes a perfect escape from the crowds and hotels of Daytona's beach strip.

# DeLand✧

**ⓘ DeLand Chamber of Commerce** *336 N Woodland Boulevard; tel: (904) 734-4331. Open Mon–Fri 0830–1700.*

**ⓘ Henry A DeLand House** *137 W Michigan Avenue; tel: (904) 734-7029. Open Tue–Sat 1200–1600.*

**Gillespie Museum of Minerals** *Stetson University, 234 E Michigan Avenue; tel: (904) 822-7330. Open Mon–Fri 0900–1200, 1300–1600.*

In 1876, Henry A DeLand founded what he hoped would become the 'Athens of Florida'. Despite falling short of its founder's vision, DeLand is an agreeable place with a nicely restored centre and the Greek Revival **Henry A DeLand House**, built in 1886 and furnished in period style.

To attract settlers, Henry DeLand founded the private college that evolved into **Stetson University**, in recognition of the financial contribution made by his friend, hat-maker John Stetson. Spread across 150 acres, the campus has many attractive century-old buildings and with the **Gillespie Museum of Minerals** boasts one of the world's largest privately owned mineral collections.

## Food in Deland

**Hontoon Landing Resort & Marina** **$$** *2317 River Ridge Road; tel: (904) 734-2474 or (800) 248 2474.* In a rural setting beside the St John's River offering a choice of motel-type rooms, kitchen-equipped cottages and houseboats.

# DeLeon Springs State Recreational Area✧✧✧

**ⓘ DeLeon Springs State Park** **$** *off Hwy-17; tel: (904) 985-4212. Open daily 0800–sunset.*

Canoeing and swimming are offered in this 600-acre park built around a natural spring. From the early 1800s, the spring powered a waterwheel used to grind sugar-cane. Still in use, the machinery now grinds the flour used in the breads and biscuits made at the park's Sugar Mill Restaurant, where customers can also bake their own pancakes at the griddle-equipped dining tables.

# Ormond Beach✧✧

**ⓘ The Casements** **$** *25 Riverside Drive; tel: (904) 676-3216. Open Mon–Thur 0900–2100, Fri 0900–1700, Sat 0900–1200.*

**Ormond Memorial Art Museum and Gardens** *78 E Granada Boulevard; tel: (904) 676-3347. Open Mon–Fri 1000–1600, Sat–Sun 1200–1600.*

Connection to the railway in the 1880s made Ormond Beach a favoured winter base of the rich and famous. One who took a shine to the place was millionaire oil baron John D Rockefeller who from 1918 to his death in 1937 spent his winters at the elegant mansion known as **The Casements**. A small collection of furnishings and other items record Rockefeller's occupancy, although the building now houses Hungarian Culture Centre as well as somewhat incongruous display of Italian ceramics and boy scout paraphernalia.

Close by, the art exhibitions of the **Ormond Memorial Art Museum** are of less interest than its 4-acre **gardens**, a profusion of tropical trees and plants set along shady walkways that lead to pleasant gazebo and a turtle-inhabited pond.

## Food in Ormond Beach

**Barnacle's Restaurant and Lounge $$** *869 S Atlantic Avenue; tel: (904) 673-1070.* Fresh seafood served beside the beach and a help-yourself salad bar; dinner only.

# PONCE INLET*

**Ponce de Leon Inlet Lighthouse $**
*4931 S Peninsula Drive. Open May–Labor Day, daily 1000–2000; rest of year daily 1000–1600.*

**Right**
Ponce de Leon Inlet
Lighthouse

Ponce de Leon Inlet was known as Mosquito Inlet until 1927 when the name was deemed a deterrent to would-be settlers. At the southern extremity, the restored outbuildings of the 1887 **Ponce de Leon Inlet Lighthouse** provide an intriguing history of Florida's lighthouses and record some of the many shipwrecks they failed to prevent. The reward for clambering up 203 steps is a coastal view from 175ft high.

## Food in Ponce Inlet

**Down the Hatch $–$$** *4849 Front Street; tel: (904) 761-4831.* A riverside location and an impressively lengthy menu that includes oysters, lobster tails and grouper sandwiches amid mostly fish-based lunches and dinners.

# SUGAR MILL GARDENS*

**Sugar Mill Gardens**
*Old Sugar Mill Road, Port Orange; tel: (904) 226-0446. Open daily dawn–dusk.*

Footpaths weave through the magnolia and holly trees of this 12-acre park to the substantial ruins of the buildings at the heart of an 1804 sugar plantation. The plantation produced molasses (using the juice of crushed sugar-cane) and during the Civil War was used by Confederate troops to extract salt from seawater. During the 1950s, the grounds made an unlikely setting for a dinosaur theme park, a few bizarre remnants of which remain.

# Suggested tour

## Accommodation

Although this route is designed as a day-trip from Orlando, accommodation is plentiful in Daytona Beach but varies greatly in price and availability according to season and local events. Sleeping on a houseboat is an option at DeLand.

**Length:** Main tour 115 miles; detours: Ponce Inlet, 22 miles; DeLand and De Leon Springs State Recreation Area, 25 miles; Cassadaga, 4 miles; Blue Springs State Park, 22 miles.

**Duration:** Main tour 3 hours; detours: Ponce Inlet, 1 hour; DeLand and De Leon Springs State Recreation Area, 40 minutes; Cassadaga, 20 minutes; Blue Springs State Park, 45 minutes.

**Links:** Orlando and its theme parks (*see pages 180–91*).

This is designed as a day-long tour but if your preference is to sunbathe at the beach then there will be little time left for detours, although Ponce Inlet makes a simple and worthwhile excursion from Daytona Beach. For wildlife and nature, take one of the state park detours, and for sheer strangeness do not miss Cassadaga.

Leave Orlando heading east on I-4, after 48 miles joining Hwy-92. As it reaches the outskirts of **DAYTONA BEACH** ❶, Hwy-92 passes the **Daytona International Speedway.** Continue east on Hwy-92. A right turn 3 miles ahead along Nova Road leads to the **Museum of Arts and Sciences.** From the museum, return to Hwy-92 and turn right. At the junction with Hwy-1 (Ridgeway Avenue), turn right for the heart of mainland Daytona Beach and the **Halifax Historical Society Museum,** two blocks east on Beach Street.

Return to Hwy-92 to cross the Halifax River. Directly ahead is the **Pier,** the focal point of Daytona Beach. A concrete boardwalk running three blocks north from the pier provides a chance to sample the seaside atmosphere without getting sand between your toes. Drive north along the hotel-lined Atlantic Avenue for 3 miles to reach **ORMOND BEACH** ❷.

**Detour:** One of the area's nicest oceanside drives runs 11 miles south from the Daytona Beach pier. Tourist-dominated areas give way to quiet residential communities and the sands become steadily les crowed. At the end of the route is **PONCE INLET** ❸ and its redbric' **lighthouse.** Returning north, turn left on to Dunlawton Avenue after 5.5 miles reaching the mainland at **Port Orange.** Turn righ on to Nova Road and shortly after right into Herbert Road. Old Sugar Mill Road forks to the left and holds the entrance to **SUGAI MILL GARDENS** ❹.

**Detour:** The placid and welcoming town of **DELAND** ❺ is reached on Route 44, off I-4, and by Hwy-92 from Daytona Beach. Seven mile north of DeLand, **DE LEON SPRINGS STATE RECREATION AREA** ❻ is at the end of a signposted turning off Hwy-17.

**Detour:** The spiritualists' community of **CASSADAGA** ❼ can b reached using Exit 54 from I-4, 35 miles from Orlando and 25 mile

**Tomoka State Park**
$ *2099 N Beach Street; tel: (904) 676-4050. Open daily 0800–sunset; museum daily 0930–1630.*

from Daytona Beach. Continue by turning right on to Route 4139. Nestled in undulating hillsides, the village lies 1.75 miles ahead.

**Detour:** BLUE SPRING STATE PARK ❽ is close to the aptly named citrus-producing community of **Orange City**, 5.5 miles south of DeLand on Hwy-92 and 4 miles from I-4 using Route 472. The signposted park lies 2.6 miles west of the town, off W French Avenue, reached with a right turn 1.5 miles south of the Hwy-92 and Route 472 junction.

### Also worth exploring

Occupying an oak and magnolia-studded peninsula at the meeting point of the Halifax and Tomoka rivers, **Tomoka State Park** lies 4 miles north of Ormond Beach off Route 5A (Old Dixie Highway). The verdant park makes an appealing spot for a picnic and ramble along its trails, and also has a small **museum** remembering the Timucuan people, the pre-European inhabitants of the area, and Fred Dana Marsh.

Although an award-winning painter, Marsh made his name with art deco murals depicting working people and in the 1920s designed a striking modernist house for himself and his wife in Ormond Beach. Photographs of the house, his murals and other items from his life are displayed. The park also holds Marsh's sculpture, *Legend of Tomokie*, completed in 1957 four years before his death.

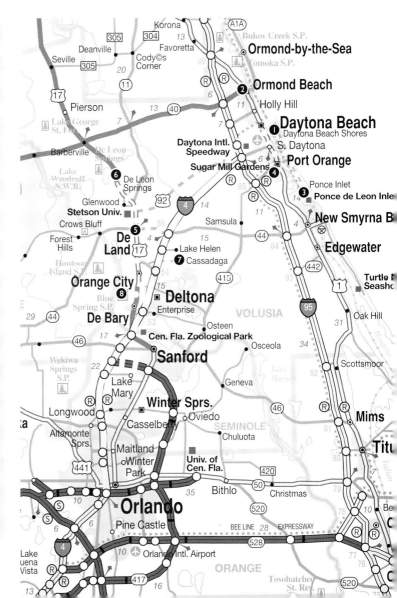

# The Space Coast

**Ratings**

| | |
|---|---|
| Beaches | ●●●●● |
| Science | ●●●●● |
| Children | ●●●● |
| Nature | ●●●● |
| Scenery | ●●●● |
| Museums | ●●● |
| Surfing | ●●● |
| History | ●● |

It was from Florida's Space Coast that the first moon landings were launched and it is here that the space shuttle lifts off and returns to earth. Even for locals, the excitement of watching a launch, be it the shuttle or satellite-carrying rockets, never pales and this predominantly flat area has endless vantage points for doing so. The pivot of the Space Coast is the Kennedy Space Center, its exhibition areas illustrating NASA's greatest achievements and its future aspirations.

Strangely, though, nature rather than technology is likely to be your lasting impression of the Space Coast. NASA's launch pads rise from the alligator-patrolled fringes of one the nation's largest wildlife refuges and the Space Center marks one end of a series of barrier-island beach communities. Some, such as Cocoa Beach, are heavily developed while others are set amid lush rows of pine trees with small beach parks often used more by residents than tourists.

## ASTRONAUT HALL OF FAME*

**Astronaut Hall of Fame** $$ *Route 405, west of Kennedy Space Center, Titusville; tel: (407) 269-6100. Open daily 0900–1700.*

Remembering the early days of the US's manned space programme with exhibits on and memorabilia from the Mercury and Gemini flights of the early and mid-1960s, this entertaining collection brings home how low-tech and gung-ho the early years of space exploration were.

Any would-be astronauts can have their physical mettle tested by being strapped into a centrifuge and whisked around until experiencing gravity at three times its normal force. Another simulated adventure, *Shuttle to Tomorrow*, provides an entertaining if not particularly inspired look at the future of space travel. Elsewhere, multimedia and virtual reality displays allow visitors to pilot the space shuttle on a simulated landing and sample weightlessness.

## CANAVERAL NATIONAL SEASHORE**

Between the Atlantic Ocean and Mosquito Lagoon (aptly named especially so in summer) and overlooked by the launchpads of the

:al Park

82 ● Scottsmoor

CANAVERAL NATL.
SEASHORE

46 81 ◉ **Mims**

*ATLANTIC*

MERRITT ISLAND
N.W.R.

80 Astronaut
Hall of Fame
35 50
Christmas

**.tusville**

KENNEDY
SPACE
CENTER

CAPE
CANAVERAL
AIR FORCE STA.

*OCEAN*

79

78 10 ● Bellwood

BEE LINE EXPRESSWAY ◉ **Port St. John**

Cape Canaveral

Sharpes

28 77

Tosohatchee
St. Res.

76

13 ◉ **Cape Canaveral**

75 **Cocoa**

**Merr.. Island**

**Rockledge** 74 1 **Cocoa Beach**

532 26

A1A

419

73 Pineda

**Patrick
A.F.B.**

South Patrick Shores

**Satellite Beach**

23 **Indian Harbour Beach**

72

.ndialantic

24 192

71

**Melbourne**

Deer Park **W. Melbourne** 6 **Palm Bay**

70 Malabar

441

34 Valkaria

Grant

● Kenansville

507

34

Micco

Sebastian Inlet
St. Rec. Area

Roseland **Sebastian**

32 ■ Pelican Island N.W.R.

*Blue
Cypress
Lake*

Fellsmere 69

510 ● Wabasso

Orchid

512

Winter
Beach

Indian River
Shores

60

193

Yeehaw
Junction

60

23

**Gifford**

68 60

8

**Vero Beach**

Oslo

14

FLORIDA©S. TPK.

95

**Lakewood Park**

18

40 67

R St. Lucie

Indrio

.ucie

0          10 Miles

68

**Fort Pierce**

Mus.

Fort Pierce
Inlet

0          10 Kilometers

609 152

5

65

S. R. A.

White City

Basinger 68

441

70

32 Indian River Estates

64

Walton

**Canaveral National Seashore** *off Hwy-1 near Titusville; tel: (407) 267-3036. Open May–Oct, 0600–2000; rest of the year daily 0600–1800.*

Kennedy Space Center, the Canaveral National Seashore comprises 24 miles of stunningly pristine protected beaches walled by sea-oat-topped sand dunes. Roads reach **Apollo Beach** and **Playalinda Beach** between which the 12-mile-long **Klondyke Beach** can only be explored on foot. Swimming is not advised due to strong currents and walkers on Klondyke Beach should be wary of high tides.

# COCOA❖

**Brevard Museum of History and Natural Science** $ *2201 N Michigan Avenue; tel: (407) 632-1830. Open Oct–Apr, Tue–Sat 1000–1600, Sun 1300–1600. Closed Sun rest of the year.*

Cobbled streets, small parks and restored buildings largely occupied by antique shops and cafés, fill the four-block **Old Cocoa Village**. The Olde World atmosphere makes a welcome contrast with the predominantly ultra-modern Space Coast. The village lies at the heart of the sprawling settlement of Cocoa, founded in the 1860s in the hope of exploiting the commercial potential of the Indian River. The town's past is cogently documented by the **Brevard Museum of History and Natural Science**.

# COCOA BEACH❖

**Cocoa Beach Area Chamber of Commerce** *400 Fortenberry Road, Merritt Island; tel: (407) 459-2200. Open Mon–Fri 0900–1700.*

**Cocoa Pier** *401 Meade Avenue; tel: (407) 783-7549.*

**Ron Jon Surf Shop** *4151 N Atlantic Avenue; tel: (407) 799-8888. Open 24 hours daily.*

Cocoa Beach, the major beach community of the Space Coast, is a long and narrow strip of beach shops and motels, with 8 miles of splendid sands sometimes buffeted by the powerful waves that make this one of the few Florida locations renowned for surfing. The pulse of the community is best felt at the 800-ft-long **Cocoa Pier** which holds several bars and restaurants, and is one of the region's best places to view space launches. The other local landmark is the **Ron Jon Surf Shop**, a vividly decorated store offering outrageously kitsch beach accessories alongside its staple stock of top-class surfboards.

## Accommodation and food in Cocoa Beach

**Sea Esta Villas** $$–$$$ *686 S Atlantic Avenue; tel: (407) 783-1739 or (800) 872-9444.* The homecooked breakfasts are a great start to the day, the comfortable rooms a welcome end to it.

**Silver Sands Motel** $ *225 N Atlantic Beach; tel: (800) 647-0761* Beachside rooms with or without cooking facilities, but with patios for space-launch watching and barbecues.

**South Beach Inn on the Sea** $–$$ *1701 S Atlantic Avenue; tel: (407) 784-3333 or (877) 546 6835.* Sunbathe and view shuttle launches from kitchen-equipped rooms a few steps from the beach.

**Bernard's Surf** $$–$$$ *2 S Atlantic Avenue; tel: (407) 783-8732.* Family owned since 1948 and a favourite of locals and astronauts for its fresh seafood and steaks in a friendly atmosphere. The adjoining Rusty's Raw Bar offers inexpensive lunches.

**Herbie K's $** *2080 N Atlantic Avenue; tel: (407) 783-6740.* Pseudo-1950s diner providing great fun for burger-and-milkshake-loving kids and nostalgic adults.

**The Pier Restaurant $–$$** *Cocoa Beach Pier, 401 Meade Avenue; tel: (407) 783-7459.* Enjoying a perfect setting on the area's most popular pier, with good-value daily specials often featuring freshly-caught seafood.

# FORT PIERCE INLET STATE RECREATION AREA✧✧

**Fort Pierce Inlet State Recreation Area $** *905 Shorewinds Drive; tel: (561) 468-3985. Open daily 0800–sunset.*

This 340-acre park, a mix of ocean beach, sand dunes and coastal tree hammock, marks the southern end of the pine-lined Hutchinson Island. Park activities include swimming, surfing, picnicking and walking the marked nature trails. Bird-watchers will find more to their liking by crossing the 300-ft concrete bridge leading to **Jack Island State Preserve**, a mangrove-dominated area abutting the Intracoastal Waterway with a mile-long trail and an observation platform likely to bring sightings of herons, ospreys and other birds.

# KENNEDY SPACE CENTER✧✧✧

*Below
Saturn rocket, Kennedy Space Center*

The undisputed highlight of the Space Coast is the Kennedy Space Center, where NASA puts its past and present on show, exhibited in and around the visitor center and on bus tours that access the far-flung reaches of this enormous complex. Complementing the displays are powerful IMAX films on themes of space travel and exploration.

The **Gallery of Space Flight** is a cornucopia of space flight memorabilia, with real and replica space craft from the Mercury, Gemini and Apollo programmes, a lunar rover, assorted space suits, moon rock and many other items accompanied by a photographic record of manned space flight. Outside, the **Rocket Garden** demonstrates how small the early space rockets were,

**Kennedy Space
Center (bus tours
$$)**; Merritt Island; tel:
(407) 452-2121. Open daily
0900–dusk.

particularly when compared to the monstrous Saturn V and the full-sized space shuttle replica adjacent to the interactive exhibits of the **Launch Status Center**, which highlights the craft's pre-launch routines.

Further afield and only accessible on a bus tour, the **Apollo/Saturn V Center** focuses on the Apollo programme that used the immense power of the Saturn V rocket to reach speeds of 25,000mph to escape the earth's atmosphere on the way to the exploration of the moon. The **Firing Room Theater** effectively re-creates the launch, including the shuddering blast of Apollo 8, the craft that carried the first astronauts to orbit the moon with footage of the event shown on towering screens. The momentous first moon landing is re-created inside the **Lunar Surface Theater**.

Also on the bus tour, the **LC39 Observation Gantry** provides an unobstructed view of the space shuttle's two launch pads, previously used by the Apollo missions, and of the 525-ft-high Vehicle Assembly Building where the shuttle is put together. Exhibits and a narrated film describe the extraordinary complex task of simply moving the shuttle, at 1mph, to its launch site.

The bus tour continues to the **International Space Station Center**, with exhibits on the current multinational space station project and teasing tasters of NASA's plans for the exploration of Mars, and to the **Cape Canaveral Air Force Station**, launch site for military and commercial rockets, and home to the **Air Force Space Museum** with its enormous collection of missiles.

# MELBOURNE*

Spick and span but rather soulless, Melbourne was originally settled by freed slaves and given its name by the Australian proprietor of the local post office. The small economic boom it enjoyed when linked to the railroad in 1894 was greatly surpassed in the 1960s when NASA's expansion brought thousands of new settlers. Across the Indian River, **Melbourne Beach** is a pleasantly low-key alternative to the busier Cocoa Beach.

# MERRITT ISLAND WILDLIFE REFUGE**

**Merritt Island
National Wildlife
Refuge** eastern end of
Route 402; tel: (407) 861-
0667. Open daily
dawn–dusk; some roads
closed during space launches.

The Merritt Island National Wildlife Refuge fills 220 square miles around the Kennedy Space Center and holds more endangered species than any other refuge in the US. Within a landscape dominated by marshes but studded with hardwood hammocks and pine woods are alligators, bobcats, otters, marsh rabbits and even a few wild pigs among a long list of regularly sighted creatures.

Above the refuge, particularly during winter migrations, the skies teem with herons, gulls, terns and pelicans, while wading birds such as wood storks and ibis are often spotted feeding at the water's edge. Majestic bald eagles and colourful roseate spoonbills make less frequent appearances. Also occasionally sighted overhead, the space shuttle uses a landing strip adjacent to the refuge.

The 6-mile **Black Point Wildlife Drive** provides an excellent introduction to the refuge and is lined by marked stops with displays highlighting aspects of the landscape, be they bald eagle habitats or mudflats. The drive also accesses the **Cruickshank Trail**, a 5-mile foot trail with an observation tower a few minutes' walk from the car-park.

The salt marsh mosquitoes that gave Mosquito Lagoon its name and prevented human settlement of the area can still make summer visits very unpleasant. The best time to spot wildlife is during the winter, in the early morning and as dusk approaches.

# SEBASTIAN INLET STATE RECREATION AREA❖❖

**Sebastian Inlet State Park $** *9700 S Hwy-A1A, between Melbourne Beach and Vero Beach; (561) 984-4852. Open daily 0800–sunset.*

**McLarty Treasure Museum $** *1380 N Hwy-A1A, between Melbourne Beach and Vero Beach; tel: (561) 589-2147. Open daily 1000–1630.*

Spanning both sides of Sebastian Inlet, where the Indian River meets the Atlantic Ocean, this 587-acre park is much admired by anglers for the snook, redfish and Spanish mackerel that surrender themselves to hooks, and by surfers for the powerful breakers that make this Florida's premier wave-riding location.

Also in the park, the **McLarty Treasure Museum** tells the dramatic story of the Spanish fleet that floundered in Sebastian Inlet during a hurricane in 1715 and the attempts by the 1500 survivors to salvage the gold and silver, essential to the economy of Spain, that had gone down with the ships. Some of the recovered booty was subsequently raided by British pirates.

# VERO BEACH❖

**Center for the Arts**
*3001 Riverside Drive;*
*tel: (561) 231-0707. Hours*
*vary according to exhibitions.*

Although it has little to detain visitors, Vero Beach is among Florida's most attractive small coastal towns and has compounded its affluent and culturally aspiring image with the $2.5 million **Center for the Arts**, an art museum and teaching facility that is the largest of its kind in the state. Despite its ramshackle form, a longer-standing structure of note is the splendid **Driftwood Inn**, constructed from odd bits of timber during the 1930s and serving as a hotel until being converted to apartments.

# YEEHAW JUNCTION❖

At dot-on-the-map Yeehaw Junction, the **Desert Inn** can trace its roots to the 1880s when it became a supply stop for timber-carrying trains and cattle-driving cowboys. The inn's bar and dining-room is a wonderful evocation of bygone Florida, and also serves traditional Florida food (*see below*). If asked nicely, the owner will lead guided tours of the upper floor, giving customers a glimpse of the state's only restored bordello.

## Accommodation and food in Yeehaw Junction

**Disney's Vero Beach Resort $$$** *9250 Island Grove Terrace, Vero Beach; tel: (561) 224-2000.* Disney fans who love the beach will relish this luxurious Disney-owned oceanside property, styled as an old Florida resort complete with replica Spanish galleon.

**Desert Inn $** *5570 S Kenansville Road; tel: (407) 436-1054.* A genuine slice of old Florida that offers gator tail and frogs' legs among more common delights.

**Left**
Vero Beach

## NASA and the Space Coast

In May 1961, President Kennedy's pledge that the US would land a man on the moon and return him safely to earth by the end of the decade sparked a massive influx of technicians, engineers, astronauts and other NASA (National Aeronautics and Space Administration) personnel into a thinly populated citrus and cattle-farming area around the Air Force missile base of Cape Canaveral, soon to become known as the Space Coast.

Through the 1960s, the Apollo programme, climaxing with the first manned moon landing in 1969, brought world attention to the region. Declining public enthusiasm and a reduction in NASA's funding prompted the development of the reusable space shuttle, its success tempered by the *Challenger* disaster of 1986. With the current International Space Station project and a long-term objective of a manned Mars landing, NASA continues to be a major employer in a region where developments in space exploration are perhaps more keenly observed than any other place in the world.

# Suggested tour

**Length**: Main tour 162 miles; Merritt Island detour, 20 miles; Sebastian Inlet detour and return to Orlando, 150 miles.

**Duration**: Main tour 3 hours; Merritt Island detour, 45 minutes; Sebastian Inlet detour and return to Orlando, 3.5 hours

**Links**: Orlando and its theme parks (*see pages 180–91*).

Designed as a day tour from Orlando but with the option of spending a night on the coast, this tour focuses on the Kennedy Space Center and explores the surrounding communities with a scenic drive along a portion of the coast. The first detour is the unspoilt beaches and wildlife areas adjacent to the Kennedy Space Center. The second extends the idea of coastal touring but also branches inland to one of Florida's more unusual places of interest.

The Bee Line Expressway is the most direct route from Orlando to the **KENNEDY SPACE CENTER ❶**, 50 miles east. Exit on to Route 407 and after 6.6 miles join Route 405 following the well-signposted route that continues across the Indian River. From the Kennedy Space Center, head south from Route 405 on Hwy-1, continuing for 13 miles to **COCOA ❷** and its atmospheric historic area, Old Cocoa Village. This is on the banks of the Indian River, just south of the junction with Route 520.

Return to Route 520, which becomes the Merritt Island Causeway as you turn right and cross the Indian River and a section of Merritt Island before sweeping over the broad Banana River. After 7 miles, the route reaches the ocean-hugging Hwy-A1A and **COCOA BEACH ❸**. This expansive beachside community extends for many miles along Hwy-A1A, though its spiritual centre is the **Cocoa Pier**, half a mile ahead after turning north on to Hwy-A1A.

**Below**
Ron Jon Surf Shop, Cocoa Beach

From the pier, head south along Hwy-A1A, passing myriad motels, beach accessory and souvenir shops, and oceanside small parks. Possessing a lengthy runway and the laboratories where military rocket technology was developed, the **Patrick Air Force Base**, 6.5 miles south of Route 520 junction, provides the first major variation in the view. The route continues through shoulder-to-shoulder beach towns such as **Satellite Beach** and **Indian Harbour Beach**, each with their own small beach parks.

Four miles south of Indian Harbour Beach, turn right on Hwy-192 and re-cross the Banana River to reach MELBOURNE **4**, 2.8 miles ahead. Continue on Hwy-192 to return to Orlando, 60 miles further.

Detour: Turn right turn on to Hwy-1 after leaving the Kennedy Space Center. After 6.5 miles, this passes through Titusville where there's a right turn on to Route 406 leading to the MERRITT ISLAND NATIONAL WILDLIFE REFUGE **5**. Within the refuge, Route 402 branches from Route 406 to provide access to Playalinda Beach marking the southern edge of the CANAVERAL NATIONAL SEASHORE **6**.

Detour: Instead of turning inland off Hwy-A1A towards Melbourne, continue on the scenic coast course for 19 miles, reaching the SEBASTIAN INLET STATE RECREATION AREA **7**. The route continues across the inlet and after a further 16 miles meets the junction with Route 60, which heads inland to VERO BEACH **8**. Continue inland on Route 60 from Vero Beach for 31 miles and the tiny crossroads settlement of YEEHAW JUNCTION **9**. The Desert Inn stands by the junction of Route 60, Hwy-441 and the Florida Turnpike. Travel north on the latter (toll) for 84 miles to reach Orlando.

## Also worth exploring

Overlooking cruise and cargo ships and the launch pads of the adjacent Cape Canaveral Air Force Base, **Jetty Park** is a 35-acre patch of sand-dune-lined greenery in Port Canaveral, immediately north of Cocoa Beach off Hwy-A1A. Popular with anglers and surfers, the park also makes an excellent picnic stop and is a fine place to view space launches.

# St Augustine

## Ratings

| | |
|---|---|
| History | ●●●●● |
| Ambience | ●●●●○ |
| Architecture | ●●●○○ |
| Children | ●●●○○ |
| Museums | ●●●○○ |
| Arts and crafts | ●●○○○ |
| Beaches | ●●○○○ |
| Nature | ●○○○○ |

St Augustine is a pocket-sized town that speaks volumes about Florida's colonial past. It's an immediately welcoming place and one of the few towns in the state that can be comprehensively explored on foot. The short, narrow streets are lined by palm trees and 200-year-old houses whose plaster-coated walls and wooden verandas would evoke an atmosphere akin to a sleepy Mediterranean village were it not for the many tourists who flock to this deservedly popular destination.

Founded by the Spanish in 1565, St Augustine is the oldest permanent European settlement in the US. Swapping Havana, Cuba, for Florida in 1763, the British arrived here and stayed for 20 years until Florida returned to Spanish rule, prior to being ceded to the US in 1821. From the town's oldest house to the old county jail, it showcases all these periods with the kind of authenticity that Walt Disney World might spend a fortune trying to re-create.

## Sights

**❶ St Augustine Visitor Information Center**
*10 Castillo Drive; tel: (904) 825-9000. Open June–Labor Day, daily 0800–1930; Apr, May, Sept and Oct, daily 0830–1830; rest of the year 0830–1730.*

**❶ Castillo de San Marcos $ / Castillo**
*Drive; tel: (904) 829-6506. Open daily 0845–1645.*

Castillo de San Marcos❖❖❖

If a single feature symbolises St Augustine's battled-scarred past, it is Castillo de San Marcos. The castle was completed around 1695, with pointed triangular bastions at each corner, and is the oldest masonry fort in the US. The 12-ft-thick coquina (limestone formed by compacted sea shells) walls were able to resist a 27-day British bombardment in 1740 by absorbing the arriving cannon balls.

The 35-ft-high ramparts provide a good view over the town and many of the castle's atmospheric rooms carry historical displays. Free guided tours and the periodic 'living history' demonstrations by period-attired volunteers explain much more about the castle's history and architecture.

Bridarin Street

Old Jail

Williams Street

San Marco Avenue

Magnolia Avenue

Fountain of Youth
Archaeological Park

0                    300 metres
0                    300 yards

Myrtle Avenue

Sebastian Avenue

Ocean Avenue

Old Mission Avenue

Mission de Nombre de Dios

1

Pine Street

Water Street

Rhode Avenue

5

Shenandoah Street

Matanzas
River

Castillo Drive

Ponce De Leon Boulevard

Riberia Street

Old City Gate

Castillo de San Marcos

Orange Street

Oldest Wooden Schoolhouse

Cordova Street

Cuna Street

St George Street

Charlotte Street

Avenida Menendez

Spanish Quarter
History Museum

Riberia Street

Sevilla Street

Treasury Street

Pena-Peck House

Malaga Street

1

Valencia Street

Flagler
College

Cordova Street

Sevilla Street

Plaza de la Constitución

Cathedral Place

Bridge of Lions

A1A

King Street

Spanish Military Hospital

King Street

Zorayda Castle

Lightner Museum

Granada Street

Ximenez-Fatio
House

Cadiz St

Avenida Menendez

M L King Avenue

Bridge Street

Riberia Street

Cordova Street

St George Street

Charlotte Street

Marine St

Avenida Menendez

San
Sebastian
River

Tovar House

Oldest House

St Francis Street

### Flagler College❖❖

Flagler College occupies the former Ponce de León Hotel, opened by oil and transportation magnate Henry Flagler in the 1880s to accommodate the wealthy vacationers brought to St Augustine by his railway.

Named for the first European to land in Florida and intended to be the last word in luxury lodgings, the hotel sought to replicate the grandeur and elegance of the finest European architecture with a profusion of spires, masses of terracotta ornamentation and two bell towers. The renowned Louis Comfort Tiffany provided stained-glass windows and lampshades in a design overseen by fledgling architects, Carrere & Hastings, later to find fame with the New York Public Library.

**Flagler College** *74 King Street; tel: (904) 829 6481. Ground floor open daily 1000–1600; more viewable by guided tour, phone for details.*

The extension of the Flagler railroad to create the new resort of Palm Beach contributed to the decline of the hotel, which became a college in the 1970s, although many interior features can still be admired on guided tours.

**Fountain of Youth Archaeological Park** $
*155 Magnolia Avenue; tel: (904) 829-3168. Open daily 0900–1700.*

### Fountain of Youth Archaeological Park❖

When Ponce de León and his crew made the first European landing in Florida in 1513, their agenda included discovering gold and silver, converting natives to Catholicism and finding the secret of eternal life which modern-day visitors are led to believe consists of drinking the slightly sulphurous water issuing from the well around which this park is built. The park has greater significance, however, for the archaeological excavations which have yielded evidence of the Timucuan settlement, thought to have been the first point of contact for Spanish Pedro Menéndez de Avilés, who landed in the vicinity in 1565 having been appointed first governor of Florida.

**Lightner Museum** $
*75 King Street; tel: (904) 824-2874. Open daily 0900–1700.*

### Lightner Museum❖❖❖

Only slightly less posh than the Ponce de León (*see Flagler College, above*), the Alcazar was another Flagler-owned hotel with an exuberant Spanish-Moorish design. Many of the original architectural features have been maintained and create an impressive backdrop for the outstanding collection of mostly 19th-century decorative arts amassed by publisher Otto Lightner, who bought the dilapidated hotel as a home for his collection in 1948.

Over three copiously-filled floors are Tiffany windows, crystal glass, Meissen porcelain, musical instruments, furnishings, clocks paintings, stamps, buttons, dolls and dolls' houses, and all manner of *objets d'art*, mostly acquired from the estates of wealthy Chicagoans as they sought to raise money during the Depression. On a lower level once the site of the world's largest indoor swimming-pool, is an antiques mall.

**Above**
Flagler College

 **Mission de Nombre Dios** *San Marco Avenue; tel: (904) 824-3045. Open daily 0800–sunset.*

**Old Jail** *$ 167 San Marco Avenue; tel: (904) 829-3800. Open daily 0830–1700.*

**Oldest House** *$ 14 St Francis Street; tel: (904) 824-2874. Guided tour only, daily 0900–1700.*

**Oldest Wooden School House** *$ 14 St George Street; tel: (904) 824-0192. Open daily 0900–1700.*

## Mission de Nombre Dios*

The first Mass in what became the US was held on these grounds in 1565. The fact is marked by a 208-ft stainless steel cross rising above the Tolomato River, marking the alleged landing site of the ship carrying first Florida governor Pedro Menéndez de Avilés and Father Lopez de Mendoza Grajales, who conducted the Mass in front of Timucuan villagers. A re-creation of the original chapel makes an atmospheric addition to the pleasant, tree-filled grounds where the US's first Spanish mission was erected and which now hold an uninteresting modern church.

## Old Jail**

This county jail and sheriff's quarters was built in 1892 and remained in service until 1953. Now a museum, the jail gives surprisingly intriguing insights into Florida's one-time penal system, not least the fact that the prisoners, segregated by race as well as gender, ate food cooked by the sheriff's wife (some inmates apparently considered this part of their punishment). Assorted weapons, a gallows and an electric chair complete the picture.

Personal items belonging to Flagler and the story of his railway form the best sections of the **Florida Heritage Museum**, in a building adjoining the jail.

## Oldest House***

The strongest evocation of daily life in early St Augustine is provided by this inauspicious dwelling, the oldest parts of which are the coquina walls, built around 1702. A tabby floor and spartan furnishings suggest the deprivations of artilleryman Tomás González and his family who lived here during the first period of Spanish rule. The British take-over of Florida in 1763 saw an increase in comfort, with glass windows and fireplaces, plus the addition of an upper storey complete with balcony.

Operated for a time as a tavern and occupied by Joseph and Maria Peavett (inspiration for the main character in Eugenia Price's best-selling novel, *Maria*) until being sold at auction in 1790, the house spent the second period of Spanish rule and the early years of US control under the ownership of Gerónimo Alvarez and his descendants. These years are remembered by the Alvarez family dining-room and the four-poster bed once occupied by General Joseph Hernández, a leader in the US's war against the Seminoles.

## Oldest Wooden School House*

This rickety-looking structure was probably built in the mid-1700s, its cedar and cypress planks held together by wooden pegs and handmade nails. Classes were conducted on the ground floor, the teacher and family living above.

**ℹ️ Peña-Peck House $**
*143 St George Street; tel: (904) 829-5064. Guided tour only, daily 1230–1600.*

**Cathedral-Basilica of St Augustine** *Plaza de la Constitución; tel: (904) 824-2806. Open daily 0900–1700.*

**Spanish Military Hospital $** *(entrance free with Spanish Quarter Museum ticket) 3 Aviles Street; tel: (904) 825-6380. Open daily 0900–1700.*

**Spanish Quarter Museum $** *33 St George Street; tel: (904) 825-5033. Open daily 0900–1700.*

**Tovar House $** *(included with Oldest House admission; shared entrance) 14 St Francis Street; tel: (904) 824-2874. Guided tour only, daily 0900–1700.*

**Below**
Blacksmith working in the Spanish Quarter Museum

## Peña-Peck House✧✧

Originally the residence of Juan de Peña, St Augustine's Spanish royal treasurer, and probably built in the 1740s, this house has an elegant appearance accentuated by a second storey added after its purchase by Seth Peck, a doctor from New England, in 1837. Peck, his wife and their descendants amassed the fine collection of paintings, antiques and furnishings that now fill the house.

## Plaza de la Constitución✧

The Spanish influence in St Augustine is compounded by this tree-studded plaza, laid out in 1589 to provide the settlement with an administrative and business centre. On the west side of the plaza, **Government House**, restored to its 1764 appearance, marks the site from where St Augustine has been run since the 16th century. A small **museum** uses archaeological finds and other items to document the town's history.

On the plaza's north side, the **Cathedral-Basilica of St Augustine** dates largely from 1887 when the transept and bell tower were added, although there are a few items, such as the marble altar, that survived the fire that destroyed the 1790 original.

## Spanish Military Hospital✧✧

This 1960s reconstruction depicts the apothecary's office and a ward of the Spanish-built hospital erected here in the late 1700s. The hospital's rules and records, surgical instruments and a selection of medicinal herbs, strongly suggest that 18th-century St Augustine was not a good place in which to fall ill.

## Spanish Quarter Museum✧✧

The St Augustine of the 1740s is kept alive in this series of restored homes, gardens and workshops in which period-attired guides take the roles of locals and craftspeople, such as blacksmiths, weavers and carpenters, and go about their chores with period tools. Describing and demonstrating the ups and downs of everyday life in the Spanish colony, the quarter is entertaining and extremely informative, and a good place to keep children amused.

## Tovar House✧

Occupied by infantryman José Tovar from 1763 and subsequently by a Scottish merchant, this two-storey house now contains the **Museum of the Florida Army**, with displays of uniforms worn by Florida

**Ximenez-Fatio House** $ 20 Aviles Street; tel: (904) 829-3575. Guided tour only, Mon and Thur–Sat 1100–1600, Sun 1300–1600.

**Zorayda Castle** $ 83 King Street; tel: (904) 843-3097. Open daily 0900–1700.

soldiers during the Spanish and British periods, and through the Seminole and Civil wars to the present day.

### Ximenez-Fatio House**

This inviting coquina house was built around 1798 for Spanish merchant Andres Ximenez, and has a typically St Augustine blend of Spanish and British architecture. It gained a second storey after being purchased in 1830 by an American, Margaret Cook.

Cook ran the extended property as a boarding house and, prior to the arrival of Flagler's railway and his luxury hotels, it became one of the town's most popular lodgings for wealthy and adventurous northerners. Guided tours tell the story of the house, its design and its owners, and pass through the rooms maintained in the style that Florida tourists enjoyed in the mid-1800s.

### Zorayda Castle***

Millionaire Bostonian Franklin W Smith was so enamoured of the Alhambra on a visit to Spain that he commissioned a scaled-down replica of one wing of the 13th-century Moorish palace to be built in St Augustine. With its square towers, archways, and 40 windows all of differing size and colour, the building was completed in 1883. The castle was purchased by a former Egyptian consul in 1913 and, despite being used as a casino during the 1920s, continues to display its second owner's remarkable stash of Far and Middle Eastern decorative arts.

# Accommodation and food

**Cedar House Inn** $$–$$$ 79 Cedar Street; tel: (904) 829-0079 or (800) 233-2746. Each of the five rooms in this bed-and-breakfast inn is named after, and decorated with memorabilia of, the owner's grandparents.

**Coquina Gables** $$$ 1 F Street, St Augustine Beach; tel: (904) 461-8727. Ocean-facing bed and breakfast in a plushly furnished 1920s house.

**Old Powder House Inn** $$–$$$ 38 Cordova Street; tel: (904) 824-4149 or (800) 447-4149. Bed and breakfast in an 1899 house in the heart of the historic district; guests enjoy complimentary sherry and home-made sweets.

**Casa de Tacos** $ 48 Spanish Street; tel: (904) 810-6865. Burritos and tacos, and other inexpensive Mexican food, for a quick, filling feed.

**Churchill's Attic** $–$$ 20 Avenida Menendez; tel: (904) 810-1919. Good general menu, strong on seafood and steaks; eat inside or out on the patio.

**Harry's Seafood Bar & Grill** $$ 46 Avenida Menendez; tel: (904) 824-7767. New Orleans-style cuisine, including jambalaya and shrimp remoulade, and live entertainment in the courtyard.

**Old City House** $$$ 115 Cordova Street; tel: (904) 826-0781. Highly regarded for its creative menu and subdued setting; dinner only.

# Suggested tour

**Oldest Store Museum** $ *4 Artillery Lane; tel: (904) 829-9729. Open Mon–Sat 0900–1700, Sun 1200–1700; open at 1000 on Sun June–Aug.*

**St Augustine Lighthouse** and **Museum** $ *Old Beach Road, Anastasia Island; tel: (904) 829-0745. Open daily 0900–1730; extended hours May–Sept.*

**Length:** Main tour, 0.7 miles; 1 mile with American era detour and 2.5 miles with the Fountain of Youth Archaeological Park detour.

**Duration:** Main tour, 30 minutes' walk; 45 minutes with American era detour; 1.5 hours with Archaeological Park detour.

Begin at the **Old City Gate ❶**, the only access to the city after the British bombardment of 1702. To the left is the **CASTILLO DE SAN MARCOS ❷**; directly ahead is the palm-lined and pedestrianised St George Street with the **OLDEST WOODEN SCHOOLHOUSE ❸** on the right. The main entrance to the homes and workshops of the **SPANISH QUARTER MUSEUM ❹** is ahead on the left.

Cross the junction with Treasury Street for the **PENA-PECK HOUSE ❺**, then continue along St George Street to reach **PLAZA DE LA CONSTITUCION ❻**. East of the plaza, the decorated 1926 **Bridge of Lions ❼** carries traffic across Mantanzas Bay toward the beaches.

On the south side of the plaza, the **SPANISH MILITARY HOSPITAL ❽** is to the left on Aviles Street. Ahead on the right is Artillery Street holding the **Oldest Store Museum ❾**, a well-stocked general store in early-1900s style. Return to Aviles Street where the **XIMENEZ-FATIO HOUSE ❿** is ahead on the right. From here, turn left on to Cadiz Street then right on to Charlotte Street, walking south for St Francis Street and the neighbouring **TOVAR HOUSE ⓫** and **OLDEST HOUSE ⓬**.

**Detour:** To discover the key sights of St Augustine's American era walk west along King Street from Plaza de la Constitución. The strikingly ornate forms of **FLAGLER COLLEGE ⓭**, to the right, and the **LIGHTNER MUSEUM ⓮**, to the left, loom across Cordova Street. The no-less imposing **ZORAYDA CASTLE ⓯** is ahead on the left.

**Detour:** A contrast to the narrow and mostly traffic-free streets of the old centre, busy San Marco Avenue runs north from the Old City Gate. Half-a-mile ahead is the **MISSION DE NOMBRE DIOS ⓰**. Continue north, along Myrtle and Magnolia avenues to reach the **FOUNTAIN OF YOUTH ARCHAEOLOGICAL PARK ⓱**. From the park, Williams Street runs west and meets San Marco Avenue directly opposite the **OLD JAIL ⓲**.

## Also worth exploring

Cross the Bridge of Lions and the ocean is just 2 miles distant on Anastasia Boulevard, a local section of the coastal route, Hwy-A1A, which continues along the slender and scenic **Anastasia Island**. The 11-mile-long island is flanked by a glorious beach. For a bird's-eye view of the island and St Augustine itself, climb the 214 steps to the top of the **St Augustine Lighthouse** on Old Beach Road.

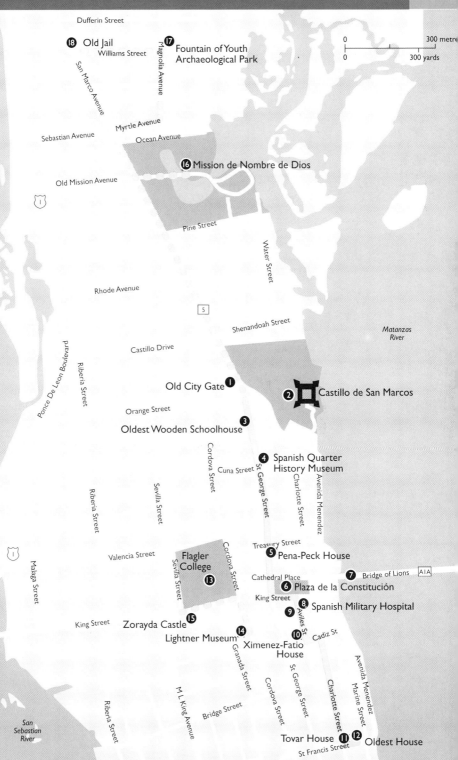

Dufferin Street

**18** Old Jail
Williams Street

**17** Fountain of Youth
Archaeological Park

0        300 metres
0        300 yards

San Marco Avenue

Magnolia Avenue

Myrtle Avenue

Sebastian Avenue

Ocean Avenue

Old Mission Avenue

**16** Mission de Nombre de Dios

Pine Street

Water Street

Rhode Avenue

Ponce De Leon Boulevard

Shenandoah Street

Matanzas
River

Castillo Drive

**1** Old City Gate

**2** Castillo de San Marcos

Orange Street

**3** Oldest Wooden Schoolhouse

Riberia Street

Cordova Street

Cuna Street

St George Street

Charlotte Street

Avenida Menendez

**4** Spanish Quarter
History Museum

Riberia Street

Sevilla Street

Treasury Street

**5** Pena-Peck House

Valencia Street

Flagler
College

**13**

Cordova Street

Cathedral Place

**7** Bridge of Lions    A1A

**6** Plaza de la Constitución

King Street

**8** Spanish Military Hospital

Malaga Street

King Street

**15** Zorayda Castle

Sevilla Street

**14** Lightner Museum

**9**

Aviles St

**10**

Cadiz St

Ximenez-Fatio
House

Granada Street

M L King Avenue

Bridge Street

Cordova Street

St George Street

Charlotte Street

Avenida Menendez
Marine Street

San
Sebastian
River

Riberia Street

**11** Tovar House

**12** Oldest House

St Francis Street

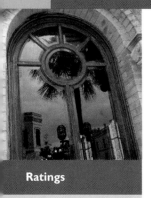

# Amelia Island and the northeast corner

**Ratings**

| | |
|---|---|
| Beaches | ●●●●● |
| Nature | ●●●●○ |
| Scenery | ●●●●○ |
| History | ●●●○○ |
| Sport | ●●●○○ |
| Surfing | ●●●○○ |
| Children | ●●○○○ |
| Museums | ●●○○○ |

Florida first-timers can be forgiven for being unaware of the charms of the state's northeast corner. A glance at the map suggests the area is consumed by sprawling Jacksonville and an enormous naval air force base. Old hands know better, however, and this tour makes a point of showing why many of them make repeated visits to the area, happy in the knowledge that much of it remains secret from the vacationing hordes.

From commercially developed surfer-friendly beach communities, the route strikes into less developed areas of old shrimping villages and state parks that consume entire islands. With Fernandina Beach, the end of the road is literally reached in a time-locked port town of hundred-year homes and dune-lined beaches. Throughout are echoes of earlier times: from the pre-European Timucua people and a 16th-century French Huguenot settlement to a slave-worked plantation and a dramatic re-creation of life in a Civil War fort.

## AMELIA ISLAND ❖❖❖

**ⓘ Amelia Island Chamber of Commerce** *102 Centre Street, Fernandina Beach; tel: (904) 261-3248 or (800) 226-3542. Open Mon–Fri 0900–1700.*

**ⓒ Amelia Island Plantation $$$** *3000 First Coast Highway; tel: (904) 261-6161 or (800) 864-6878. A sybaritic retreat spread across 1250 acres; besides faultless rooms and service it boasts golf courses, tennis courts and several miles of beach.*

Mixing verdant greenery with 12 miles of sparkling beaches, Amelia Island is the gem of Florida's northeastern corner. Although its perfectly contoured golf courses and champion-frequented tennis courts attract many regular visitors, this is still one of the few places in Florida where horses can be ridden bareback along the sands.

The peace and tranquillity of the present day conceal the island's lively past. Becoming the Atlantic terminal of a cross-state railway to Cedar Key made Amelia a transit point for slaves and liquor. The decline of the railway left the island high and dry, particularly as newer railways carried tourists to more southerly sections of the state. The largest settlement, Fernandina Beach (*see page 220*) is a wonderfully preserved Victorian town; the excellent Fort Clinch State Park (*see page 221*) marks the island's northern tip.

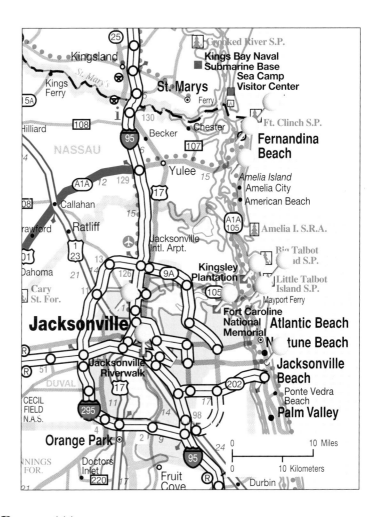

# FERNANDINA BEACH ✧✧✧

**Amelia Island Museum of History**
$ 233 S 3rd Street; tel: (904) 261-7378. Guided tour only, Mon–Sat 1100 and 1400.

A sheltered estuary and the US's ban on foreign shipping in 1807 helped Fernandina Beach (then under Spanish control) become a multinational port with merchants, pirates and smugglers all looking to exploit illicit trade routes into the US. The outlaw days were ended by US rule in Florida and Fernandina's relocation to a site adjacent to the cross-state railway, which boosted the local economy as it brought the first major influx of American tourists and settlers.

Remarkably, some 450 structures dating mostly from the last quarter of the 19th century still remain in the heart of Fernandina Beach, forming part of a 50-block **historic district** on and around Centre

**Eight Flags Shrimp Festival** The first weekend in May finds 100,000 people heading to Fernandina Beach to eat shrimps in familiar and unfamiliar ways and watch a variety of strange shrimp-related events.

Street. The predominantly Queen Anne and Italianate architectural features of the carefully maintained homes, such as bay windows, corner turrets, wraparound porches and all manner of decorative carpentry, bring considerable charm to the town.

The island's eventful past is outlined at the **Amelia Island Museum of History**, housed in a former gaol. The museum also details the shrimping industry that developed on the Amelia River in the 1850s and is still among the most important in the US, celebrated each May with the **Eight Flags Shrimp Festival** around the docks at the west end of Centre Street.

## Accommodation and food in Fernandina Beach

**The Bailey House $$** *28 S 7th Street; tel: (904) 261-5390 or (800) 251 5390.* One of the most photographed homes in the historic district offers bed and breakfast in antique-filled rooms with a wealth of period features, not least the claw-foot bathtubs.

**Florida House Inn $$** *20 & 22 S 3rd Street; tel: (904) 261-3300 or (800) 258-3301.* Dating from 1857 and one of Florida's oldest hotels, this 11-room bed-and-breakfast inn has handmade quilts and rugs; the pricier rooms have fireplaces and Jacuzzis. The inn's downstairs restaurant serves black-eye peas, catfish, mashed potato, pork chops, meatloaf and other staples of Deep South cuisine from help-yourself bowls.

**Beech Street Grill $$–$$$** *801 Beech Street; tel: (904) 277-3662.* Offers an enticing range of imaginatively prepared seafood from the blackboard's daily specials.

# FORT CAROLINE NATIONAL MEMORIAL*

**Fort Caroline National Memorial** 12713 Fort Caroline Road, Jacksonville; tel: (904) 641-7155. Open daily 0900–1700.

This reconstructed fort faces a mile-wide section of the St John's River and remembers one of the bloodiest episodes in colonial-era Florida: the Spanish decimation of the 300-strong French Huguenot settlement here in 1565. After storming the triangular earthen and timber fort, built a year earlier, the Spanish soldiers pursued the fleeing French to the coast off St Augustine where, despite being unarmed and having surrendered, they were attacked and killed.

A visitors' centre describes the rise and fall of the French colony, the subsequent French revenge mission, and much more of the human and natural history of an area that now forms part of the National Park-run Timucuan Ecological and Historic Preserve.

# FORT CLINCH STATE PARK**

**Fort Clinch State Park $** 2601 Atlantic Avenue, Fernandina Beach; tel: (904) 277-7274. Park open daily 0800–sunset; fort daily 0900–1700; candle-lit tours (separate fee $) May–Labor Day, Fri–Sat, phone for reservations and times.

Fort Clinch, started in 1849, was used by both sides during the Civil War although the cannons mounted on its ramparts saw little action: Confederate forces took the fort without opposition in 1861 and abandoned it to the Union a year later. The Union occupation is convincingly portrayed with candle-lit re-enactments led by guides dressed as soldiers who act in character as they lead visitors around the restored outbuildings.

Aside from the fort, the 1100-acre park has sand dunes, tidal marshes, maritime hammocks and an alligator-inhabited pond to be explored on marked trails. A beach lines the park's eastern edge, while directly across the Cumberland Sound to the north are views of Georgia.

# JACKSONVILLE*

**Jacksonville and the Beaches Convention & Visitors Bureau** 3 Independent Drive; tel: (904) 798-1948 or (800) 733-2668. Open Mon–Fri 0830–1700.

Jacksonville is named after Andrew Jackson, governor of Florida before becoming the US's seventh president. It is the state's largest city in terms of area and one of its major financial centres. High-rise glass and steel offices reflect its commercial importance while visitor attention focuses on the Riverwalk and the city's beaches (see below).

# JACKSONVILLE BEACH**

**American Lighthouse and Maritime Museum** 1011 N 3rd Street; tel: (904) 241-8845. Open Tue–Sat 1100–16.00.

A 983-ft-long **pier** lined by snack stands and anglers encapsulates the seaside mood of Jacksonville Beach, one of a string of oceanside communities that form the city's eastern edge. While the beach itself is the main point of note, the **American Lighthouse and Maritime Museum** provides a brief diversion with paintings, models and other items relating to the nation's coastal beacons.

# JACKSONVILLE RIVERWALK❖

**Jacksonville Historical Center**
*Riverwalk; tel: (904) 438-3901. Open Mon–Sat 1000–1700, Sun 1200–1700.*

**Museum of Science and History** $ *1025 Museum Circle; tel: (904) 396-7062. Open Mon–Fri 1000–1700, Sat 1000–1800, Sun 1300–1800.*

**River City Brewing Company** $–$$ *835 Museum Circle; tel: (904) 398-2299. Usefully placed beside the Riverwalk with steak and seafood dishes, a river view and quality beers brewed on the premises.*

In the heart of Downtown Jacksonville, the Riverwalk runs for 1.2 very pleasant miles along the south bank of the St John's River. On the route are the **Friendship Fountain**, where jets of water reach 100ft, and the **Jacksonville Historical Center** tracing the growth of the city with simple but informative displays.

The much larger **Museum of Science and History** has interactive exhibits aimed at youngsters and covers topics such as Florida's pre-European inhabitants and the coast's endangered marine life. An adjoining planetarium has space and laser shows. Crossing the river to the north bank by bridge or river taxi leads to **Jacksonville Landing**, a popular conglomeration of shops and restaurants with live open-air entertainment.

**Right**
Local marine life: roseate spoonbills

# KINGSLEY PLANTATION❖❖

**Kingsley Plantation** $ *11676 Palmetto Avenue, King George Island; tel: (904) 251-3537. Open daily 0900–1700.*

Set on 25 acres beside the Fort George River, the Kingsley Plantation flourished in the early 1800s producing sugar and cotton. The plantation was owned by Zephaniah Kingsley, a Scots-born member of Florida's legislative council during its territorial period (prior to full statehood). Kingsley's belief that slaves should be treated well, if only to make them more efficient workers, made him a thorn in the side of his slave-owning peers and he defied convention still further by marrying an African woman.

Florida's oldest extant plantation home, Kingsley's nine-room house dates from 1817 and has furnishings typical of the time. The adjacent kitchen, barn and 23 slave cabins have also been restored. Exhibits detail many aspects of plantation life and Kingsley's pioneering agricultural work.

# LITTLE TALBOT ISLAND STATE PARK✥

**Little Talbot Island State Park $** *11435 Fort George Road; tel: (904) 251-2320. Open daily 0800–sunset.*

Long and narrow Little Talbot Island is entirely consumed by a 2500-acre state park. Five miles of dune-lined beach mark the ocean side, woods of holly, oak and magnolia fill much of the interior, while tidal creeks and salt marshes define the island's mainland-facing edge. Wildlife spans river otters, bobcats and rabbits, and the multitude of shore birds that bring legions of bird-watchers during spring and autumn migrations. There are picnic areas and an excellent nature trail weaving through the park's diverse terrain.

# MAYPORT FERRY✥

**Jacksonville River Taxi ($)** *makes a 10-minute trip across the St John's River linking the Riverwalk and Jacksonville Landing; crossings are continuous throughout the day and early evening.*

Launched in November 1950 to carry cars and pedestrians across the St John's River between Fort George Island and the shrimp-fishing village of Mayport, this ferry earned such local affection that attempts to end the service in the 1990s were successfully resisted. The diminutive size of the craft makes a vivid contrast with the cargo ships and naval vessels that regularly use the river.

**Jacksonville Beach Pier** *Eastern end of 6th Avenue, Jacksonville Beach; tel: (904) 246-6001. Open daily 0600–2000; extended hours in summer.*

# Suggested tour

**Length:** Main tour 65 miles; 97 miles with detours.

**Duration:** Main tour 1.5 hours; 3 hours with detours.

**Links:** This route assumes you arrive in the Jacksonville area on I-95, although it can also, and far more scenically, be joined by using the coastal Hwy-A1A north from St Augustine (*see pages 210–17*).

Take any route to **JACKSONVILLE BEACH ❶**, its effervescent mood contrasting with that of the commercially important city of Jacksonville 12 miles inland. Dotted by high-rise hotels and beach accessory shops, and with the **pier** at the foot of 6th Avenue South, Jacksonville Beach is the most popular and lively of a string of beach communities. The waves close to the pier often draw surfers.

Third Street, the local section of Hwy-A1A, is the main traffic artery parallel to the beach. Follow this north through **Neptune Beach**. Just ahead, turn left on to Atlantic Boulevard then very shortly right on to

**Pablo Historical Park** *425 Beach Boulevard, Jacksonville Beach; tel: (904) 246-0093. Open Mon–Sat 1000–1600, Sun 1300–1600.*

**Horse Riding** Ride a horse bareback along Amelia Island's beaches by contacting **Sea Horse Stables** *5700 First Coast Highway; tel: (904) 261-4878.*

Mayport Road. For 5 miles Mayport Road skirts the tidal marshlands of the St John's River and then reaches the 300-year-old shrimping village of **Mayport**.

The still-thriving shrimping fleet is dwarfed by the aircraft carriers, frigates, destroyers and other craft commonly seen in and around the vast **Mayport Naval Station**, one of the US's largest naval bases. From Mayport, the **MAYPORT FERRY** ❷ carries cars on to Fort George Island.

Using Hwy-A1A, the 52-mile route from Fort George Island to Amelia Island is among the most scenic coastal drives in the US, officially called the **Buccaneer Trail**. After 2.4 miles, a signposted turn-off leads to the **Huguenot Memorial Park**, an oceanfront park ideal for a picnic stop. Directly north, Hwy-A1A crosses **LITTLE TALBOT ISLAND** ❸ passing the entrances to the state park of the same name before reaching Big Talbot Island.

Winding through forests and beside wildlife-rich marshes, Hwy-A1A crosses Nassau Sound to reach **AMELIA ISLAND** ❹, first passing the Amelia Island Plantation, a sprawling luxury resort which occupies much of the island's southern tip. Eleven miles ahead is the island's largest settlement, **FERNANDINA BEACH** ❺.

**Detour**: On Fort George Island, look for the signposted left turning for **KINGSLEY PLANTATION** ❻, on Hwy-A1A 5 miles north of the Mayport Ferry crossing. The approach to the plantation is a 3-mile course along a bumpy, gravel road. Rows of stately sabal palms mark the entrance to the plantation.

**Detour**: When leaving Jacksonville's beaches, keep to Atlantic Boulevard rather than turning right for Mayport. Ten miles ahead is **Downtown Jacksonville**. Follow signs for the **JACKSONVILLE RIVERWALK** ❼ on the river's south bank. Alternatively, cross the river and park on the north bank at Jacksonville Landing. Between the beaches and the city, the **FORT CAROLINE NATIONAL MEMORIAL** ❽ can be reached on a signposted 5-mile loop off Atlantic Boulevard.

## Also worth exploring

Prior to 1925, Jacksonville Beach was known as San Pablo and it grew around a railway network that formed part of Henry Flagler's East Coast Railroad. At the **Pablo Historical Park**, the railroad days are remembered inside the 1880s station building and outside with a 28-ton steam locomotive. Exhibits also document the almost forgotten aviation achievement of Army Air Corps Lieutenant James 'Jimmy' Harold Doolittle, who in 1922 took off from San Pablo and 21 hours 28 minutes later landed in San Diego, California, completing the US's first single-day, coast-to-coast flight.

## Amelia Island's eight flags

Much is made locally of Amelia Island's unusual past which has seen it under the rule of eight different flags. After it was landed by French Huguenots in 1562, control of the island switched between Spain and Britain (Amelia takes its name from the daughter of King George II) as did the rest of Florida. The island also saw the one-day reign of the Patriots of Amelia Island (locals who overthrew the Spanish), the raising of the Green Cross of Florida (a more sustained overthrow of Spanish rule) and a Mexican rebel flag hoisted by a Scotsman and French pirate. In 1821, Amelia came under US control, subsequently joining the Confederacy at the start of the Civil War.

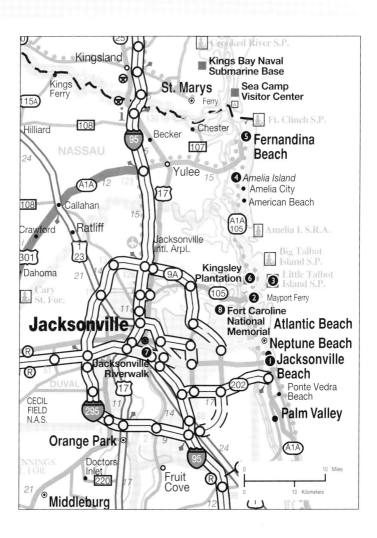

# Tallahassee

**Ratings**

| | |
|---|---|
| History | ●●●●● |
| Architecture | ●●●●○ |
| Art | ●●●○○ |
| Museums | ●●●○○ |
| Scenery | ●●●○○ |
| Sport | ●●○○○ |
| Children | ●○○○○ |
| Nature | ●○○○○ |

Staples of the Sunshine State such as theme parks and crowded beaches seem far removed from Tallahassee, a small city easily explored on foot that has been the seat of Florida's government since 1823. With its streets lined by oak and magnolia trees and everything, including local accents, moving at subdued pace, Tallahassee's mood and manners are much more akin to the US's Deep South than the brash Florida epitomised by Orlando and Miami.

Many early Tallahassee fortunes were earned from plantations, the owners sinking some of their wealth into elegant homes in fashionable areas in what was still very much a frontier settlement. Their neighbours were the financiers and politicians who shaped Florida through its early years of US rule. Two restored historic areas and several museums keep Tallahassee's past on view, while the contrasting old and new capitol buildings illustrate the gulf between the state's rough-and-ready past and modern Florida's power and influence.

## Sights

**Black Archives Research Center and Museum** *FAMU Campus, junction of Martin Luther King Boulevard and Gamble Street; tel: (850) 599-3020. Open Mon–Fri 0900–1600.*

**Calhoun Street Historic District** *On and around Calhoun Street between Tennessee and Georgia streets.*

**Black Archives Research Center and Museum**✣✣
Housed in the 1907 Carnegie Library, the oldest building on the FAMU (Florida Agricultural and Mechanical University) campus, this museum's collection spans half-a-million manuscripts, paintings, photos, taped oral histories and many other artefacts relating to the history of Black people in Florida and beyond. The regularly changing exhibitions focusing on topics as diverse as African-American slavery and the tribal art of Ethiopia are imaginatively constructed and invariably thought-provoking.

**Calhoun Street Historic District**✣✣
In 1840s Tallahassee, the discerning professional lived in or around Calhoun Street, dubbed 'gold dust row' for its wealthy reputation. Surviving a road-widening scheme in the 1940s and social decay in the 1970s, the area is now a designated historic district where oak-lined streets hold some of the finest gatherings of antebellum and territorial-period homes in Florida.

**ℹ Tallahassee Chamber of Commerce** *100 N Duval Street; tel: (850) 224-8116. Open Mon–Fri 0900–1700.*

**Tallahassee Visitor Information Center** *Plaza Level, New Capitol, entrance on N Duval Street; tel: (850) 914-8200 or (800) 628-2866. Open Mon–Fri 0800–1700, Sat–Sun 0900–1500.*

**🏠 Brokaw-McDougall House** $ *329 N Meridian Street; tel: (850) 488-3901. Open Mon–Fri 0800–1700.*

**The Columns** *100 N Duval Street; tel: (850) 224-8116. Open Mon–Fri 0900–1700.*

**FSU Campus** *Visitor Information Center, 100 S Woodward Avenue; tel: (850) 644-3246. Open Mon–Fri 0800–1630; extended hours during summer semester.*

**FSU Museum of Fine Arts** *Fine Arts Building, junction of Tennessee and Copeland streets, FSU Campus; tel: (850) 644-6836. Open Mon–Fri 1000–1600, Sat–Sun 1300–1600.*

**Governor's Mansion** *700 N Adams Street; tel: (850) 4884661. Open Mar–May, 1000–1200; closed rest of the year.*

The only example open to the public is the excellent **Brokaw-McDougall House**, completed in 1860 for a livery stable owner. Mixing Italianate and Classical Revival styles, a full-width second-floor porch supported by six Corinthian columns adds elegance to the exterior, as does the cupola which crowns the house. Inside, tall ceilings and period furnishings evoke the well-heeled Florida lifestyle of a time when much of the state was still swamp.

### The Columns*

Now occupied by the Chamber of Commerce, the Columns is the oldest extant house within Tallahassee's original boundaries, built around 1830 for prominent banker William 'Money' Williams. At the heart of high finance and political intrigue in Florida's formative years, the Columns, named for the four two-storey high columns supporting its porticoed entrance, spent many ignominious decades serving as a boarding house and a restaurant before being restored and furnished in the style of the 1840s.

### FSU Campus*

The array of collegiate Gothic (the architectural style pioneered at Princeton University and adopted by US academic institutions during the early decades of the 1900s) buildings that dominate the eastern section of the 347-acre campus of Florida State University can be admired from shady pathways lined by oak, palm, pine, dogwood and azalea trees.

Founded in 1857 as a womens' college, the university now has 30,000 students, two of the world's most powerful computers, and an alumni that includes actor Burt Reynolds. The **Museum of Fine Arts** features work by top names in temporary exhibitions and holds end-of-year student art shows.

### Governor's Mansion*

One of the perks of being elected governor of Florida is you get to use this redbrick official residence, built in the 1950s on the site of

**Knott House
Museum** $ *301 E Park
Avenue; tel: (850) 922-2459.
Open Wed–Fri 1300–1600,
Sat 1000–1600.*

the 1907 governor's mansion. The antebellum home of Andrew Jackson (Florida's first governor, later US president) in Tennessee provided the design inspiration for the house whose front door bears the state seal. Inside, guided tours pass through formal rooms decorated with a disparate collection of paintings and antiques.

### Knott House Museum❖❖❖

Knott House, built around 1843, is deeply entwined with Tallahassee's history. The emancipation proclamation freeing Florida's slaves was read from its steps in 1865, and its occupants included several Supreme Court judges and Tallahassee's first Black physician. While successive owners steadily enlarged the original house, it was the arrival of newly appointed state treasurer William Knott and his wife, Luella, in 1928 that added the Classical Revival portico and most of the Victorian furnishings that the sumptuous dwelling retains.

The restored house evokes both luxury living and the trials and tribulations of the turbulent 1920s and 1930s, when William Knott became one of Florida's most influential politicians. Luella, meanwhile, was a leading Tallahassee society figure, a campaigner in

**Below**
Knott House Museum

the Temperance Movement (her efforts led to a 50-year alcohol ban in Tallahassee), and author of the twee poems that are attached to pieces of furniture and other domestic items, earning the dwelling a nickname of 'the house that rhymes'.

## Why Tallahassee?

In colonial times, Pensacola to the west and St Augustine to the east enjoyed periods as Florida's centre of government. When Florida became part of the US in 1821, both contested for the honour of becoming capital of the new territory. The result was a compromise: representatives from both sides agreed that they would meet halfway. Tallahassee, then an empty plot of land accessed by dirt track, was chosen in 1823 and a log cabin erected for the meetings of the legislature.

**Museum of Florida History** 500 S Bronough Street; tel: (850) 488-1484. Open Mon–Fri 0900–1630, Sat 1000–1630, Sun 1200–1630.

## Museum of Florida History**

The proof that Florida existed before Walt Disney World arrived is contained within this comprehensive but very easily toured museum which charts the region's development from uninhabited swamp to one of the US's fastest-growing states.

The exhibits, from a 12,000 BC mastodon skeleton (sporting a ferocious set of tusks) to temporary displays on contemporary themes outline Florida's geology and chart the lifestyle and customs of its native cultures, particularly the Paleo-Indian peoples of the Panhandle. The native decline was largely due to the European diseases that arrived with the Spanish, whose expeditions and first settlements are described and colonial exploits illustrated with an array of early maps, cannons, nautical paraphernalia and gold and silver coins recovered from sunken galleons.

Florida's brief period under British rule and subsequent acquisition by the US is covered, and the state's role in the Civil War is described with a mock-up of a Confederate camp. The wars between the US and the Seminoles are told beneath a series of portraits of the Seminole chiefs who frequently outwitted their opponents but were ultimately unable to outgun them.

The removal of the Seminoles (many to Oklahoma, some to the Everglades) cleared the way for the exploitation of Florida as a cattle and citrus producing region, and as a vacation destination for newly mobile car-owning Americans, nicknamed the 'tin can tourists' during the 1920s and remembered here with photos and early Florida travel souvenirs.

**New Capitol**
*S Adams Street; tel: (850) 413-9200. Open Mon–Fri 0800–1700, Sat–Sun 0900–1500; guided tours on the hour, Mon–Fri 0900–1100, 1300–1500, Sat–Sun 0900–1500.*

**Old Capitol** *S Monroe Street; tel: (850) 487-1902. Open Mon–Fri 0930–1600.*

**Old City Cemetery**
*Corner of Park Avenue and Martin Luther King Boulevard; tel: (850) 891-8711. Open daily sunrise–sunset.*

**Park Avenue Historic District** *Park Avenue between Meridian and Macomb streets.*

**Lewis House** *316 E Park Avenue; tel: (850) 224-6048.*

## New Capitol*

The site of Florida's legislature and executive, the remarkably unattractive 307-ft-high New Capitol building has been a concrete blot on the city's skyline since 1977. The best way to experience the building is by escaping to its interior where, from the 22nd-floor observation deck there are wonderful views across Tallahassee and the tree-filled hillsides that surround it. Paintings and murals on Florida themes are found throughout the building. From March to May, the Florida legislature can be seen in action from public galleries.

## Old Capitol**

Ugly though it may be, the New Capitol was a necessary replacement for the Old Capitol, completed in 1845 to mark Florida's acquisition of statehood but since 1911 lacking the space to keep the expanding state's organs of government under one roof. The Old Capitol's copper dome that brings considerable gravitas was added in 1902, as were the wings and the distinctive red-and-white striped awnings protecting the interior from excessive sunlight.

Stepping inside reveals the splendidly restored interior, where a grand staircase rises toward the stained-glass dome and rooms such as the dainty Supreme Court, the governor's office and the legislative chambers.

Several side rooms are packed with absorbing memorabilia among it the documents and weapons with which Florida's leader sought to steer a course through the traumatic years of the Civil War Reconstruction, and the 'Bourbon era' from the 1870s which re-defined the politics and economies of the southern states.

## Old City Cemetery*

Florida was still in its pre-statehood territorial phase when this 11-acre cemetery was laid out in 1829. The graves are arranged on a grid-style system, adopted following a yellow fever outbreak that claimed several hundred lives in 1841 and providing a simple method for racial segregation: Whites being buried in the eastern half, Blacks in the west. The full roll-call includes an ex-state governor, the dead from both sides in the Civil War (buried in separate sections), and many more who are described in the walking tour leaflet available from kiosk near the entrance.

## Park Avenue Historic District**

Once marking the northern edge of the city, Park Avenue began as dirt track probably intended to deter Indian attack. When the dirt was re-shaped into a series of small parks, Park Avenue evolved into a address favoured by the city's social élite during the 1840s.

Noted residences include the Columns (*see page 227*) and Knott House (*see page 226*); the **Lewis House**, bought by the founder of the Lewis State Bank and periodically open for public tours of its restored interior

**Right**
Tallahassee's Old and New
Capitols

**Right**
Tallahassee's Old and New
Capitols

**First Presbyterian
Church** *110 N Adams
Street; tel: (850) 222-4504.
Usually closed except for
services.*

**Federal Courthouse**
*110 W Park Avenue.*

and the **First Presbyterian Church**, dating from the 1830s and
Tallahassee's oldest extant church, now restored to its neo-classical
form after being gothicised during the late 1800s. A more recent
addition to the street is the 1930s **Federal Courthouse**, a WPA
(Works Project Administration, a Depression-era government body
intended to create employment) initiative, decorated with murals
depicting Florida's history.

On Park Avenue's south side, the 1838 **Murphy House** is said to have
been a billet for government troops during the Reconstruction period,
while legend has it that the 1841 **Chittenden House** was financed by
winnings on the Louisiana state lottery.

St John's Episcopal
Cemetery *North side
of Call Street, facing Old City
Cemetery; tel: (850) 222-
2636. Open daily
dawn–dusk.*

**Union Bank Building**
*219 Apalachee Parkway; tel:
(850) 487-1902. Open
Mon–Fri 0930–1630.*

The Old City Cemetery (*see page 230*) anchors the district's west side. Behind it is **St John's Episcopal Cemetery**; its graves include that of Prince Murat, exiled son of the King of Naples and a nephew of Napoleon Bonaparte, and his wife, Catherine, a great-grandniece of George Washington. Murat owned a 100-acre plantation north of Tallahassee and his writings have provided valuable information about 1820s Florida.

**Union Bank Building**⁕
Florida's oldest commercial structure, the Union Bank Building, dates from 1841, but the financial institution it housed, one of the most important of the time, failed a few years later due to crop failure and the Seminole wars. Beneath its vaulted ceiling the restored bank now carries exhibits on Florida banking and remnants from its time as a National Freedmen's bank, set up during Reconstruction to financially assist freed slaves, and less distinguished periods when it served as a shoe factory and beauty parlour.

## Accommodation and food

During the March to May sitting of the Florida legislature and home games of the FSU's well-supported football team, the Seminoles, accommodation can be scarce in Tallahassee. At any other time, the few centrally located properties and scores of hotels and motels on the periphery offer good-priced lodgings.

**Calhoun Street Inn $$** *525 N Calhoun Street; tel: (850) 425-5095.* Within easy walking distance of Downtown Tallahassee and in the heart of a celebrated historic district, this cosy property promises home baking and has a golden retriever available for walks.

**Governor's Inn $$–$$$** *209 S Adams Street; tel: (850) 681-6855 or (800) 342 7717.* Much loved by visiting politicians for its luxurious rooms and suites named after Florida governors; serves a complimentary breakfast.

**The McFarlin House $$–$$$** *305 E King Street, Quincy; tel: (850) 875-2526.* An atmospheric bed-and-breakfast inn in the small town of Quincy, 23 miles north of Tallahassee on Hwy-90, offering a choice of individually furnished rooms.

**Andrew's Second Act $$–$$$** *228 S Adams Street; tel: (850) 222-3444.* Stylish setting for classy food, be it veal, beef or seafood; the lunches are less expensive but equally good.

**Barnacle Bill's $–$$** *1830 N Monroe Street; tel: (850) 385-8734* Generous portions of smoked, steamed, boiled and fried seafood and other dishes, to eat inside or out.

**El Chico $–$$** *2225 N Monroe Street; tel: (850) 386-1133.* A cut above the average Mexican restaurant with tasty, well-prepared dishes.

**The Mill $–$$** *2329 Apalachee Parkway; tel: (850) 656-2867.* The menu spans steaks, seafood, pastas, pizzas and home-baked pastries; the very drinkable beers are brewed on the premises.

**Silver Slipper $$$** *531 Scotty's Lane; tel: (850) 386-9366.* A favourite of Florida legislators for its steaks, seafood and Greek specialities, all served in a sophisticated atmosphere

**Right**
Florida State University,
Tallahassee

# Suggested tour

**Length**: Main tour 1 mile; Calhoun Street Historic District and Governor's mansion detour 0.75 mile; Museum of Florida History and Black Archives Research Center and Museum detour, 2 miles.

**Duration**: Tallahassee is compact and its streets very easy to walk, though crossing them can be slow especially during rush hours. Main tour walking time is 40 minutes. The Calhoun Street Historic District and Governor's Mansion detour will add a further 40 minutes; the detour to the Museum of Florida History will add only an additional few minutes; but continuing to the Black Archives Research Center and Museum is best done by car and will take 10 minutes driving time.

**Links**: Around Tallahassee: the Old South (*see pages 236–43*) and Tallahassee to the Forgotten Coast (*see pages 244–53*).

**Above**
Tallahassee's Capitol complex

The **NEW CAPITOL ❶** is far and away the tallest building in Tallahassee, and is easy to find as it lies at the heart of the Capitol Complex, a grouping of state administrative offices that occupies a large chunk Tallahassee's compact centre. The main entrance is on Duval Street, and in the lobby is a useful tourist information centre. Adjacent is the elevator to the 22nd-floor observation level.

Directly east stands the **OLD CAPITOL ❷**, recognised by its dome and stripped awnings, its entrance facing Monroe Street. A block further east, on the right side of Apalachee Parkway, a major traffic route into the city, stands the **UNION BANK BUILDING ❸**. To the right on Monroe Street, the 40-ft-high black marble pylons of the **Vietnam Veteran's Memorial ❹** are etched with the names of Floridians dead or missing in the Vietnam War.

Walk north along Monroe Street to the junction with Park Avenue. Formerly McCarthy Street, Park Avenue gained its name in 1905 for the series of parks in its centre and the wish of a local resident for a 'more sophisticated' address for her son's wedding invitations. This section forms the **PARK AVENUE HISTORIC DISTRICT ❺**. Turn right, passing the 1903 **Walker Library ❻** and crossing Calhoun Street, for the **KNOTT HOUSE MUSEUM ❼**, neighboured by the **Murphy ❽** and **Chittenden ❾** houses. Cross to the north side of

**Mission San Luis**
2020 W Mission Road; tel: (850) 487-3711. Open Mon–Fri 0830–1630, Sat 1000–1630, Sun 1200–1630.

**Old Town Trolley** The Old Town Trolley is a free service that includes a taped commentary on the historic sights of Tallahassee and makes 15 central stops. The service operates Mon–Fri 0700–1800; tel: (850) 574-5200.

**Festival** For four weeks over March and April, the Springtime in Tallahassee Festival finds parades, concerts and many other special events throughout the city, one of the southeast US's largest annual events.

Park Avenue and walk east for five blocks. This route passes the **Lewis House** ⑩, the **Federal Courthouse** ⑪, the **First Presbyterian Church** ⑫ and the **Columns** ⑬.

Directly ahead across Copeland Street is the **OLD CITY CEMETERY** ⑭, created five years after Tallahassee formally became a city. Behind it across Call Street is **St John's Episcopal Cemetery** ⑮, with graves dating from 1840. Further west along Park Avenue are the fraternity and sorority houses lining the approach to the **FSU CAMPUS** ⑯, its eastern side marked by early-1900s collegiate Gothic buildings.

**Detour:** If Park Avenue stimulates a thirst for more historic buildings, walk two blocks north along Adams Street, turning right along Tennessee Street and left on to Calhoun Street. Ahead is the oak- and magnolia-lined heart of the **CALHOUN STREET HISTORIC DISTRICT** ⑰. The **Brokaw-McDougall House** ⑱ stands two blocks east facing Virginia Street, surrounded by a small park. Rejoin Adams Street and continue north to the **GOVERNOR'S MANSION** ⑲.

**Detour:** Housed in the Gray Building, which also stores the state archives, is the **MUSEUM OF FLORIDA HISTORY** ⑳, two blocks west of the New Capitol and entered from Bronough Street. Martin Luther King Junior Boulevard is the most direct route to the FAMU campus, a mile south, site of the **BLACK ARCHIVES RESEARCH CENTER AND MUSEUM** ㉑.

## Also worth exploring

Remnants of a Spanish mission, established in 1567, are steadily being excavated at the 60-acre **San Luis Archaeological and Historic Site**. The mission was among the most important of the hundred established in Florida and, at its peak, housed 1400 Spanish and natives. Exhibitions and finds displayed at the visitors' centre provide a vivid picture of mission life. Children will enjoy the monthly 'living history' days, when period-attired guides take the roles of mission dwellers and describe their daily routines.

# Around Tallahassee: the Old South

## Ratings

| | |
|---|---|
| History | ●●●●● |
| Nature | ●●●●○ |
| Scenery | ●●●●○ |
| Architecture | ●●●○○ |
| Crafts | ●●●○○ |
| Food | ●●●○○ |
| Museums | ●●○○○ |
| Children | ●○○○○ |

Some of the most relaxing routes in Florida lie close to Tallahassee, the roads draped with Spanish moss and passing through hamlets where the silence is broken only by the hum of insects and the drone of farm machinery in nearby fields. Tallahassee developed as a centre for cotton and other crops grown on the many plantations that exploited the rich and fertile soils in its vicinity. The population shift to southern Florida has left much of this farmland intact, still crossed by the winding roads that once linked the plantations and provided access to the city's markets.

Many of the area's larger towns, such as Monticello and Thomasville, maintain a fine stock of 19th-century buildings. Others, like Havana, have become filled with antiques shops. Elsewhere, the area holds evidence of major prehistoric settlements, the sites of battles between White settlers and natives, and a celebrated store where devoted locals have been buying their sausages for years.

## BRADLEY'S COUNTRY STORE*

**ⓘ** **Bradley's Country Store** *Route 3, Centerville Road, 12 miles from Tallahassee; tel: (850) 893-1647. Open Mon–Fri 0800–1800.*

Promising the 'best country smoked sausage money can buy', Bradley's Country Store has been in business since 1927. The tin-roofed, wood-framed building was erected to capitalise on the fame of Grandma Bradley's sausages, which were first cooked, smoked and

sold from her kitchen in 1910. The sausages, seasoned with black and red pepper, sage and salt to a recipe handed down through the generations, have no artificial preservatives and are sold alongside other rural Florida specialities such as hog's head cheese, liver pudding, cane syrup and grits. Each November, the Bradley Farm Days festival, based here, celebrates rural craft and cuisine.

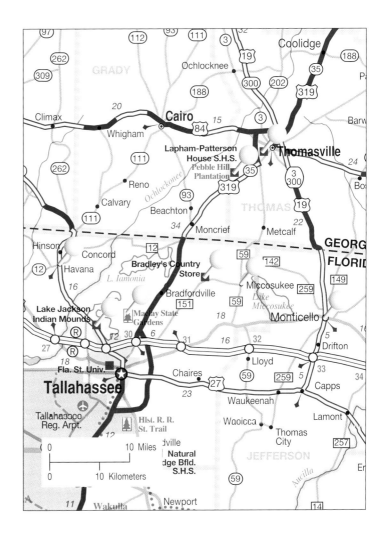

# HAVANA*

Like the Cuban capital after which it is named, Havana once enjoyed a flourishing cigar industry and was noted for producing a broad-leafed tobacco used in their production. Nowadays, the concentration of antiques shops set in the compact turn-of-the-century Downtown district is the reason Havana's 2000-strong permanent population is swamped every weekend by a mixture of serious collectors and casual browsers. Havana's dainty size and its setting amid pine forests brings a measure of rural charm although there is little to savour beyond the antique outlets.

## Accommodation and food in Havana

**Historic Havana House $–$$** *301 E 6th Avenue; tel: (850) 539-5611.* Two-room bed and breakfast in a 1907 house; the 'country gourmet' breakfast can be eaten inside or out on the carpeted porch.

**The Gazebo $** *310 N Main Street; tel: (850) 539 6285.* Perfect for a simple, filling lunch when exploring the adjacent antiques shops and art galleries.

**Nicholson Farmhouse $$–$$$** *Route 12, 3 miles west of Havana; tel: (850) 539-5931.* Beef is the speciality and it comes in large portions at this former farmhouse complex; chicken and seafood are also on offer.

# LAKE JACKSON INDIAN MOUNDS❖❖

**Lake Jackson Indian Mounds** *3600 Indian Mounds Road, Tallahassee; tel: (850) 922-6007. Open daily dawn–dusk.*

One of Florida's most important archaeological sites occupies a quiet setting on the banks of Lake Jackson. From AD 1000 to 1500, the site is believed to have been a religious and administrative centre of the Apalachee culture. Native inhabitants of the Panhandle, the agriculture-based Apalachee people had an advanced political system and spiritual beliefs that included the building of temple mounds. Three such mounds, the tallest 26ft-high, are visible at the site and once formed part of a large village built around a central plaza.

Copper breastplates, badges and axes decorated with elaborate ritual figures are among the finds that indicate the historic significance of the site and also suggest the Apalachees' links with other native groups across the Southeast: part of the 'Southern Cult', at its height around 1200. Other discoveries reveal trading links with native peoples as distant as the Great Lakes and Oklahoma. For unknown reasons, the Apalachee abandoned the Lake Jackson area around 1500; by the early 1800s it was occupied by a cotton plantation.

# MACLAY STATE GARDENS❖❖❖

**Maclay State Gardens** *$ 3540 Thomasville Road, Tallahassee; tel: (850) 487-4556. Gardens open daily 0800–sunset.*

In 1923, New York financier Alfred B Maclay purchased 1900 acres on the shores of Lake Hall as a winter retreat and set aside 28 acres for formal gardens, designed to be in bloom from December to April. With pines and oaks set alongside dogwoods and redbuds, the gardens mix native and exotic flora, and include 150 types of camellia and 50 azalea species. Among the gardens' wildlife is the flying squirrel, a nocturnal species born with a loose fold of skin that enables it to glide through the air.

Overlooking the gardens, the **Maclay House** dates from 1905 and holds many of the Maclay family's furnishings and personal items.

Though the house is only open when the gardens are at their best, from January to April, the gardens and the lakeside area are worth a visit at anytime. There are designated swimming and picnic areas, and the **Big Pine Nature Trail**, which picks a short course trail through wooded hillsides.

# MICCOSUKEE✧

**Monticello Chamber of Commerce** *420 W Washington Street; tel: (904) 997-5552. Open Mon–Fri 0900–1700.*

The village of Miccosukee was inhabited by Miccosukee people until 1818 when it was attacked by 3000 US troops under Andrew Jackson, who arrived from Georgia without official sanction ostensibly to repel a British incursion into Spanish-ruled Florida, but actually setting in place the events that would culminate in the US take-over of the region and the removal of its natives. Burning the village to the ground, Jackson became known as 'Sharp Knife' among the Miccosukee, who fled to central and southern Florida. The village was subsequently occupied by White settlers.

# MONTICELLO✧

Monticello thrived on the cotton trade from the 1820s but was later by-passed by the rail routes that opened up the rest of the Florida. As a result, 27 central blocks are made up almost exclusively of 19th-century buildings, a mixture of wood-framed homes in Classical Revival and Italianate style, and brick-built commercial buildings.

The most eye-catching structure, however, is the 1909 **Jefferson County Courthouse**, modelled after Thomas Jefferson's home,

Monticello, in Virginia, around which the main traffic arteries flow. Close by, the splendidly restored **Opera House** was built in the 1890s and made Monticello the cultural centre of northern Florida. The Chamber of Commerce offers a free guide detailing walking and driving tours of the town.

### Accommodation in Monticello

**The Clarke House $–$$** *580 W Washington Street; tel: (850) 997-1348.* In the heart of this small town's historic centre with just two guest rooms.

**Palmer Place $–$$** *625 W Palmer Mill Road; tel: (850) 997-5519.* Extremely comfortable and well-priced bed and breakfast in a restored antebellum home; one of the five guest rooms is a two-bedroom suite.

# PEBBLE HILL PLANTATION❖❖

**Pebble Hill Plantation $**
*Thomasville Road (Hwy-319), south of Thomasville; tel: (912) 226-2344. Open Oct–Labor Day, Tue–Sat 1000–1700, Sun 1300–1700.*

Around the Florida-Georgia border is the US's largest concentration of plantation homes. One of the few open to the public is Pebble Hill, where lanes of live oak and magnolia lead to the two-storey, 40-room mansion occupied, until her death in 1978, by Elisabeth Ireland Poe, better known to her staff as Miss Pansy.

Although the plantation was founded as a working cotton farm in 1820, it became a winter home for the affluent Cleveland-based Hanna family for whom the present mansion was erected in 1936, replacing a less opulent home destroyed by fire. Antiques, silverware, porcelain and crystal decorate the house, as do an extraordinary number of hunting and wildlife paintings including several valuable Audubon bird study prints.

The former cow barn serves as a visitors' centre with exhibits on family and farm history; other outbuildings include the log cabin school for the children of plantation workers.

# THOMASVILLE❖❖

**Thomasville Welcome Center**
*135 N Broad Street; tel: (912) 227-7099 or (800) 704-2350. Open Mon–Fri 0830–1700, Sat 0900–1200.*

Situated 330ft above sea-level, Thomasville earned a reputation during Victorian times as a health resort, its comparatively high elevation sparing it the disease-carrying mosquitoes common to lower-lying marsh areas. Wealthy northerners wintered in the town's hotels while some built the 'winter cottages' that lie within a few blocks of Thomasville's enjoyable commercial centre, the well-preserved Broad Street.

The only such cottage open for tours is the Queen Anne-style **Lapham-Petterson House**. This yellow-painted structure was completed

**Lapham-Petterson House** $ *626 N Dawson Street; tel: (912) 226-0405. Open Tue–Sat 0900–1700, Sun 1300–1700.*

**Thomas County Museum of History** $ *725 N Dawson Street; tel: (912) 226-7664. Open Tue–Sat 1000–1200, 1400–1700.*

in 1885 and has 26 windows and 19 rooms but not a single right angle due to a superstition of its owner, a Chicago shoe merchant.

The **Thomas County Museum of History** records Thomasville's health resort era with photographs and assorted memorabilia, stocks a formidable display of ladies fashions from 1825 to 1947, and has a pioneer-era log cabin and, oddest among many odd exhibits, a single-lane bowling alley from 1893.

## Accommodation and food in Thomasville

**Serendipity Cottage** $$ *339 E Jefferson Street; tel: (912) 226-81111 or (800) 383-7377.* Decorated with antiques, wicker furniture and potted ferns, the three guest rooms include modern features such as VCRs and cable TV.

**Susina Plantation Inn** $$ *1420 Meridian Road; tel: (912) 377-9644.* This 1841 Greek Revival plantation home makes an ultra-elegant setting for bed and breakfast, and is handily placed on Route 151 between Thomasville and Tallahassee.

**Izzo Pharmacy** $ *122 N Broad Street; tel: (912) 226-4411.* Historic drugstore diner, complete with soda fountain and menu of burgers and milk shakes.

**The Market Diner** $$ *502 Smith Avenue; tel: (912) 225-1777.* Fresh produce is a certainty at this friendly restaurant which shares the site with the local farmers' market.

## Suggested tour

**Length:** Main tour 83 miles. If driving a rental car, ensure that crossing from Florida into Georgia is permitted. Detours 25 miles each.

**Duration:** Main tour 2.5 hours. First detour 45 minutes; second detour 1 hour.

**Links:** Tallahassee (*see pages 226–35*), Tallahassee to the Forgotten Coast (*see pages 244–53*).

Take Hwy-319 (Thomasville Road) north from Tallahassee. A mile north of the junction with I-10, the entrance to **MACLAY STATE GARDENS** ❶ is on the left. Continue north for 14 miles, crossing the state border into Georgia, where the winding two-lane route becomes appreciably straighter and wider. After 13 miles, the entrance to **PEBBLE HILL PLANTATION** ❷ is on the left and 3 miles further is **THOMASVILLE** ❸.

Leave Thomasville heading south on Hwy-19, re-entering Florida and after 31 miles reaching **MONTICELLO** ❹. Hwy-19 (called Jefferson

The route is intended as a day-trip from Tallahassee but there are a number of distinctive bed-and-breakfast inns in the area, often offering accommodation for much lower prices than more heavily touristed areas.

Street locally) passes through the centre of this largely Victorian-era town; the junction with Hwy-90 forms the commercial centre and holds the unmistakable **Jefferson County Courthouse.**

West from Monticello, much of the 25-mile length of Hwy-90 to Tallahassee is known as **Fred Mahan Drive**, remembering the local nursery owner who donated some 40,000 plants to beautify highways, churches and cemeteries during the 1930s. For 30 cents an hour, labourers spent eight years planting the palms, arbor vita, crape myrtle and other flowering vegetation whose summertime blooms bring colour to the edge of the highway.

**Detour:** Looping off Hwy-90 between Tallahassee and Monticello, this detour explores the quiet, moss-draped roads along which horse-drawn wagons once transported cotton from local plantations to Tallahassee. From Monticello, Hwy-90 skirts the southern edge of Lake Miccosukee and, just under 5 miles ahead, is the junction with Route 59. Route 59 heading north passes through the hamlet of **Concord** and reaches **MICCOSUKEE ❺** at the junction with Route 151. Turn right here, left at the next junction and right again soon for **Reeve's Landing**, a popular fishing and picnic spot on the edge of tranquil **Lake Miccosukee.**

Return to Miccosukee and continue west on Route 151. After 5 miles, this tree-lined route bends to the south and passes **BRADLEY'S COUNTRY STORE ❻**. A further 5 miles ahead on the left, a gravel driveway leads to the white wooden form of **Old Pisgah United Methodist Church**, built in 1858. Route 151 continues into Tallahassee forming one of the city's celebrated 'canopy roads', overhung by Spanish moss from the branches of live oaks.

**Detour:** A better detour for antique seekers is to return to Tallahassee from Monticello on Hwy-90, joining I-10 east of the city and continuing to the Hwy-27 exit. Follow Hwy-27 north for 12 miles until it reaches **HAVANA ❼**. The town's antiques shops line the highway and adjoining streets. If browsing takes less time than expected, stop on the way back to Tallahassee at the **LAKE JACKSON INDIAN MOUNDS ❽**, signposted from Hwy-27 on the approach to Tallahassee.

## Also worth exploring

Nine miles west of Monticello, Hwy-90 passes the southbound Route 59. After dipping beneath I-10 Route 59 reaches **Lloyd**, a tiny settlement with a disproportionately large brick-built railway station. The station was raised in 1858 during a period when the town enjoyed prominence for its connection to the Seaboard Coast Line Railroad. The building is now restored and much fussed over by the county historical society.

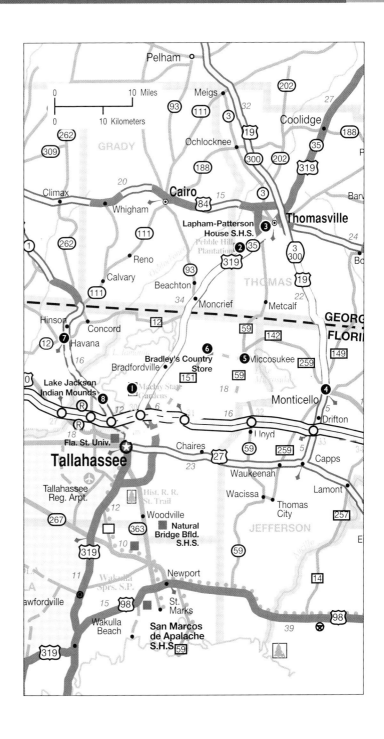

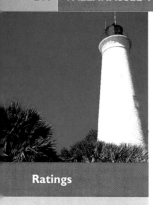

# Tallahassee to the Forgotten Coast

## Ratings

| | |
|---|---|
| Beaches | ●●●● |
| Food | ●●●● |
| History | ●●●● |
| Nature | ●●●● |
| Architecture | ●●● |
| Scenery | ●●● |
| Children | ●● |
| Museums | ● |

The area between the state capital and the Gulf of Mexico, one of Florida's least known but most rewarding corners, is a landscape rich in natural sights: freshwater springs, forests of oak and pine, and numerous rivers around which the lack of modern development allows the sense of history to be strong, bolstered by the remnants of a 16th-century Spanish fort and the site of the Civil War battle that kept Tallahassee in Confederate hands.

At the coast, too, the scenery has changed little in decades. The so-called Forgotten Coast is studded with once-thriving towns whose growth was stunted as transport patterns changed (in one case, a town was simply abandoned), leaving behind Victorian-era wood-framed buildings and local economies more dependent on oysters than tourism. For good measure, the region has some of the least crowded beaches in the state and unpretentious eateries serving the best seafood for miles.

## APALACHICOLA✦✦✦

**ⓘ Apalachicola Chamber of Commerce and Visitors Center** *99 Market Street; tel: (850) 653-9419. Open Mon–Fri 0930–1600, Sat 1000–1500.*

It's hard to believe on first sight, but in the early 1800s Apalachicola was a thriving port and rivalled New Orleans as a transportation centre, sending cotton to New England and Europe. Many of the elegant homes of cotton merchants still stand in the now sleepy and thinly populated town, as do those of the 1920s lumber barons who moved in following the decline of cotton, staying until the local cypress forests were decimated.

When railway travel surpassed ships, Apalachicola turned to the 6000 acres of oysters beds that lie in the nearby estuaries to the shore and now produces 10 per cent of all those consumed in the US. The estuaries and the broad Apalachicola River make fruitful territory for nature-orientated river trips, many of which operate from the small marina.

The most instantly noticeable of the town's many historic buildings is the 1907 **Gibson Inn**, complete with wraparound veranda. Through the 1980s, the inn set the trend for the stylish restoration that is

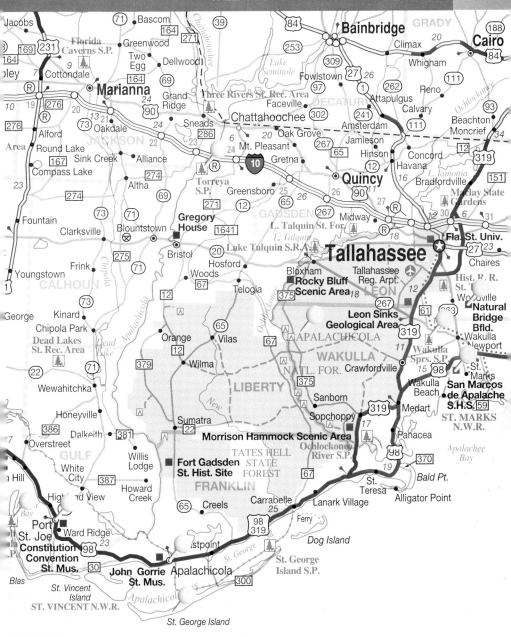

GULF OF MEXICO

0          10          20  Miles

0      10      20      30  Kilometers

**John Gorrie State Museum $** *Corner of 6th Street and Avenue D; tel: (850) 653-9347. Open Thur–Mon 0900–1700.*

**River Trips** Apalachicola makes a good base for excursions on the river of the same name. Nature-watching trips are operated by **Eco Ventures Inc** *(tel: (850) 653-2593)*, more general sight-seeing voyages by **Captain Tony** *(tel: (850) 653-3560)*, and paddlewheel boat trips by **Paddlewheel Riverboat Tours** *(tel: (850) 653-9502)*.

**Festivals** The only time when accommodation may be at a premium in Apalachicola is during the November Seafood Festival, when the local oysters, shrimps, clams and other succulent marine creatures are consumed by the bucketful.

steadily rejuvenating many local buildings. A useful free walking tour map is provided by the Chamber of Commerce.

A prominent figure in 1840s Apalachicola was John Gorrie. At times post master, treasurer and bank director, Gorrie is best remembered as a physician. Seeking a way of cooling his patients' rooms during an outbreak of yellow fever in 1841, he developed an ice-producing machine that formed the basis of modern air-conditioning. His work is remembered in the one-room **John Gorrie State Museum**, where a replica of the ice machine takes pride of place.

## Accommodation and food in Apalachicola

**Brigitte's Romantic Retreat $$** *101 6th Street; tel: (850) 653-3270.* Exceedingly cosy bed and breakfast in a wonderfully furnished house, complete with friendly hosts.

**Coombs House Inn $–$$** *80 6th Street; tel: (850) 653-9199.* The largest of several antique-filled old homes offering bed-and-breakfast accommodation, this three-storey 1905 dwelling also offers free bicycles for local exploration.

**The Boss Oyster Bar $–$$** *123 Water Street; tel: (850) 653-9364.* Oysters are what Apalachicola is famous for and this rustic dockside eatery is among the most enjoyable places to sample them, served in a variety of styles. Shrimp, scallops, clams and other fare is also offered.

**Chief Eddie's Magnolia Grill $$$** *133 Avenue E; tel: (850) 653-8000.* Draws discerning diners from near and far. It's owned by one of Florida's best chefs, who spends as much time chatting to customers as preparing the excellent food.

**Tamara's Cafe Floridita $–$$** *17 Avenue E; tel: (850) 653-4111.* Well-priced lunch and dinner fare featuring seafood and meat dishes given a Latin-American twist.

## Apalachicola's oysters

Seafood of many kinds is plentiful throughout Florida but Apalachicola can justly claim to have the region's best oysters; the local waters yield 90 per cent of all the state's oysters and 10 per cent of those harvested in the entire US. Offered raw, steamed and in numerous other styles, oysters are a mainstay of many restaurants in the area and are popularly consumed with ample quantities of beer. Occasionally oysters take second place to scallops, which appear roughly every seven years as thick, floating 'islands' off the coast.

Above right
Black-crowned night heron

# APALACHICOLA NATIONAL FOREST*

Spanning 565,000 acres, Apalachicola National Forest is easily the largest of Florida's three federally protected forests. The canoe-friendly rivers, swamps, savannahs, pine woods and glades of cypress, oak and magnolia within it are all accessed by walking and horse-riding trails. Among the more popular sections is the **Silver Lake Recreation Area** with boating, swimming and a small beach.

# NATURAL BRIDGE BATTLEFIELD SITE**

**Natural Bridge Battlefield Site**
*Natural Bridge Road, tel: (850) 922-6007. Open daily 0800–sunset.*

Its present-day peace interrupted only by birdsong, the 7-acre Natural Bridge area made an unlikely setting for the battle in March 1865, shortly before the end of the Civil War, which enabled Tallahassee to become one of the few Confederate capitals not to fall to the Union. In a five-day battle that claimed 24 lives, some 500 advancing Union soldiers were forced back towards the coast by 700 Confederate troops made up of teenage students (who required their mothers' permission to fight) and elderly men. Displays beside a monument indicate the progress of the conflict, re-enacted on its anniversary.

# PORT ST JOE*

**Constitution Convention State Museum $** *200 Allen Memorial Way; tel: (850) 229-8029. Open Thur–Mon 0900–1700.*

**Whispering Pines $$** *Star Route 1, Port St Joe; tel: (850) 227 7252. Cottages enclosed by oak, pine and palm trees with views of St Joseph's Bay, just a few minutes' walk from the beach; guests have free use of canoes and, in season, can scoop their own scallops from the nearby shoreline.*

Hard-working Port St Joe, set on a sheltered bay, is noted for its paper mills and scallop fishing, and occupies the site of the vanished city of St Joseph. Flourishing as a port during the 1830s, St Joseph enjoyed a brief period as Florida's capital but was abandoned when it lost its political role to Tallahassee and was decimated by disease and hurricane. Its houses were destroyed or reassembled in Apalachicola and only the town cemetery remained.

The strange story of St Joseph is outlined at the **Constitution Convention State Museum**, which also details the 34-day convention that led to the drafting of the first Florida constitution in 1839, a step on the road to statehood that was acquired six years later. The convention delegates are rather unflatteringly represented by speaking mannequins.

**Right**
Wetland egrets

# ST GEORGE ISLAND***

St George Island is one of three barrier islands that protect Apalachicola Bay and allow its oyster beds to thrive, and is the only one accessible by road. At the eastern end, **St George Island State Park** protects 9 miles of beaches, dunes, pine woods and live oak hammocks. The park is the best place to spot the island's abundant birdlife, particularly the ospreys which are frequently seen plucking fish from the water and whose nests adorn many pine trees. During spring and autumn the park provides an important stop for migratory birdlife. Besides swimming and picnic areas, the park has a 2.5-mile hiking trail and two observation decks providing excellent views of the island and beyond.

## Accommodation and food in St George Island

**Inn on St George Island** $$ *119 Franklin Boulevard; tel: (800) 824-0416.* This wood-framed hostelry is a long-serving local landmark; the simple but comfortable rooms open on to balconies with views of the bay or the Gulf.

**The Captain's Table** $$ *49 W Pine Avenue; tel: (850) 927-3923.* Fare such as seafood gumbo and bacon-wrapped shrimp feature on the menu in this tastefully furnished dinner-only restaurant.

# ST JOSEPH PENINSULA STATE PARK❖❖

**St Joseph Peninsula State Park** $ *Eastern end of Route 30E, near Port St Joe; tel: (850) 227-1327. Open daily 0800–sunset.*

Named for the long-gone city whose site is now occupied by Port St Joe (*see opposite*), this long and slender park has water on both sides and looms as a mirage-like string of white-sand dunes and beaches. The ocean beaches are used for swimming and fishing; the bay side has a picnic area and two nature trails.

# ST MARCOS DE APALACHE HISTORIC SITE❖❖

**St Marcos de Apalache Historic Site** *1022 De Soto Boulevard, near St Marks; tel: (850) 925-6216. Open Thur–Mon 0900–1700.*

**Sweet Magnolia Inn** $$ *803 Port Leon Drive, near St Marks; tel: (850) 925-7670. In an unlikely rustic setting, offering excellent seven-course dinners.*

This site, one of Florida's oldest reminders of its Spanish past, was chosen for a fort by Pánfilo de Narváez in 1528 because of its strategic importance at the confluence of the Wakulla and St Marks rivers. The series of wood and stone forts built here were regularly attacked by pirates and natives, and switched hands frequently as control of Florida passed from Spain to Britain and back again. Future Florida governor and US president Andrew Jackson occupied the fort during his illegal incursion into Florida in 1818.

Using stones from the Spanish-built foundations, a sailor's hospital was constructed here in 1857 and now holds a small **museum** outlining the fort's eventful past. A signposted **walking tour** links many of the main points of interest, including the thick-walled Spanish bombproof fort, the cemetery holding members of Jackson's expedition, and the hillock constructed by Confederate troops to hold a gunpowder magazine during the Civil War.

# TORREYA STATE PARK❖❖

**Torreya State Park** $ *Near Bristol; tel: (850) 643-2674. Open daily 0800–sunset.*

Hills of any kind are rare in Florida, which makes this park, set round the 150ft-high limestone bluffs that rise from dense forests above a bend in the Apalachicola River, seem all the more spectacular. The park is named after the torreya tree, a rare species of yew found only here.

From 1840 to the 1920s, the river was an important steamboat trading route and strategically significant during the Civil War. The remains of

**Gregory House $**
Guided tour only,
Mon–Fri 1000, Sat–Sun
1000, 1400 and 1600.

Confederate gun placements, dug into the bluffs to attack Union shipping, can still be seen on the dramatic **Apalachicola River Bluffs Trail**, which passes through a hardwood forest before emerging high above the river. Another walk, the **Weeping Ridge Trail**, explores one of the deep ravines carved by the river's tributaries over many centuries.

The importance of the river and the ups and downs of a cotton planter's life in the run-up to the Civil War are revealed during the guided tours of the **Gregory House**. The two-storey house, with its period fixtures and fittings, was built in 1849 for a successful planter and, perched above the river, enjoys one of the finest back garden views in Florida.

# WAKULLA SPRINGS STATE PARK✦✦✦

**Wakulla Springs
State Park $** 550
Wakulla Park Drive; tel:
(850) 224-5950. Open daily
0800–sunset; boat trips ($)
operate Apr–Oct.

**Lodge $** / Spring
Drive; tel: (850) 224-
5950. Peace, quiet and a
slice of Florida history are
all provided by this 1930s
hotel where every room
has a marble bathroom
and fireplace.

At the heart of this 2860-acre park is one of the world's largest and deepest freshwater springs. An average day brings 561 million gallons of crystal clear water from a source as yet undiscovered amid the intricate network of caves which lie hundreds of feet below the springs' deceptively calm surface.

The discovery of a fossilised mastodon skeleton here in 1850 prompted scientific interest in the springs. A few fossils can still be spotted, along with a multitude of colourful fish, on the glass-bottomed boat trips which provide a commentary on the mysteries of the spring and offer views reaching 100 feet down.

A 6-mile hiking route penetrates the park but a less demanding form of exploration are the river trips venturing for 3 miles along the cypress-lined Wakulla River. Park wildlife includes alligators, turtles and deer, and a bird population of turkeys, herons, egrets, vultures, ospreys and the occasional bald eagle. The setting provided the backdrop for the 1954 film *Creature from the Black Lagoon* and several early *Tarzan* films.

# Suggested tour

**Length**: Main tour 190 miles; St Joseph Peninsula State Park detour 50 miles; Torreya State Park detour 19 miles.

**Duration**: Main tour 4 hours. Taking one or both detours will require dropping something from the main tour unless it is spread over two days. If nature is preferred to history, ignore the San Marcos de Apalachee and Natural Bridge battlefield sites in favour of Wakulla Springs and Torreya State Park (the latter adding 45 minutes' driving time). If isolated beaches appeal, be sure to include the St Joseph Peninsula State Park detour (30 minutes' driving time).

**Links**: Although designed as a day-trip from Tallahassee, stopping overnight in Apalachicola or near by makes this an easy link with Crossing the Panhandle (*see pages 254–63*).

**Above**
Wakulla Springs State Park

Leave Tallahassee on Hwy-363. As it proceeds south, this route parallels the **Tallahassee-St Marks Railroad**, completed in 1837 and the first railway in Florida. The line, on which wagons were originally pulled by mules, saw 147 years of commercial use until being abandoned and redeveloped in the 1990s as a cycling, walking and skating route.

Six miles south of Tallahassee at **Woodville** is a left turn for Natural Bridge Road which, after 6.2 miles, reaches the **NATURAL BRIDGE BATTLEFIELD SITE ❶**. Just beyond the battlefield site are two natural springs. Return to Woodville and continue south for 6 miles on Route 363, to a far larger spring within **WAKULLA SPRINGS STATE PARK ❷**. The park's entrance is on Route 267, 4.8 miles from the junction with Route 363. Ahead on Route 363, **ST MARCOS DE APALACHE HISTORIC SITE ❸** is 3.5 miles from the Route 267 junction, close to the village of **St Marks**. The remains of the old fort enjoy a bucolic setting above the meeting point of the Wakulla and St Marks rivers.

The main coastal route, Hwy-98, crosses Route 363 2.5 miles north of the historic site. Join Hwy-98 heading west. The route is uneventful until, after 17 miles, it passes through **Panacea**, built around one of the many coastal inlets which now become a feature of the tour and here mark the start of the 'forgotten coast'. The road continues through numerous hamlets and the relatively large **Carrabelle**, from which **Dog Island**, accessible only by boat, is visible.

A further 16 miles along the coast, Hwy-98 passes the access road to the 5-mile bridge linking **ST GEORGE ISLAND ❹** to the

**St Marks National Wildlife Refuge $**
Tel: (850) 925 6121. Open daily dawn–dusk; visitors' centre Mon–Fri 0815–1615, Sat–Sun 1000–1700.

mainland. Cross the bridge into the heart of the island; the main beach is directly ahead. A left turn along Gulf Beach Drive continues for 11 miles into the sand-dune-dominated **St George Island State Park** and the island's eastern tip.

Back on the mainland, Hwy-98 continues west across the 5-mile-long John Gorrie Memorial Bridge, crossing a large bay fed by the Apalachicola River and touching ground at the time-locked town of **APALACHICOLA ❺** with the stately **Gibson Inn** directly ahead. As it steers through the town, Hwy-98 passes the only traffic light in the county. Hwy-98 continues for 26 miles, bringing views of **St Vincent Island**, an offshore wildlife refuge, before passing the right turn to the **State Constitution Museum** on the outskirts of **PORT ST JOE ❻**.

In the centre of Port St Joe, Hwy-98 forms a junction with Route 71. Take the latter north to return to Tallahassee. For 51 miles the route passes riverside hamlets and crosses bridges bringing views of cypress swamps before reaching Bfrom reaching Blountstown and the junction with Route 20. Turn right, heading east for 26 miles passing through **Bristol** and meeting the junction with Route 267. Continue on Route 20 for a direct 18-mile course to Tallahassee, or join Route 267 skirting the **APALACHICOLA NATIONAL FOREST ❼** before meeting Hwy-319 near Wakulla Springs State Park, 12 miles south of Tallahassee.

**Detour:** Eight miles west of Apalachicola on Hwy-98 is a left turn on to Route 30A. The latter skirts the north bank of the Indian Lagoon and after 16 miles sweeps northwards along the slender arm of land that holds **ST JOSEPH PENINSULA STATE PARK ❽**.

**Detour:** From Bristol, head north on Route 12 for 6.5 miles, then take the left turn on to Route 271. After 5.5 miles, passing through tiny **Rock Bluff**, is the entrance road to the isolated **TORREYA STATE PARK ❾**.

## Also worth exploring

Covering 66,000 acres of the marshy shoreline of Apalachicola Bay, the **St Marks National Wildlife Refuge** is studded with roadside wildlife look-out points from which patience and luck may result in sightings of racoons, white-tailed deer and otters. A visitors' centre documents the area and its denizens. Also within the refuge is the still-functioning **St Marks Lighthouse**, constructed in part with bricks from San Marcos de Apalache (*see page 249*) and completed in 1831. The adjacent **observation tower** brings views of the coastline and the wide variety of birdlife inhabiting it.

Reach the refuge by turning right on to Hwy-98 after leaving the St Marcos de Apalache Historic Site, passing through **Newport** and, after 2.5 miles, making a right turn on to Route 59, the only road into the refuge and one which continues to the lighthouse.

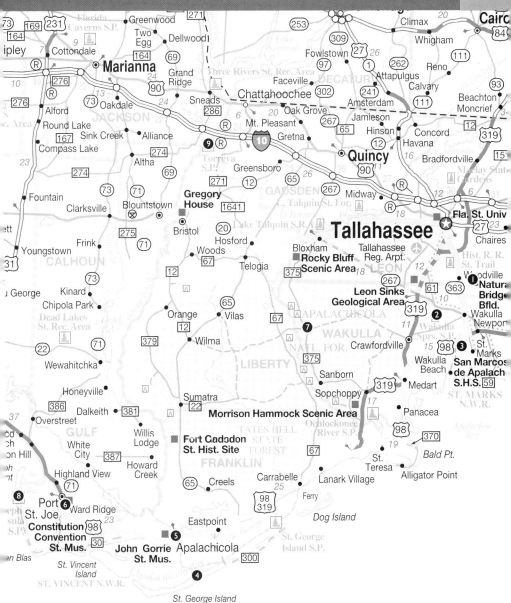

```
0              10              20  Miles
|-------|-------|-------|-------|
0      10      20      30  Kilometers
```

# Crossing the Panhandle

## Ratings

| | |
|---|---|
| Beaches | ●●●●● |
| Architecture | ●●●○○ |
| Fishing | ●●●○○ |
| Nature | ●●●○○ |
| Scenery | ●●●○○ |
| Children | ●●○○○ |
| History | ●●○○○ |
| Museums | ●○○○○ |

As it crosses the central section of the Panhandle, this route encounters Florida beach towns of every kind. They range from Seaside, a planned community fresh off the designer's drawing board, to rustic hamlets such as Grayton Beach and the commercially excessive Panama City Beach. What they all share, however, is proximity to intensely white-sand beaches (due to the powdered quartz washed up here over thousands of years from the Appalachian Mountains) and a section of the Gulf of Mexico where the near-shore waters are a gorgeous emerald colour.

Deep-sea fishing is a major draw, particularly around Destin, where charter boats for novice anglers are as plentiful as the seafood restaurants that serve the best of the day's catch. Away from the coast, old Florida asserts itself in sleepy rural towns, often decorated by Confederate flags of which De Funiak Springs is by far the most distinctive.

## DE FUNIAK SPRINGS❖❖

**ⓘ Beaches of South Walton Visitors Center** *junction of Hwy-98 and Hwy 399, Santa Rosa Beach; tel: (850) 267-1216 or (800) 822-6877. Open daily 0800–1730.*

**ⓗ Walton-De Funiak Library** *3 Circle Drive; tel: as Chamber of Commerce, (see page 256). Open Mon–Wed, Fri–Sat 0900–1500 or later.*

If local lore is to be believed, De Funiak Springs is set around one of the world's two naturally circular lakes. The beauty of the spring-fed lake, discovered in a forest by a railway survey party, encouraged the founding of the town as a transportation base in the 1880s and it gained *élan* as the winter base of the Chautauqua Alliance. Founded to promote educational values in rural areas, the alliance raised an imposing domed **auditorium** beside the lake in 1909 and made this small town one of the cultural hot spots of the southeastern US.

Ringed by live oaks and magnolias, the lake forms a magnificent centre-piece to the town and is overlooked by the best examples of the community's Victorian homes: a rich confection of turrets, dormer windows, gingerbread carpentry, fluted columns and two-storey verandas that line the mile-long and aptly named **Circle Drive**. Also on Circle Drive is the dainty 1886 **Walton-De Funiak Library**, among the oldest libraries in Florida and the only one to display medieval armour and weaponry alongside its books.

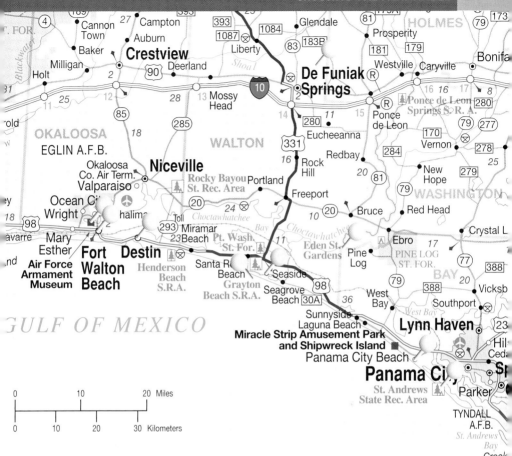

**De Funiak Springs-
Walton County
Chamber of
Commerce** *Circle Drive,
De Funiak Springs; tel: (850)
892-3191. Open Mon–Fri
0900–1700.*

The Panhandle was more deeply involved in the Civil War than any other region of Florida and in 1871, having raised a collection of $250, De Funiak Springs became the area's first town to erect a monument to its Confederate dead. The **Confederate Monument** still stands outside the county courthouse beside Hwy-90.

## Accommodation and food in De Funiak Springs

**Sunbright Manor $–$$** *606 Live Oak Avenue; tel: (850) 892-0656.* Splendidly atmospheric Queen Anne home, once occupied by a state governor, now offering three antique-filled bed-and-breakfast rooms.

**The Busy Bee $** *2 N 7th Street; tel: (850) 892-6700.* Except for the food and the staff, everything in this enjoyably odd lunch-only spot seems to date from Victorian times.

# DESTIN*

**ⓘ Destin Chamber of Commerce** *1021 Hwy-98; tel: (850) 837-6241. Open Mon–Fri 0900–1700.*

**ⓜ Museum of Fishing** *$ 20009 Emerald Coast Parkway. Open Mon–Sat 1100–1600.*

Destin began as a fishing village and is now a major centre for sportsfishing thanks to the 100-ft-deep De Soto Canyon – a lair of tuna, marlin, tarpon and other denizens of the deep that put up a fight when snagged by an anglers hook – which is within easy reach of the charter and private fishing boats berthed at the town's busy marina.

Unappealing high-rise condominiums diminish Destin's visual appeal, even though there is a very fine **beach** on its eastern edge. Otherwise, the core of the town is a functional but unattractive string of petrol stations and shopping malls, in one of which the **Museum of Fishing** has an entertaining assortment of vintage fishing tackle and stuffed fish, and countless photos of satisfied anglers grasping their catch.

## Food in Destin

**Back Porch** $–$$ *1740 Hwy-98 E; tel: (850) 837-2022.* Appealing beachside setting for seafood that comes steamed, grilled, chargrilled and fried.

**Lucky Snapper Grill & Bar** $–$$ *76 Hwy-98 E; tel: (850) 654-5441.* Squid, shrimp fritters and gator tail are among the options at this seafood eatery, with a menu as long as your arm.

# EDEN STATE GARDENS**

**ⓜ Eden State Gardens** *$ Port Washington; tel: (850) 231-4214. Gardens daily 0800–sunset; house by guided tour only Thur–Mon 0900–1600.*

Though his company laid waste to the Panhandle's forests from the 1890s, lumber baron William Henry Wesley made some amends by building this charming white-columned Greek Revival mansion in 1897. The architecture reveals some of the features of living in Florida in the days before air-conditioning. Raised above ground level, the house allows air to circulate beneath while preventing flood damage; large windows embrace whatever breeze may appear during the humid summer and allows the air to flow through a lofty central hallway dividing the rooms on both floors of the two-storey structure.

The Wesley family occupied the house until the 1950s. Subsequently, New York journalist Lois Maxon expanded it and added the cornucopia of family heirlooms and antiques, among them a Chippendale cabinet and Louis XVI mirror, that remain. Even when the house is closed, the splendid gardens justify a visit. Moss-draped oaks fringe the lawns, while masses of camellias and azaleas blossom throughout the winter, reaching their colourful peak in mid-March.

# EGLIN AFB ARMAMENT MUSEUM

**Eglin AFB Armament Museum** *Route 85, near Valparaiso; tel: (850) 882-4062. Open daily 0930–1630.*

Within Eglin Air Force Base, which covers 720 square miles and dominates the economy of nearby Fort Walton Beach (*see page 258*), this collection of planes, missiles and other weaponry that has determined the course of history from World War I to the 1991 Gulf War will convince anyone of the US's technological superiority in global conflict. Among the planes that can be inspected at close quarters are a B-52 bomber, a F16 fighter and a SR17 spy plane.

Other exhibits include a replica of *Fat Boy*, the atomic bomb dropped on Nagasaki in 1945, a variety of cruise missiles, accounts of the Korean and Vietnam wars focusing on the role of the air force, and a collection of duelling pistols and early revolvers decidedly at odds with the high-tech implements of death arranged all around.

# FORT WALTON BEACH✤

**Greater Fort Walton Beach Chamber of Commerce** *34 Miracle Strip Parkway; tel: (850) 244-8191. Open Mon–Fri 0900–1700.*

The sand dune-lined beach that fringes Okaloosa Island is one reason to linger in Fort Walton Beach. Another is the engaging **Indian Temple Mound Museum** $ (*139 Miracle Strip Parkway; tel: (850) 243-6521. Open Sept–May, Mon–Fri 0900–1600; June–Aug, Mon–Sat 0900–1600*) which documents the Native American cultures of the region over a period of 10,000 years. Facing the museum is an Indian-built mound, believed to date from 1400 and topped by a reconstructed temple.

Beside the Gulf of Mexico, the **Gulfarium** $$ (*1010 Miracle Strip Parkway; tel: (850) 244-5169. Open spring and summer, daily 0900–1800; rest of the year daily 0900–1600*) is among the better of the Panhandle's marine parks with displays by dolphins and sea lions, and glass tanks full of sharks, eels, sea turtles and other creatures.

## Florida in the Civil War

The Panhandle was Florida's most populated region during the Civil War (1861–5), when the state aligned with the Confederacy though most of Florida's coastal fortifications were occupied by Union forces. The battles that took place in Florida were mostly in the Panhandle, the largest being the Battle of Olustee (near Live Oak) in February 1864, which involved 10,000 men and left 300 dead. Overall, the conflict took the lives of a third of the 15,000 Floridians who fought in it.

# GRAYTON BEACH❖❖❖

Despite its beach constantly being rated among the best in the US, Grayton Beach remains largely unspoilt and seemingly does little to encourage large-scale tourism. Unlike many of its neighbours where high-rise resort hotels are two-a-penny, this appealing place finds hammocks strung across porches, surfboards resting against garage doors, vibrant murals, and art galleries and small cafés lining its short main street.

The town's greatest asset is the **Grayton Beach State Recreation Area $** (*357 Main Park Road; tel: (850) 231-4210. Open daily 0800–sunset*) with a mile-long white-sand beach flanked by sea-oat-topped dunes. Swimming, sunbathing and surfing are all popular pursuits here, while a nature trail penetrates the scrub and pinelands beside a large brackish lake on the inland side.

**Above**
Grayton Beach

### Accommodation and food in Grayton Beach

**Hibiscus Coffee & Guesthouse $** *85 De Funiak Street; tel: (850) 231-2733.* Bed and a vegetarian breakfast in four simple rooms enclosed by gardens on the main approach road into Grayton Beach. By day, it operates as a coffee-house serving gourmet blends and simple snacks.

**Criolla's $$$** *North side of Hwy-30A, near junction with Route 283; tel: (850) 267-1267.* Coffee-scented duck breast, wood-grilled swordfish and salmon steamed in bamboo are among the succulent and creative offerings that blend Creole and Caribbean cookery.

# PANAMA CITY BEACH❖

**☾ Sugar Beach Motel $–$$** *(16819 Front Beach Road; tel: (800) 528-1273.* A heated pool, a shuffleboard court and a choice of regular and kitchen-equipped rooms put this a cut above the many motels lining the beach road.

Panama City Beach is not a place to find peace and solitude. With every seaside amusement imaginable – go-karting, mini-golf, game arcades and lots more – plus an influx of 600,000 hedonistic students during the February to Easter Spring Break, the town is devoted to mass market tourism and earning as much revenue as possible from a powdery beach that stretches more than 20 miles.

The tackiness is so unrelenting that it almost becomes appealing in itself. The only escapes from the highly developed beach strip are diving and sportsfishing (both well provided for by boat trips from the local marinas) and visiting the unspoilt St Andrews State Recreation Area (*see below*).

# ST ANDREWS STATE RECREATION AREA❖❖

**🛈 St Andrews State Recreation Area $** *4607 State Park Lane; tel: (850) 233-5140. Open daily 0800–sunset.*

This deservedly popular park is a welcome antidote to the unrelenting commercialism of Panama City Beach and fills over 1200 acres on a finger of land that extends eastwards from the busy beach city. Facing the emerald-coloured Gulf of Mexico, a glorious sugar-sanded beach is ideal for swimming; other park areas offer snorkelling, diving, canoeing and kayaking. Many locals catch a fish dinner from the park's piers and jetties.

An inland nature trail leads to Gator Lake and a vantage point for gazing at wildlife that includes alligators, racoons, deer and a multitude of birds. Another trail explores the pine woods and marshlands of the park's northern section and passes a reconstructed pioneer-era turpentine still. The turpentine industry flourished here in the late 1800s and accounts for the scars still borne by some pine trees.

Another rewarding section of the park is 700-acre **Shell Island**, accessible only by boat (shuttle trips depart during spring and summer), with 7 pristine miles of beach coated with a fresh layer of shells with each tide.

# SEASIDE❖❖

Looking at first glance like a New England coastal town, complete with picket fences and clapboard cottages, Seaside was created from scratch in the 1980s. With cottages for rent or purchase and a number of shops and restaurants linked by brightly painted porches, Seaside hoped to acquire an instant smalltown atmosphere and sense of community. Some find Seaside a sentimental, theme park-like creation, while others, such as those who return year after year, regard it as idyllic. Love it or loathe it, Seaside has won numerous architectural awards for its 'nouveau-Victorian' style and is definitely worth a look.

## Suggested tour

**Length:** Main tour 64 miles; first detour 10 miles; second detour 70 miles.

**Duration:** The main tour is a scenic coastal route taking about 4 hours of driving time. The Eden State Gardens detour will add 30 minutes and should be ignored if you are taking the second detour to De Funiak Springs, which will add 90 minutes.

**Links:** Tallahassee to the Forgotten Coast (*see pages 244–53*), The Pensacola Area and its beaches (*see pages 272–81*).

From the east, the main coastal route, Hwy-98, passes through the industrial port town of **Panama City** before crossing Hathaway Bridge above St Andrews Bay and entering **PANAMA CITY BEACH ❶**. To check the pulse of this heavily developed vacation town, take the left fork on to Alt Hwy-98. This continues past 15 miles of restaurants, shopping malls and motels. To re-discover the coast as nature intended it, take the left turn on to Route 3031 (Joan Avenue) soon after crossing the bridge and follow signs for **ST ANDREWS STATE RECREATION AREA ❷**.

On the western edge of Panama City Beach, Alt-Hwy 98 rejoins Hwy-98. After 2.5 miles, take the left turn on to Route 30A at tiny **Inlet Beach**. This coast-hugging road brings views of dune-walled beaches and the emerald waters of the Gulf of Mexico; large brackish lakes appear on the inland side. The first community reached is **Rosemary Beach**, an architect-planned coastal village still under construction. After 7 miles, the route passes through **SEAGROVE BEACH ❸** and then reaches the spick-and-span cottages of **SEASIDE ❹**.

In contrast to Seaside's award-winning but rather soulless appearance is the rustic beach community at **Grayton Beach**. Reach it by passing through Seaside and turning left at the junction of Route 30A and Route 283. The latter proceeds into Grayton Beach, passing

wooden bungalows and expiring at the little beach town's main street, parallel to an excellent and easily accessed beach. The main entrance to **Grayton Beach State Recreation Area** is signposted on Route 30A, just east of the Route 283 junction.

Nine miles west of Grayton Beach, having passed through the quiet coastal villages of **Blue Mountain Beach** and **Dune Alley Beach**, Route 30A rejoins Hwy-98. Take this route for 4.4 miles, passing through the high-rise developments of Sandestin where the two-lane road expands into a six-lane highway, and turn left on to Route 2378, returning to the coast. For the next 7 miles, the route passes holiday condos and high-rise hotels facing a commendable beach.

**Chautauqua Vineyards** *Hwy-331, one mile south of De Funiak Springs; tel: (850) 892-5887. Free tastings Mon–Sat 0900–17.00, Sun 1200–1700.*

**Ponce de Leon State Park $** *Route 181A, east of De Funiak Springs; tel: (850) 836-4281. Open daily 0800–sunset.*

The route returns to Hwy-98 on the eastern edge of **DESTIN ❺**. For 3 miles, the route passes through the commercialised section of the town with Destin Harbor to the left, lined by fishing boats and seafood restaurants. By bridge, the route crosses the **East Pass** that separates the vast Choctawhatchee Bay from the Gulf of Mexico.

Hwy-98 touches ground on **Okaloosa Island**, a slender strip of sand dune and beach owned by the US Air Force that stretches nearly 5 miles. Hwy-98 crosses the island and continues over a high bridge into the centre of **FORT WALTON BEACH ❻**, where many residents are employed at the nearby Eglin Air Force Base. Look for the **Indian Temple Mound Museum** on the right beside this busy stretch of Hwy-98.

**Detour:** From Hwy-30A, turn right on to Route 395 at Seagrave Beach, crossing Hwy-98 and continuing towards the one-time logging community of **Port Washington**. After 4.8 miles is the entrance on the left to **EDEN STATE GARDENS ❼**.

**Detour:** From Grayton Beach or Eden State Gardens, return to Hwy-98 and continue west to the junction with Hwy-331. This makes a 3.3-mile crossing of Choctawhatchee Bay, along which logs were floated during the late-1800s Florida timber boom. Some invitingly shaded picnic tables stand on the bridge's northern end.

Hwy-331 continues north for 4.5 miles and meets Route 20. Turn left and, shortly ahead at the crossroads town of Freeport, turn right on to the continuation of Hwy-331. For the next 17 miles, the route is intermittently enlivened by small villages. At the junction with I-10, a signposted driveway leads to the **Chautauqua Vineyards** where there are complimentary tastings of some of Florida's finest wines. Continue on Hwy-331 for a mile into **DE FUNIAK SPRINGS ❽**, following signs for the Historic District which lead to Circle Drive.

Leave De Funiak Springs heading west on Hwy-90 or I-10. After 14 miles is the junction with the southbound Route 285. Take this to return to the coast, crossing Eglin Air Force Base, founded in the 1930s when a golf course was donated as a gunnery and bombing range, and after 18 miles reaching **Niceville**, a dormitory town for Air Force personnel. Follow signs for Fort Walton Beach, joining Route 85. The entrance to **EGLIN AFB ARMAMENT MUSEUM ❾** is 5.7 miles ahead on the left. To rejoin Hwy-98, continue to Fort Walton Beach, 6 miles south.

## Also worth exploring

Named after the 16th-century Spaniard who arrived in Florida searching for the Fountain of Youth and was greatly encouraged by the region's plethora of natural springs, the **Ponce de León Springs State Recreation Area**, 12 miles east of De Funiak Springs

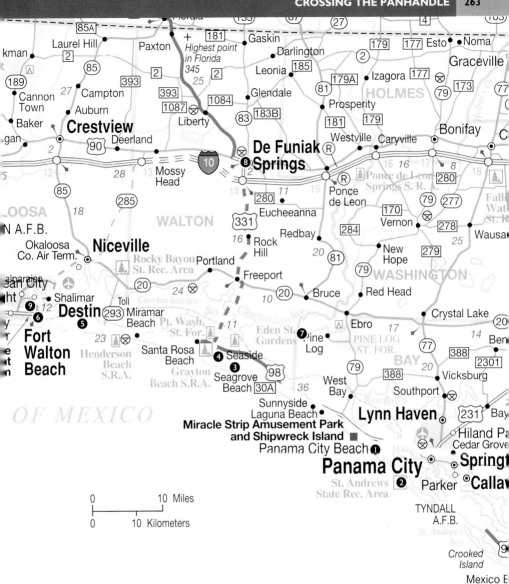

off Route 181A, is the perfect spot to cool off on a hot day. The major spring here is fed by 14 million gallons of water pumping daily from a deep limestone cavity. With a constant temperature of 68°F, the spring invites a dip and there is a designated swimming area. Picnic tables and a nature trail through pine woods encourage a longer stay.

# Pensacola

Anyone hankering for history will find Pensacola much to their liking. While the nearby beaches and islands are the main attraction for most visitors, the city itself has done an impressive job of preserving and restoring its past. Entire streets are still lined by the early-1800s buildings whose ethnically diverse occupants laid the foundations of the modern city. Another area retains turn-of-the-century commercial façades, while a third leafy neighbourhood still boasts the sumptuous middle-class homes that set the tone for gracious Pensacola living through the early 1900s.

Adding spice is the fact that while Pensacola now occupies a relatively remote corner of the state, Florida's destiny was shaped by the events that unfolded here. The Spanish and British established forts and challenged each other for supremacy of this important sea base until both were unceremoniously removed by future president Andrew Jackson, who oversaw Florida's admission to the US here.

## Sights

### Blount Building*

Replacing an earlier building destroyed by fire, the 1907 Blount Building turned many heads on the northern approach to the commercial centre of Pensacola. The beaux arts features such as copper cornices and terracotta arches were regarded as daring, while the fire-proof steel-girder construction spared it the fate that befell its predecessor.

### Civil War Soldiers Museum**

The Civil War often seems a recent memory throughout the Panhandle, a region more involved that any other part of Florida. Several rooms of maps, uniforms and weapons tell the story of the war that killed 620,000 Americans, while personal items such as letters and photos belonging to soldiers reveal its impact on everyday life.

Particularly striking are the medical exhibits that form part of a reconstructed Confederate field hospital, highlighting the difficulties

**ⓘ Fort George** *Junction of Palafox and LaRua streets.*

**Historic Pensacola Village** $ *Includes entry to museums of commerce and industry, Julee Cottage, Dorr and Lavallé houses, and TT Wentworth Museum; part of Seville Historic District; tel: (850) 444-8905. Open Mon–Sat 1000–1600.*

encountered by physicians tending the injured. Alongside some crude surgical tools are artificial limbs, crutches and a portable dental chair in which the unfortunate patient would be tethered for an emergency extraction without anaesthetic.

Much less gory is a section on Civil War music, with instruments purpose-made for battle. Alongside drumsticks from the Battle of Gettysburg is a wooden flute that could swiftly be converted into a baton.

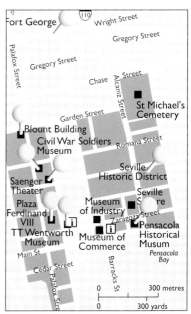

### Fort George and North Hill*

For 60 years from the 1870s, the well-to-do of Pensacola built homes in North Hill, a 50-block area immediately north of the city's commercial district. Doctors, lawyers and bankers were among those who occupied elegant houses in styles spanning neo-classical, Queen Anne, Tudor Revival and more. Most are excellently preserved and set along the neighbourhood's quiet oak-lined streets. Another well-maintained building is **Christ Episcopal Church**, its Mediterranean Revival form intended to reflect Pensacola's Spanish past, its pebble-dash exterior topped by a 64-ft-high dome.

Although only a plaque and small park marks the spot, it was in North Hill that the British built the largest of their three Pensacola forts, **Fort George**, completed in 1778. Three years later, the Spanish regained control of the city and the fort became Fort San Miguel.

### Historic Pensacola Village***

Within the Seville Historic District (*see page 267*), Historic Pensacola Village comprises several small museums and homes and is often roamed by period-attired guides and volunteers re-enacting life in bygone times. Historical orientation is provided by a short video at the visitors' centre.

Inside a 19th-century warehouse, the **Museum of Industry** explores the fishing, lumber and brick-making industries that provided the backbone of the local economy for many years. A brick kiln (local clay proved an ideal raw material) and a re-created sawmill are among the exhibits; others detail the rise of the railways that helped Pensacola

flourish as a transportation centre. Next door, the **Museum of Commerce** enjoyably re-creates Pensacola street scenes of times past. A print shop is packed with antique presses, a pharmacy carries vintage medicines and there is more nostalgia to be found within the hardware and toy stores.

Before it joined the US, Florida provided a sanctuary for runaway slaves and allowed Black people to work and prosper in a manner not possible in neighbouring states. The 1804 **Julee Cottage** belonged to a successful Black woman, Julee Canton, and exhibits about her and Black life in Florida occupy the interior.

**Above**
TT Wentworth Museum

**Museum of Industry** *Zaragoza Street, part of Historic Pensacola Village.*

**Museum of Commerce** *Zaragoza Street, part of Historic Pensacola Village.*

**Julee Cottage** *Zaragoza Street, part of Historic Pensacola Village.*

**Pensacola Historical Museum $** *115 E Zaragoza Street; tel: (850) 433-1559. Open Mon–Sat 0900–1630.*

**Plaza Ferdinand VII** *On Palafox Street between Zaragoza and Government streets.*

**Saenger Theater** *118 Palafox Place.*

**Seville Historic District** *Bordered by Tarragona, Florida Blanca and Wright streets, and Bayfront Parkway.*

**TT Wentworth Museum $** *(included in Historic Pensacola Village admission); 330 S Jefferson Street; tel: (850) 444-8586. Open Memorial Day–Labor Day, Mon–Sat 1000–1600, Sun 1300–1600. Closed Sun rest of the year.*

**Pensacola Historical Museum***

A better setting for an historical museum is harder to imagine than Old Christ Church, built in 1823 and among Florida's oldest churches. Inside the sturdy redbricked structure, which served as a barracks for Union troops during the Civil War and spent many years as a public library, the exhibits comprehensively trace Pensacola's development from Native American times onwards.

**Plaza Ferdinand VII***

It was in the palm-studded Plaza Ferdinand VII in 1821 that Florida formally became part of the US. A statue of future president and Florida's first territorial governor, Andrew Jackson, who drove the British out of Pensacola stands in the centre of the plaza, which was laid out by the Spanish and used by the British as a drill field.

**Saenger Theater***

Regaining its role as an entertainment venue in the 1980s, the Saenger Theater dates from the era of vaudeville and silent movies: Cecil B De Mille's *The Ten Commandments* was the attraction on opening night in 1925. The Spanish baroque details, inside and out, now make an atmospheric setting for Broadway shows, Pensacola Symphony Orchestra concerts and other cultural events.

**Seville Historic District***

Still an important cargo terminal, the harbour triggered large-scale settlement of Pensacola. By the late 1700s, the nascent city was a thriving multicultural trading post where French, Spanish, British and freed slaves (some escaping across the border from the US) lived and prospered side by side. On streets laid out by the British but named by the Spanish, the Seville District still has many wood-frame homes of the early days intact, some now housing museums, shops, restaurants and cafés. The district, a strange mixture of Victorian and Creole architecture, includes Historic Pensacola Village (*see page 265*) and the **Seville Quarter**, a popular nightlife complex.

**TT Wentworth Museum***

The three-storey yellow brick creation in Renaissance Revival style that rises in eye-catching manner beside Plaza Ferdinand VII was built in 1908 as Pensacola's City Hall. The building's architecture alone merits viewing, with red-tiled towers, overhanging eaves and a triple-arched entrance, but the contents also warrant closer inspection.

Reflecting the eclectic collecting passions of a local property dealer, TT Wentworth, the museum boasts an amazing array of antlers, shrunken heads, coke machines, car licence plates, telephone paraphernalia and seemingly whatever else Wentworth, who began his collection aged eight with a gold dollar coin in

1906, could lay his hands on. Alongside are strong displays on local history; the top floor is a hands-on educational area intended for children.

## Accommodation and food

Pensacola has an abundance of chain motels and hotels on its main approach roads. The selections below are limited to those in and around the historic core of the city, adjacent to the suggested tour. The same applies to restaurants, with those listed all within walking distance of the described route. If neither accommodation nor food appeal it is a simple drive to find many other options, such as those described in the Pensacola area and its beaches route (*see pages 272–81*).

**Marsh House $$–$$$** *205 Cevallos Street; tel: (850) 433-4866.* Cross the white-painted wraparound veranda and spacious armchair-filled lobby to find several distinctively furnished bed-and-breakfast rooms.

**Noble Manor $–$$** *110 W Strong Street; tel: (850) 434-9544.* Bed and breakfast in a 1905 Tudor Revival house in the elegant North Hill neighbourhood is an excellent way to immerse yourself in Pensacola's past; the gardens invite a stroll.

**Pensacola Grand Hotel $$–$$$** *200 E Gregory Street; tel: (850) 433-3336.* Modern high-rise hotel, often hosting conventions, at odds with its historic surrounds but within easy walking distance of the city's attractions, dining and nightlife.

**Pensacola Victorian Bed & Breakfast $$–$$$** *203 W Gregory Street; tel: (850) 434-2818 or (800) 370-8354.* A Queen Anne home built for a ship's captain who also founded the Pensacola Symphony Orchestra. Private bathrooms, cable TV and home-baked snacks.

**Seville Inn $–$$** *223 E Garden Street; tel: (850) 433-8331 or (800) 227-7275.* Hard to better for good-priced accommodation in a central location.

**Barracks Street Fish House $–$$** *600 Barracks Street; tel: (850) 470-0003.* Probably the only reason to visit the Pensacola docks is this friendly restaurant serving excellent fresh seafood, plus steaks, sandwiches and salads, with freshly made desserts to follow.

**McQuire's Irish Pub** *600 E Gregory Street; tel: (850) 433-6789.* Steaks, seafood and substantial burgers are among the fare of this pseudo-Irish bar serving lunch, dinner and own-brew beers.

**Spanish Quarter** *130 E Government Street; tel: (850) 434-6211.* Replicating the Church Street Station dining and nightlife complex of Orlando, the Seville Quarter provides a downtown focal point for evening entertainment. Included is the **Palace Oyster Bar**, serving seafood and local specialities.

**Right**
Pensacola's Historic District

**Barklay House** *410 S Florida Blanca Street.*

**Seville Square** *Bordered by Zaragoza, Government, Alcaniz and Barracks streets.*

**Dorr House** $ *(included in Historic Pensacola Village admission), 311 S Adams Street.*

**Lavallé House** *205 E Church Street, part of Historic Pensacola Village.*

**Pensacola Museum of Art** *407 S Jefferson Street; tel: (850) 432-6247. Open Tue–Fri 1000–1700, Sat 1000–1600.*

The 1912 *Pensacola Grand Hotel, 200 E Gregory Street; tel: (850) 433-3336.* Good-quality lunch menu; by night it becomes a slightly more formal and highly rated dinner restaurant.

## Suggested tour

**Length:** Main tour, 0.75 miles; detour 1.5 miles and best undertaken by car.

**Duration:** 3–4 hours on foot including viewing time; add 30 minutes for the detour.

**Links:** Pensacola lies within the area described in the Pensacola area and its beaches tour *(see pages 272–81).*

The oldest quarter of the city, the **SEVILLE HISTORIC DISTRICT ❶** makes a good beginning to an exploration of Pensacola. At the foot of Florida Blanca Street, the 1825 **Barklay House ❷**, built for a British merchant, is one of the oldest masonry homes in Florida and still enjoys a splendid view over Pensacola Bay despite the busy highway which runs close by. Walk to Zaragoza Street and turn left, passing more early-1800s homes before reaching **Seville Square ❸**, a block ahead and overlooked by Old Christ Church, which now holds the **PENSACOLA HISTORICAL MUSEUM ❹**. The museum collections help make sense of the city's turbulent and complicated history.

The next step is to purchase a ticket for the homes and museums of **HISTORIC PENSACOLA VILLAGE ❺** from the visitors' centre, a block ahead at the junction with Barracks Street. The wooden **Julee Cottage ❻** stands directly opposite the visitors' centre; the **Museum of Commerce ❼** and the **Museum of Industry ❽** face each other on Zaragoza Street just across Barracks Street.

Within the village are several former homes with historic exhibits. The most substantial, both viewed by guided tour, are the sumptuously appointed 1871 **Dorr House ❾**, across Church Street facing Seville Square, and the 1805 **Lavallé House ❿**, co-built by a French woman fleeing a slave rebellion in the Caribbean. The latter is a good example of the French Creole architectural style, complete with overhanging porch, while the interior suggests life in 1820s Pensacola.

Continue west along Church Street to reach **PLAZA FERDINAND VII ⓫**, on the east side of which the former City Hall is now taken up by the **TT WENTWORTH MUSEUM ⓬**. Among the museum's exhibits are those describing the archaeological dig which has unearthed parts of the British fort which occupied the Seville area in the 1700s. A still-expanding **trail ⓭**, beginning behind the museum, links several points of interest from the old fort. A block south on Main Street, the

**North Hill Historic District** *Bordered by Wright, Blount, LaRua and Palafox streets.*

**St Michael's Cemetery** *Alcaniz Street, opposite junction with Garden Street.*

Pensacola Museum of Art ⑭ is less notable for its exhibitions than its setting: a two-storey Mediterranean Revival structure that formerly held the city jail.

A block west is the 1892 **Bear Block** ⑮, an ornate neo-classical structure marking the southern end of **Palafox Street** ⑯, the commercial core of Pensacola during the booming early 1900s, with many buildings of the time remaining. Walk north along Palafox Street. The 1887 **Escambia County Courthouse** ⑰ rises on the left immediately beyond Government Street. Cross Palafox Street to admire the Spanish Revival details of the

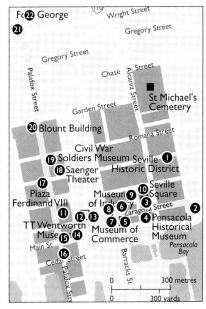

**SAENGER THEATER** ⑱. On the same block is the **CIVIL WAR SOLDIERS MUSEUM** ⑲. A block north on the corner with Garden Street is the **BLOUNT BUILDING** ⑳.

**Detour:** Those who grew rich as Pensacola thrived built homes immediately north of the Palafox district in North Hill, which rises steadily away from the bay filling a 50-block area. Although none are open to the public, many of North Hill's historic houses remain in excellent condition and collectively suggest the affluent local lifestyles of the 1870s to the 1930s. Palafox Street continues across Garden Street into North Hill, oak trees decorating its centre. On the junction of Wright Street is the distinctive domed form of **Christ Episcopal Church** ㉑. Two blocks further, near the junction with LaRua Street, is the site of the British-built **Fort George** ㉒.

## Also worth exploring

On the northern edge of the Seville Historic District and announced with its name theatrically emblazoned on an iron grille above its entrance, **St Michael's Cemetery** was laid out under the orders of the Spanish in the late 1700s. Among the 3000 internees, many of them in masonry tombs raised above the ground, are slaves, settlers, priests and merchants; a glance at the inscriptions reveals old Pensacola's ethnically diverse make up.

# The Pensacola area and its beaches

## Ratings

| | |
|---|---|
| Beaches | ●●●○ |
| Canoeing | ●●●● |
| History | ●●●● |
| Nature | ●●●● |
| Scenery | ●●●● |
| Children | ●●●○○ |
| Museums | ●●○○○ |
| Architecture | ●○○○○ |

Intensely white sand dunes and beaches are a common sight around Pensacola. The local shoreline includes several federally protected untamed expanses between heavily developed sections dominated by the motels, vacation condos and beach supply stores that attest to the popularity of the area. The barrier islands that hold the beaches form a natural shelter for Pensacola harbour, as do the long, thickly-forested peninsulas that jut from the mainland.

On one such peninsula is Gulf Breeze, a name familiar to UFO buffs throughout the world; on another is a vast Naval Air Station which displays the US's foremost collection of naval aircraft. Dotted throughout are historical markers such as Spanish-era forts and the former jail cell that held the famed Native American leader, Geronimo. The combination of beaches, nature and history makes for a varied and interesting route with many spectacular views. Venture inland and the reward is some of Florida's best canoeing.

## FORT BARRANCAS✤

**ⓘ** **Pensacola Beach Visitors Center** *735 Pensacola Beach Boulevard, Pensacola Beach; tel: (850) 932-1500 or (800) 635-4803. Open Mon–Sat 0900–1700, Sun 0900–1500.*

**ⓗ** **Fort Barrancas** *in grounds of US Naval Air Station; tel: (850) 455-5167. Open Apr–Oct, daily 0930–1700; rest of the year daily 1030–1600; guided tours in summer 1100 and 1400.*

Following Florida's acquisition by the US, Pensacola was selected as a naval base. With the aid of 400 slaves, the Spanish-built Fort Barrancas was extended and completed in 1845. The site's strategic importance below a series of bluffs to conceal it from attackers had been noted by early Spanish settlers who raised the first fortification here in 1698 and by the British who, in the 1770s, erected the Royal Naval Redoubt adjacent to the existing fort.

The fort and its interior can be explored though there is little to view, save for the brickwork galleries and the battery from where Spanish cannonballs could be bounced off the sea to strike enemy ships on their waterline.

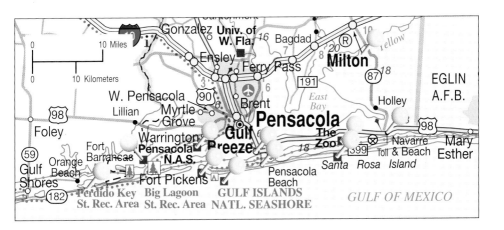

# FORT PICKENS❖❖

**Fort Pickens National Park $**
*Western end of Fort Pickens Road, Santa Rosa Island; tel: (850) 9342635. Open Apr–Oct, 0930–1700; rest of the year, daily 0830–1600.*

Pentagonal-shaped Fort Pickens was completed in 1834, the largest of a group of fortifications designed to protect Pensacola's naval shipyard. With its 40ft-high, 12ft-thick walls, the slave-built fort still has an air of invincibility, even though advances in weaponry rendered it obsolete soon after its completion. A small museum describes the fort's history and construction, and the Gulf Islands National Seashore (*see page 274*) of which it forms a part. A walk around the former storage rooms and along slender passageways to the gun placements overlooking the bay makes for an atmospheric hour.

While the fort saw no action of consequence, it did for two years incarcerate the legendary Native American, Goyahkla, popularly known as Geronimo. Leading Native resistance to enforced resettlement, Geronimo and the other Apache held with him became reluctant tourist attractions in the 1880s, before being moved, eventually to Oklahoma.

# GULF BREEZE❖

**Barnhill's Country Buffet $** *3075 Gulf Breeze Parkway, Gulf Breeze; tel: (850) 932-0403. Although it can vary in quality, the food is usually good and there is always lots of it at this all-you-can-eat restaurant.*

With its balmy climate, great fishing, affordable homes and much more to lure would-be settlers, Gulf Breeze would be just another comfortable Florida coastal community were it not for the fact that, since the 1980s, it has become one of the world's most celebrated UFO-sighting locations.

Photos of an unidentified craft taken here in 1987 and published by a local newspaper were the start of what quickly escalated into hundreds of eye-witness accounts of unusual aerial activity, sometimes captured by photography and video. While sceptics are quick to point out the proximity of Pensacola's US Naval Air Station and the Eglin Air Force

Base, a short distance east, as an explanation for unusual sightings, some video footage shot here continues to defy rational explanation.

Armed with cameras, camcorders and binoculars, many would-be UFO-spotters regularly gather at **Shoreline Park**, undeterred by the notoriety that seems to bring as many hoaxers as believers.

# GULF ISLANDS NATIONAL SEASHORE✧✧✧

**Gulf Islands National Seashore** 1801 Gulf Breeze Parkway (Headquarters), Hwy-98; tel: (850) 934-2600. Open daily 0800–sunset. Separate hours and fees for forts and other areas.

Spanning 135,000 acres of beaches, barrier islands, marshes and bayous (and forts Barrancas and Pickens, see pages 272–3) in Florida and Mississippi, the Gulf Islands National Seashore is a federally administered area protecting the natural landscape and providing environmentally friendly recreation facilities. Park ranger-led activities and guided tours, most frequent throughout the summer, are highly recommended.

The headquarters and main visitors' centre for the area is within the 1378-acre **Naval Live Oaks Reservation**. Producing a dense, disease-resistant wood, live oaks were ideal material for shipbuilding and it was here in 1828 that the government acquired a tract of land and started an experimental farm, aiming to cultivate a live oak species tailored to the needs of the navy.

The centre's displays detail the links between live oaks and shipbuilding, and document the natural and human history of the area, a site of prehistoric habitation holding one of Florida's first roads, the Pensacola-St Augustine mail route opened in 1824. A short nature trail loops from the centre through a section of the forest and to several slender beaches lining Santa Rosa Sound.

# MILTON✧

**Blackwater River State Park** $ Holt, 15 miles northeast of Milton; tel: (850) 623-2363. Open daily 0800–sunset.

Once known as Scratch Ankle for the effect the local scrub had on visitors' legs, Milton has a deserved reputation as a centre for canoeing. With several creeks and the tannin-stained Blackwater River close by, canoe rental outlets are abundant in and around the town. Further north, the Blackwater River flows through **Blackwater River State Park**, forming a section of the excellent Florida Canoe Trail, meandering through forests of oak and cypress and passing sandbanks that invite a picnic stop.

# NATIONAL MUSEUM OF NAVAL AVIATION✧✧✧

Opposite
National Museum of Naval Aviation

In 1914, long before the creation of the US Air Force, Pensacola became the country's first naval air station and remains its major training centre for naval pilots. This overwhelming museum fills

**National Museum of Naval Aviation** *In grounds of US Naval Air Station, signposted from Navy Boulevard; tel: (850) 452-3604. Open daily 0900–1700.*

300,000 square feet with the aircraft, spacecraft and various other craft flown by the US Navy and Coast Guard over the years.

A large section is devoted to World War II, including a full-sized reconstruction of an aircraft carrier flight deck, lined by planes of the period with a below-decks area complete with a shop selling 1940s shaving cream and soft drinks. The use of naval pilots in the US space programme is illustrated with the command module from the first skylab mission in 1973, crewed by naval personnel. Among many hands-on exhibits are the cockpit simulators used to train fighter and helicopter pilots.

Short of being airborne, the best way to experience the thrills and spills of cutting-edge flight is with the ultra-realistic films shown in the IMAX cinema. A more sombre side of naval pilotry is provided by a reconstruction of Hoa Lo Prison, housing captured American pilots during the Vietnam War, the misery of their incarceration suggested with photos and possessions of former inmates.

# NAVARRE BEACH✢

Narvarre Beach, among the smallest of the area's coastal settlements, has many homes raised on stilts to avoid flooding and a strip of white-sand beach from which extends a busy fishing pier. Sailing, parasailing, water-skiing, jetskiing, scuba-diving, snorkelling, fishing and canoeing are among the activities which can be enjoyed here. Immediately west begins a 17-mile stretch of sand dunes that divides the town from Pensacola Beach.

# PENSACOLA BEACH✢✢

The most developed portion of the 20-mile-long Santa Rosa Island (*see page 278*), Pensacola Beach has numerous restaurants, hotels and beach supply outlets. Commercial growth does little to dent its appeal, however, because the beach is superb and easily accessible. Though it may be hard to hear above the sound of the surf, the sand, due to its composition, squeaks as you walk on it.

### Accommodation and food in Pensacola Beach

**Clarion Resort & Suites $$** *20 Via de Luna Drive; tel: (850) 932-4300.* Kitchen-equipped suites adjacent to the beach and local amenities; free continental breakfast.

**The Dunes $$** *333 Fort Pickens Road; tel: (850) 932-3535 or (800) 83DUNES.* With two pools, penthouse rooms and a 24-hour café this is among the better-equipped of the area's lodgings.

**Left**
Gulf Islands National Seashore

**Five Flags Inn $–$$** *299 Fort Pickens Road; tel: (850) 932-3586.* All the rooms of this good-value motel face the Gulf of Mexico, tempting a pre-breakfast swim.

**Surf and Sand Cottages $$–$$$** *12 Via de Luna Drive; tel: (850) 932-2291.* One- to four-bedroomed cottages with kitchens, cable TV and views of the bay or the Gulf.

**Flounder's Chowder & Ale House $$** *800 Quietwater Beach Road; tel: (850) 932-2003.* Charboiled seafood is the speciality of this intentionally rustic eatery which extends on to a patio bar overlooking Santa Rosa Sound.

**Peg Leg Pete's Oyster Bar $–$$** *1010 Fort Pickens Road; tel: (850) 932-4139.* Oysters are but one item on a menu that includes Cajun fried catfish, blackened grouper and many more seafood and meat dishes.

# PERDIDO KEY❖❖

**Perdido Key State Recreation Area $** *Perdido Key; tel: (850) 492-1595. Open daily 0800–sunset.*

**Flora-Bama Lounge $** *Hwy-299, Perdido Key; tel (850) 492-0611.* A one-of-a-kind establishment with live music, drinks and oysters served on the Florida-Alabama border.

Perdido Key is a long, slender barrier island connected by road bridge to Florida in the east and Alabama in the west. It has its share of high-rise condos and holiday homes, but much of its beach is protected within the **Perdido Key State Recreation Area**.

Along the island's most easterly 5 miles, the beaches and sand dunes form part of the Gulf Islands National Seashore (*see page 274*). Here, the short **Johnson Beach Nature Trail** picks a route beside salt marshes supporting a rich variety of birdlife, through maritime forests and over sand hills. Facing the far-better preserved Fort Pickens (*see page 273*) across the bay, the 1830s **Fort McRee**, accessible only by foot or boat, marks Perdido Key's eastern tip.

# SANTA ROSA ISLAND❖❖❖

Almost 50 miles long, this narrow finger of land reaches from Fort Walton Beach (*see page 258*) in the east to Fort Pickens (*see page 273*) in the west. Although it holds several beach communities, the largest being Pensacola Beach (*see page 277*), many sections are undeveloped and provide a matchless setting for sunbathing, swimming and beachcombing. The whiteness of the sands, intensely bright in strong sunshine, is due to the grains being almost pure quartz, lacking the crushed seashell or feldspar that forms darker and less powdery sand.

# THE ZOO❖

This manageably sized zoo includes lions, tigers, zebras, giraffes and what is claimed to be the world's largest gorilla. The zoo can be explored from

**The Zoo** $ *5701 Gulf Breeze Highway, Gulf Breeze; tel: (850) 932-2229. Open daily 0900–1700.* atop an elephant or on the **Safari Line**, which carries passengers on a miniature railway through a 30-acre plain where rhinos, hippos, alligators and many other creatures roam comparatively freely. The children's section has a full complement of cuddly, furry creatures available for hugging and stroking.

# Suggested tour

**❶ Pensacola Convention & Visitors Information Center** *1401 E Gregory Street (foot of Three Mile Bridge), Pensacola; tel: (850) 343-1234 or (800) 874-1234. Open daily 0800–1700.*

**Length**: Main tour 78 miles; Perdido Key detour 37 miles; Milton and Blackwater State Park detour 92 miles.

**Duration**: Main tour 2.5 hours; 1 hour for the Perdido Key detour. Detours to Milton and Black Water State Park will add 2 hours' driving time but are only worthwhile if a canoe trip is included, therefore allocate at least half a day.

**Links**: Crossing the Panhandle (*see pages 254–63*), Pensacola (*see pages 264–71*).

Arriving from the east, Hwy-98 reaches the small bayside community of **Navarre**. Turn left here on to Route 399 which crosses Santa Rosa Bay (toll) to **SANTA ROSA ISLAND ❶** and **NAVARRE BEACH ❷**, consisting of a few shops, a fishing pier and a brilliantly white-sand beach with dunes topped by coarse vegetation. A similar outlook fills the next 17 miles to **PENSACOLA BEACH ❸**, the area's largest beach town. Motels, shops and restaurants become increasingly plentiful along Via de Luna (the local name for Route 399), the heart of the community.

West of the junction with Pensacola Bridge Road, signs of development thin and 2.6 miles ahead is the **Fort Pickens State Park** section of **GULF ISLANDS NATIONAL SEASHORE ❹**. The road picks through 7.5 miles of wooded picnic and camping areas before expiring close to the substantial remains of **FORT PICKENS ❺**, overlooking the seaborne approach to Pensacola.

### Canoeing

A number of specialist canoe companies operate in and around Milton. Most will provide everything for a canoe trip, including transportation to and from the launch site. Some have guided canoe tours. Two of the longest established are **Adventures Unlimited** *tel: (850) 623-6197 or (800) BE-YOUNG* and **Blackwater Canoe Rental** *tel: (850) 623-0235 or (800) 623-6789.*

Return to Pensacola Bridge Road, turning left to cross the bay (toll payable on return) to reach **GULF BREEZE ❻**. On the left immediately after the Hwy-98 junction is Shoreline Drive, which leads quickly to **Shoreline Park**, a popular site for UFO watchers. The entrance to **Naval Live Oaks** is 1.3 miles east on Hwy-98. Also on this route, after passing through the small town of **Oriole Beach**, is **Woodlawn Beach**, 8.5 miles from Gulf Breeze and site of **THE ZOO ❼**.

Some Gulf Breeze UFO sightings may be aircraft belonging to Pensacola's US Naval Air Station, located directly across Pensacola Bay from Gulf Breeze. To reach the station and its excellent **NATIONAL MUSEUM OF NAVAL AVIATION ❽**, head north on Hwy-98 as it crosses Three Mile Bridge above Pensacola Bay and swings west to pass through the city of Pensacola before becoming Navy Boulevard (Route 295) from which the museum is signposted. Signs also indicate the route to **FORT BARRANCAS ❾**, located within the Naval Air Station grounds.

**Detour: MILTON ❿**, the self-styled 'canoe capital of the world', can be reached by taking Route 87, north off Hwy-98 in Navarre. Route 87 weaves through several diminutive communities and crosses the

**Big Lagoon State Recreation Area $**
*12301 Gulf Beach Highway; tel: (850) 492-1595. Open daily 0800–sunset.*

eastern section of the Eglin Air Force Base (*see page 257*) before, after 20 miles, passing beneath I-10 and, a few miles ahead, meeting Hwy-90. Milton lies 4.3 miles west on Hwy-90, a route that crosses the Blackwater River. The river is one among many canoe-friendly waterways in the vicinity. There is more canoeing at **Blackwater State Park**, 15 heavily-forested miles north of Milton on Route 191.

**Detour:** Immediately north of the Naval Air Station, Navy Boulevard crosses Route 292 (Gulf Beach Highway, becoming Sorrento Road). Take this route west, after 10 miles passing the entrance to **Big Lagoon State Recreation Area** (*see Also worth exploring below*). Turn left on to Perdido Key Drive which continues to **PERDIDO KEY** ⑪. The route continues west, following the shoreline, passing high-rise condos and the undeveloped **Perdido Key State Recreation Area**. The even more pristine eastern section of Perdido Key, part of the Gulf Islands National Seashore, is accessed by Johnson Beach Road, off Perdido Key Drive.

## Also worth exploring

The swimming and picnicking areas of **Big Lagoon State Recreation Area** are a well-guarded secret. Even in summer, when the area's beaches are swamped by sunbathers, this 678-acre park retains much of its natural peace and tranquillity. The park's beaches flank the placid Big Lagoon, popular among anglers for its stocks of mullet and sea trout, and several walking trails pass through woodlands and around wildlife-rich salt marshes. At the east beach, an observation tower provides a panoramic overview of the park and beyond

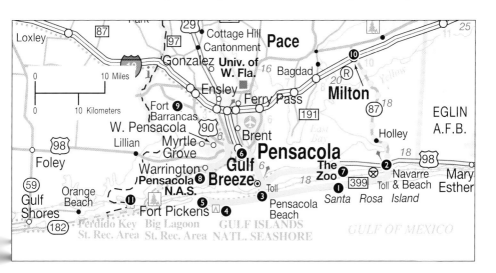

# Language

## How to talk Floridan

**Alternate:** Means 'alternative', not 'every other'– sometimes a source of confusion when reading timetables.

**Bed & Breakfast (or 'B&B'):** Overnight lodging in a private home, usually with private facilities and almost always more expensive than nearby hotels and motels.

**Brewpub:** A tavern that brews its own beer.

**Buffalo wings:** Chicken wings, usually fried and served with a spicy sauce as an appetiser or as bar food.

**California cuisine:** Anything the chef wants it to mean, as long as it's expensive, but usually based on fresh, organically grown foods.

**Chili dog or chili burger:** Hot dog or hamburger disguised with chilli, onions and cheese.

**Chimichanga:** A pseudo-Mexican concoction of a fried tortilla filled with meat, beans, cheese, tomatoes and lettuce.

**Chips:** Crisps, usually made from potatoes, but also from corn, taro, cassava, rice or other starches.

**Corn dog:** Hot dog dipped in corn meal and fried. Usually served hot on a stick.

**Dead head:** Fans of the band the Grateful Dead; also a term for hippies.

**Designer water:** Pejorative term for bottled water.

**Downtown:** City or town centre.

**Holiday:** A public holiday, such as Labor Day, not a private holiday, which is a vacation.

**Lodging:** The usual term for accommodation.

**Natural ingredients:** Food that has been grown, processed and prepared without pesticides or other chemical additives.

**Outlet shopping:** Shopping at large stores specialising in factory overruns at reduced prices. Sometimes, factory outlets are simply low-priced retail stores selling direct from the factory.

**Resort:** A fancy hotel which specialises in leisure activities such as golf, tennis and swimming.

**Road kill:** Literally, animals killed by passing cars, but usually used to describe bad restaurant food.

## Floridan driving terms

**Big rig:** A large lorry, usually a tractor pulling one or more trailers.

**Boulevard stop:** Slowing at a stop sign, but not stopping.

**CNG:** Liquified petroleum gas used as fuel.

**Crosswalk:** Pedestrian crossing.

**Connector:** A minor road connecting two freeways.

**Curve:** Bend.

**Divided highway:** Dual carriageway.

**DUI:** Driving Under the Influence of alcohol or drugs, aka Drunk Driving. The blood alcohol limit in California is 0.08% and is very strictly enforced.

**Fender:** Bumper.

**Freeway:** Motorway.

**Garage or parking:** Garage car park.

**Gas(oline):** Petrol.

**Grade:** Gradient, hill.

**Highway:** Trunk road.

**Hood:** Bonnet.

**Metering lights:** Traffic signals controlling access to bridges, freeways, etc.

**Motor home:** Motor caravan.

**Pavement:** Road surface. A UK 'pavement' is a US sidewalk.

**Ramp:** Slip road.

**Rent:** Hire.

**Rubbernecking:** Slowing down to peer while driving past the scene of an accident or some unusual event.

**RV (recreational vehicle):** Motor caravan.

**Shift (stick):** Gear lever.

**Shoulder:** Verge.

**Sidewalk:** Pavement.

**Sig-alert:** An official warning of unusually heavy traffic, usually broadcast over local radio stations.

**Switchback:** Serpentine road.

**Tow truck:** Breakdown lorry.

**Traffic cop:** Traffic warden.

**Truck:** Lorry.

**Trunk:** Boot.

**Yield:** Give way.

# Index

# Acknowledgements

**Project management:** Dial House Publishing Services
**Series design:** Fox Design
**Front cover design and artwork:** Fox Design
**Layout and map work:** Concept 5D
**Repro and image setting:** Z2 Repro
**Printed and bound in Italy by** Rotolito Lombarda Spa

We would like to thank the following photographers and organisations for the photographs used in this book, to whom the copyright in the photographs belongs:

Front cover: Miami Beach lifesaving hut (Fred Gebhart); Florida Keys sunset (Maxine Cass); The Leslie, Miami Beach (Fred Gebhart).

**Maxine Cass:** pages 3, 5, 9, 13, 14, 22, 24, 27, 30, 32, 34, 42, 45, 48, 52, 55, 56, 59, 60, 64, 67, 68, 70, 74, 77, 81, 86, 88, 91, 94, 96, 99, 103, 104, 106, 108, 111, 114, 117, 118, 120, 122, 124, 127, 128, 130, 132, 134, 136, 139, 140, 146, 148, 151, 154, 157, 162, 164, 166, 168, 172, 173, 175, 176, 179, 183, 187, 192, 195, 197, 200, 203, 205, 208, 210, 212, 218A, 218B, 220, 222, 225, 226, 228, 231, 233, 234, 244, 248, 254, 258, 261, 264, 266, 269, 272A, 272B, 275, 276, 279.

**Fred Gebhart:** pages 7, 17, 36, 41, 46, 78, 84, 85, 100, 102, 110, 144, 147, 180A, 180B, 184, 189, 191, 206, 214, 247, 251.

**Tallahassee Area Convention and Visitors Bureau:** 236A, 236B, 239.

# Feedback form

If you enjoyed using this book, or even if you didn't, please help us improve future editions by taking part in our reader survey. Every returned form will be acknowledged, and to show our appreciation we will give you £1 off your next purchase of a Thomas Cook guidebook. Just take a few minutes to complete and return this form to us.

**When did you buy this book?** ................................................................................................
....................................................................................................................................................

**Where did you buy it? (Please give town/city and, if possible, name of retailer)**
....................................................................................................................................................
....................................................................................................................................................

**When did you/do you intend to travel in Florida?** ...............................................................
....................................................................................................................................................

**For how long (approx)?** ...........................................................................................................

**How many people in your party?** ..........................................................................................

**Which cities, national parks and other locations did you/do you intend mainly to visit?**
....................................................................................................................................................
....................................................................................................................................................
....................................................................................................................................................
....................................................................................................................................................

**Did you/will you:**
❑ Make all your travel arrangements independently?
❑ Travel on a fly-drive package?
Please give brief details: ..........................................................................................................
....................................................................................................................................................

**Did you/do you intend to use this book:**
❑ For planning your trip?                ❑ Both?
❑ During the trip itself?

**Did you/do you intend also to purchase any of the following travel publications for your trip?**
Thomas Cook Travellers: Florida ..............................................................................
A road map/atlas (please specify) .........................................................................................
Other guidebooks (please specify) .........................................................................................

**Have you used any other Thomas Cook guidebooks in the past? If so, which?**
....................................................................................................................................................
....................................................................................................................................................

Please rate the following features of Signpost Florida for their value to you (Circle VU for 'very useful', U for 'useful', NU for 'little or no use'):

| | | | |
|---|---|---|---|
| The Travel Facts section on pages 14–25 | VU | U | NU |
| The Driver's Guide section on pages 26–31 | VU | U | NU |
| The Highlights on pages 40–41 | VU | U | NU |
| The recommended driving routes throughout the book | VU | U | NU |
| Information on towns and cities, National Parks, etc | VU | U | NU |
| The maps of towns and cities, parks, etc | VU | U | NU |

Please use this space to tell us about any features that in your opinion could be changed, improved, or added in future editions of the book, or any other comments you would like to make concerning the book:

..................................................................................................................................................

..................................................................................................................................................

..................................................................................................................................................

..................................................................................................................................................

..................................................................................................................................................

..................................................................................................................................................

..................................................................................................................................................

..................................................................................................................................................

..................................................................................................................................................

..................................................................................................................................................

**Your age category:**     ❏ 21-30     ❏ 31-40     ❏ 41-50     ❏ over 50

Your name: Mr/Mrs/Miss/Ms ...............................................................................................................

(First name or initials) ........................................................................................................................

(Last name) .........................................................................................................................................

Your full address: (Please include postal or zip code)

..................................................................................................................................................

..................................................................................................................................................

..................................................................................................................................................

..................................................................................................................................................

..................................................................................................................................................

Your daytime telephone number: ......................................................................................................

**Please detach this page and send it to: The Project Editor, Signpost Guides, Thomas Cook Publishing, PO Box 227, Peterborough PE3 6PU, United Kingdom.**

We will be pleased to send you details of how to claim your discount upon receipt of this questionnaire.